YOUR LIFE IS WORTH MINE

(GERMAN side of POSTER)

BEKANNTMACHUNG

Betrifft:

Beherbergung von geflüchteten Juden.

Es besteht Anlass zu folgendem Hinweis: Gemäss der 3. Verordnung über Aufenthaltsbeschränkungen im Generalgouvernement vom 15. 10. 1941 (VO. Bl. GG. S. 595) unterliegen Juden, die den jüdischen Wohnbezirk unbefugt verlassen, der Todesstrafe.

Gemäss der gleichen Vorschrift unterliegen Personen, die solchen Juden wissentlich Unterschlupf gewähren, Beköstigung verabfolgen oder Nahrungsmittel verkaufen, ebenfalls der Todesstrafe.

Die nichtjüdische Bevölkerung wird daher dringend gewarnt:

1.) Juden Unterschlupf zu gewähren,

2.) Juden Beköstigung zu verabfolgen,

3.) Juden Nahrungsmittel zu verkaufen.

Der Stadthauptmann
Dr. Franke

Tschenstochau, den 24. 9. 42.

(POLISH side of POSTER)

OGŁOSZENIE

Dotyczy:

przetrzymywania ukrywających się żydów.

Zachodzi potrzeba przypomnienia, że stosownie do § 3 Rozporządzenia o ograniczeniach pobytu w Gen. Gub. z dnia 15. X. 1941 roku (Dz. Rozp. dla GG. str. 595) żydzi, opuszczający dzielnicę żydowską bez zezwolenia, podlegają karze śmierci.

Według tego rozporządzenia, osobom, które takim żydom świadomie udzielają przytułku, dostarczają im jedzenia lub sprzedają artykuły żywnościowe, grozi również kara śmierci.

Niniejszym ostrzega się stanowczo ludność nieżydowską przed:

1.) udzielaniem żydom przytułku,

2.) dostarczaniem im jedzenia,

3.) sprzedawaniem im artykułów żywnościowych.

Częstochowa, dnia 24. 9. 42.

Translation of German Annoucement:

Concerning the Sheltering of Escaping Jews

A reminder—in accordance with paragraph 3 of the decree of October 15, 1941, on the Limitation of Residence in General Government (page 595 of the GG Register) Jews leaving the Jewish Quarter without permission will incur the death penalty.

According to this decree, those knowingly helping these Jews by providing shelter, supplying food, or selling them foodstuffs are also subject to the death penalty.

This is a categorical warning to the non-Jewish population against:

1) Providing shelter to Jews
2) Supplying them with Food
3) Selling them Foodstuffs

Dr. Franke
Town Commander
Czestochowa   9/24/42

YOUR LIFE IS WORTH MINE

How Polish Nuns Saved Hundreds of Jewish Children in German-Occupied Poland, 1939-1945

Ewa Kurek

Introduction by
Jan Karski

HIPPOCRENE BOOKS
New York

The Publisher gratefully acknowledges the Joseph B. Slotkowski
Publishing Fund of the Kosciuszko Foundation for its financial
support of this project.

All interviews, except the one with Rabbi David Kahane, have been edited
to read as uninterrupted accounts. Some have been abridged for clarity,
but no important information has been left out. Unless otherwise stated,
all interviews are part of the author's private collection residing at the
Catholic University of Lublin, 27 Chopin St., Lublin, Poland.

Originally published in Poland as *Gdy Klasztor Znaczyl Zycie*
Copyright© Znak Publishers, Cracow.

Hippocrene Books edition copyright© 1997

For information, address:
HIPPOCRENE BOOKS, INC.
171 Madison Avenue
New York, NY 10016

Library of Congress Cataloging-in-Publication Data
Kurek-Lesik, Ewa.
[Gdy klasztor znaczyl zycie. English]
Your life is worth mine : how Polish nuns in World War II saved
hundreds of Jewish lives in German-occupied Poland, 1939-1945 / Ewa
Kurek ; introduction Jan Karski.
p.   cm.
Includes index.
ISBN 0-7818-0409-4
1. World War, 1939-1945—Jews—Rescue—Poland. 2. Jewish
children—Poland. 3. Monasticism and religious orders for women-
-Poland—History. 4. World War, 1939-1945—Catholic Church.
5. Catholic Church—Poland—History—20th century. 6. Poland-
-History—Occupation, 1939-1945. I. Title
D810.J4K8313   1996
940.53'1503924—dc20   96-36226
                                                          CIP
Printed in the United States of America.

CONTENTS

Dedication

To all the Polish nuns who in the name of Christian love, and at risk to their own lives, saved those condemned by Hitler for extermination—the children of Polish Jews.

Foreword
Jan Karski

YOUR LIFE IS WORTH MINE constitutes a central part of Dr. Ewa Kurek's doctoral dissertation thus meeting academic requirements as to research, documentation and objectivity. It deals with the Polish nuns who tried or actually did save Jewish children from the Holocaust during World War II. There is no partisanship or propaganda in it. Furthermore, the book will help the reader to understand the nature and uniqueness of the Holocaust.

Destruction of the Jews was a unique phenomenon of World War II. As Elie Wiesel said: "All nations under Nazi domination were victims, but all Jews were victims."

The Jews were totally helpless. They had no country of their own, no government, no representation in the Inter-Allied war councils. They were abandoned by governments, by church hierarchies, by societal structures.

They were not abandoned by all humanity, though. Thousands upon thousands of individuals in Poland, Greece, Holland, Belgium, France, and Denmark, guided by our Lord's Commandment "love thy neighbor", tried to help although it was always difficult and dangerous. In Nazi-dominated Poland any attempt to help a Jew was punishable by death.

The story of Polish nuns saving Jewish children will fascinate the reader. Danger and defiance, fear and resoluteness; love and indifference; greed and self-sacrifice—all of them intermingle in a variety of anecdotes, testimonies, and archival documents. All of them make the book unfailingly interesting and important.

CONVENTS WHICH SAVED JEWISH CHILDREN IN WORLD WAR II

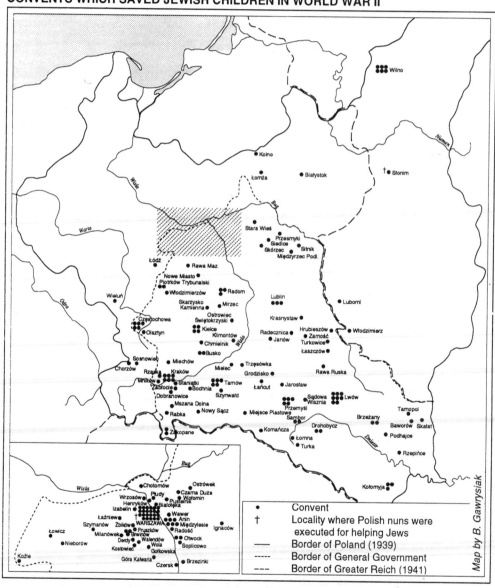

Map by B. Gawrysiak

Legend:

- •   Convent
- †   Locality where Polish nuns were executed for helping Jews
- ——   Border of Poland (1939)
- - - -   Border of General Government
- – – –   Border of Greater Reich (1941)

INTRODUCTION

THE SUBJECT OF SAVING JEWISH CHILDREN in convents in Nazi-occupied Poland during the Second World War has so far not been historically examined. Neither Polish nor Jewish historians have dealt with this issue. There are two reasons for this. Firstly, the history of the world is a history of adults. Historians have rarely noticed that what has happened in the social, political and cultural spheres down through the ages has also affected children. Secondly, a lack of documentation on the subject has hindered research. Polish nuns were threatened with the death penalty for harboring Jewish children. Death also hung over the heads of the children themselves. That is why the actions of saving them had to occur in deep secrecy, and why we must rely on the memories of the individuals involved.

I began the historical research which became the basis for the following book in the early 1980s by trying to determine how many active and contemplative woman's religious orders operated in Poland during the Second World War. Supplied by the Polish Episcopate Office with a list of contemporary convents and orders, I traveled from convent to convent, asking nuns about the history of their sisterhood. I asked them if their orders existed in Poland during World War II, and if so, had they hidden Jewish children. Besides this, I made contact with people who, as children, had been saved by the nuns, and who were now living in Israel, the United States, Poland and many other countries around the world. The accounts of both nuns and the saved Jews were recorded or videotaped. The results of my research, along with the more interesting narratives of the individuals involved on both sides of the rescue action of saving Jewish children, are presented in this book. I've also included a brief glossary of important terms necessary to a full understanding of the text.

To understand the basis of the Polish nuns' attitude toward the Jewish children sentenced to death by Hitler, one has to delve into the roots of Polish Catholicism and examine the special place held by a child in Christian doctrine.

By the end of the 13th century, Church teachings in Poland had begun to focus attention on the role of society and family in regard to children. Here two models played the most important roles: the Madonna and Child, symbolizing the absolute love of a mother for her child, and the Massacre of the Innocents, well-known from the Bible, which morally prohibited the use of force against children. Both of these models served as a basis for the Polish Catholic ethos of a child, whose chief quality is innocence.[1]

The tradition of nuns caring for children dates from the 13th century in Poland when the Bishop of Cracow, Iwo Odrowaz, brought to Poland in 1220 the Order of the Holy Spirit de Saxia, founded by Gwidon of Montpelier in 1198. A good deal of the activities of the order, both of the priests and nuns, revolved around the care of children. Article 50 of the rules clearly states: "Orphans abandoned at any time of the day are to be accepted and provided for according to the capabilities of the monastery."

Since the Middle Ages, there was a special place designated before the convent gate where a child could be deposited. A small bell would be rung informing the nuns to take the child. The nuns were not even allowed to look at the person leaving the child behind.[2]

The Polish Republic had been home to children of different nationalities: Polish, Lithuanian, White Russian, Ukrainian, Jewish, Gypsy and German. This fact, coupled with the Catholic attribute of the innocence of a child and the centuries-old convent tradition of saving children regardless of their nationality and religious beliefs, played a major factor in saving children in Poland during the Second World War. The children of all the above-mentioned nationalities needed help at some phase during the war. All found care and assistance in Polish convents. Because, according to the Polish ethos of the child, which had its roots in Catholicism, children were not responsible for the real or imagined sins of their nation, family or social group. In this sense, the fault of the Lithuanians for collaborating with the Germans was not carried over to Lithuanian children; the fault of the Ukrainians for murdering Polish families in Volhynia was not born by Ukrainian children; the fault of Germans for the hell of occupied Poland did not extend to German children; the "fault" of Gypsies, who were stereotyped in Poland as thieves, did not touch Gypsy children; the "fault" of Jews for crucifying Jesus, which Christianity had proclaimed for ages, was not shared by Jewish children. During the Second World War all these children stood at the convent gate equally innocent, defenseless and unhappy, equally needing the love and care of the convent nuns. According to the German law in effect in Poland during the years 1941-45, the nuns risked death for saving Jewish and Gypsy children. But this death threat also had a place in the ideals of convent life, for as Jesus Christ said: "Greater love has no man than this, that a man lay down his life for his fellow man." (John 15:13.)

CHAPTER I

THE TIME OF THE HOLOCAUST

WHEN WORLD WAR II BROKE OUT, Poland was the biggest Jewish center in Europe and one of the largest in the world. According to the last census taken before the war (1931), about 3.3 million Jews lived there, of which 85% gave the Hebrew or Yiddish language as their mother tongue. Jews constituted about 10% of the inhabitants of the Polish territories and more than 36% of the population of Polish towns. About 80% of Jews working in non-agricultural jobs had their own businesses or worked in other Jewish ones.

The above statistics say much about Polish Jews. Perhaps most striking is the high percentage of those who named Hebrew or Yiddish as their mother tongue. In no other European country in the first decades of the 20th century do we find similar statistics. West European Jews were very quickly assimilated because of their small number and their dispersion throughout the countries where they lived. They accepted the language and culture of the given country. They melted into the societies at large through their family connections, and social and occupational bonds.

Polish Jews, however, having lived in diaspora for ages, had created their own system of national survival. One of the most important elements of this system, applied with great success, was a conscious isolation. Jewish ghettos existed in Poland long before the German occupation, and it was not Poles who created these ghettos but the Jews themselves. Jewish memoirs and literature, as well as Polish memoirs and literature, reveal the life of the cities, towns and villages in pre-war Poland. Most of them contained quarters in which only the Jewish language was spoken. One could be born a Jew, finish school and spend one's whole adult life not knowing the Polish language and not feeling any necessity to learn it. That is why a great majority of Polish Jews spoke Polish only as far as their professional needs were concerned. It had been so for centuries, and it was so on the eve of World War II. For Polish Jews, their great number centered in urban communities, their own language, religion, clothes, customs, traditions and independent professional life constituted a culturally closed circle. Although the assimilation process existed in the years 1918-1939, it affected only a small fraction of Jewish society.

"In Warsaw," writes historian Wladyslaw Bartoszewski, "there were several thousand Jews who practiced professions in which they intermingled with Polish society—lawyers, doctors, engineers, journalists, writers, actors. On the other hand, there were more than 300,000 who worked in jobs which restricted them to their own ethnic group. Most of these Jews lived exclusively in their own circle, in a sort of a ghetto. In this area no Jew would ever rent a room to a baptized man, no matter if he was a Pole, a German or a Czech. It was impossible on principle. For pious Jews it is a sin to have someone not of their faith in their midst, in their community. A home is a community, and someone of another faith should not have access to it. The Jews built their own ghettos through this type of isolation."[1]

Excluding the polonized Jews who became strongly rooted in Polish society, as well as the small fraction of Poles of Jewish origin or those who had somehow acquired a knowledge of Polish Jewry, the two communities had little contact. Through the centuries of their co-existence in Poland a majority of Poles' knowledge of Jews boiled down to common stereotypes and rumors: Jews walked around in gaberdines, smelled of garlic, had a talent for business and an aversion to fighting, did not eat pork and needed Christian blood to make a matzoh. Jews had an equally simple-minded view of Poles. Separated by the great barrier of language, Jews and Poles formed their opinions of each other based on external observation and rumors, rather than on true acquaintanceship and knowledge. The above state of affairs was probably one of the main reasons why in the complicated historical conditions of the 19th and the first decades of the 20th century deep resentments and prejudices were growing, which resulted in the periodic increases in hostilities typical of Polish-Jewish relations until the outbreak of World War II.

Both nations, however, could have gone on living together in Poland, despite their anti-Semitism and anti-Polonism, and despite the conscious isolationism and antagonism, if Germany had not invaded Poland on September 1, 1939.

The outcome of this attack was a tragic one for Poland. Taking advantage of the German onslaught, the USSR invaded Poland from the east on September 17, and Poland's eastern territories found themselves under Soviet occupation. A Soviet-German border in Poland was fixed by the two occupants on September 28, 1939. That section of Poland under German occupation was divided into two parts. The west and northeast areas were incorporated into the Reich, and the so-called General Government was formed from the remaining territories of central Poland, an area covering 96,000 km and divided into four districts: Warsaw, Radom, Cracow and Lublin. After the outbreak of the German-Soviet war in June 1941, when Nazi troops added the territories situated far in the east to their possession, the area of the General Government grew to 145,000 km: the former Lwow, Stanislawow, and Tarnopol districts were renamed by the Germans "the Galicia district," and were included as the fifth unit in the General Government.

The Second World War began like any other war. While it was not the first war, either for Polish Jews or for Poles, no one could anticipate that it would bring holocaust to the former and great losses to the latter. They fought together in the Polish Army, they suffered together misfortunes caused by military operations and the occupier's first repressions, and thus subdued their mutual antagonisms while encouraging a united front against the Germans. This did not last long, however, and of the numerous reasons for a rather prompt return to the attitude of hostility, two seemed to have played the most important role. The first one was the Jewish communists' pro-Soviet attitude toward the occupation of the territories of eastern Poland;[2] and the other was the old "divide and conquer" strategy used quite successfully by the Germans.

In the first years of the occupation Poles were the ones whose lives were more endangered: the ratio of murdered Poles to murdered Jews was 10:1 in the years 1939-1941.[3] This led to instances of Poles putting on arm-bands with the star of David when in danger and imitating Jewish speech to avoid arrest during a round-up.[4] At this time only economic pressure was put on Jews, and so some people believed that, in the future, political pressure would be put on Poles and economic pressure on Polish Jews. Time was to show how incorrect this assumption—common in both the nations—was.

The Nazis had already conceived a policy toward the population they considered Jewish as early as September 21, 1939, during a conference in Berlin. Soon after, Reinhard Heydrich, the chief of the SD (Sicherheits Dienst), sent instructions to the commanders of the operational groups in Poland. Here are some fragments:

> In reference to today's conference in Berlin, I once again draw your attention to the fact that the jointly planned actions (in other words, the final solution) must be kept strictly a secret. You should differentiate the final solution (which will take a longer time) from the stages leading to that final solution (which will be realized in short periods of time). [...] The first foundation leading to the final solution is concentrating Jews from the provinces in bigger towns.... In each Jewish community a Jewish Council of the Seniors should be established.... The Council should be charged with all the responsibility, in the full sense of the word, for the precise and punctual execution of all orders....[5]

But neither Jews nor Poles had any idea of the aims of the German policies, either at the beginning of the occupation or for a long time afterward. On November 24, 1939 the Germans ordered Jews to wear the Star of David; later, their shops were marked in the same way. Other orders followed which blocked Jewish bank accounts, dismissed Jews from employment, restricted their right to travel and finally cut them off from the outside world within the walls of the ghetto. The first ghetto in the General Government, established already in October 1939, was the one in Piotrkow Trybunalski. The greatest centers of Jewish population were closed much later: in Warsaw in November 1940, and in Cracow only in March 1941. Like the previous orders, the order to move to the ghettos applied to all people who had three grandparents belonging to the Jewish community, no matter what religion they confessed. So the persecutions also affected those persons who did not call themselves Jewish and were not considered Jewish by Poles. The walls which surrounded ghettos in the first months or even in the first year of the occupation did not mean a complete seclusion, and contact with the outside world was not forbidden. The situation changed dramatically when on October 15, 1941, Governor General Hans Frank issued a decree which stated that there would be a death penalty for those Jews who left the ghetto and the same punishment for people giving them aid. The decree read:

> 1. Jews who without authorization leave the quarter appointed for them are liable to death penalty. Persons who knowingly give shelter to such Jews are liable to the same penalty.
> 2. Instigators and accomplices are liable to the same punishment as the perpetrator; an attempt at a deed will be punished in the same way as an executed deed. Less serious cases may be punished with close confinement or confinement.
> 3. Sentences will be passed by special courts.[6]

By confining the Jewish population within ghettos the Germans reached the most important stage of their plan to achieve the "final solution." The establishment of closed quarters involved numerous resettlements of people from smaller places to bigger towns, or within the same town. In each case great masses of people were deprived of their material possessions and forced to live in unbelievably meager conditions and at the mercy of the occupying Nazis. The poor of the Jewish nation lived in especially deplorable conditions. Their number exceeded by far the number of those who could afford to live in relative luxury owing to their wealth. Opinions on the enclosure of the Jewish population in the ghettos were varied in Jewish circles, both in Poland and abroad, and they ranged from most catastrophic visions to forecasts in every respect optimistic. Optimism was certainly characteristic of those who did not have to move into the quarters assigned for Jews. Some even thought that the ghettos had their good side too, for their administration rested in Jewish hands.[7] Among the inhabitants of the ghetto ambivalent emotions prevailed—on the one hand, a fear of being confined, and on the other, a note of satisfaction with a little pride that they had their own police, streetcars or other impressive signs of the Jewish self-government.

The law enforcement of this self-government came under the province of the Judenrats.[8] The issue of the Judenrats is an exceptionally difficult and complex one even today. The contemporary writers and poets of the ghettos evaluated the work of Judenrats very critically.

Emanuel Ringelblum wrote in January, 1942:

> All the work of the Community [Judenrats—E.K.] is one great harm done to the poor, and cries out for vengeance. If there were

a God in the world, He would destroy this seat of evil, hypocrisy and exorbitance with lightning bolts.[9]

But it is not just a question of the Judenrats. They were established by Jews who were representatives of Jewish society, and Jews worked in them. Perhaps one must consider human nature in evaluting the character that the Jewish self-government assumed. It is difficult to imagine conditions more inhuman than those created by the Germans for Jews, and not only in the sphere of material goods. Jewish society did not differ much in its structure from other societies. The war and the conditions in the ghetto created circumstances in which, among the vast majority of ordinary people, arose great heroic and just figures, as well as the most wicked types of exploiters and traitors. These contrasts could be seen on the ghetto streets where beside begging children and corpses covered with newspapers walked well-fed and elegant people, where cold, poverty-ridden homes bordered the wealth and joy of elegant apartments and restaurants. Corruption and treason existed side by side with honesty and faithfulness to human ideals; extreme poverty and wealth were neighbors. But these things had existed side by side in the world from the dawn of history. The situation in the ghettos just made it all the more conspicuous.

And the worst was coming swiftly. At the end of 1941 and in the first months of 1942 news was being received of mass executions of Jews in the east: in the districts of Bialystok, Wilno, Nowogrodek, Lwow and Tarnopol, and in Polesie and Volhynia—territories seized by Germany in the war with the USSR—as well as the start in December 1941 of the extermination camp in Chelmno on the Ner, where men, women and children from the small towns of Wartheland and from the Lodz ghetto were being killed. This news was brought by the Jewish clandestine press and the Polish underground press.[10] However, the Jewish general public did not want to believe it. One of the youth activists of the Bund in the Warsaw ghetto, Marek Edelman, wrote in 1945: "The Warsaw ghetto did not believe the news. All those people who clung onto life could not believe that this life of theirs could be taken from them in such a way."[11]

The decision to initiate the "final solution" toward the Jews—that is, to exterminate them—was made during a conference in the Chief Office of Reich's Safety in Berlin in 1942. One of the participants, the representative of the Nazi government of the General Government, Buchler, stated:

> The General Government would be glad if the solution of this problem was begun there, as the problem of transport is not complicated and the question of employment would not hinder the action. [...] My only request is that the Jewish question be solved in that territory as soon as possible.[12]

In the spring and summer of 1942 the Germans started a systematic extermination of Jews, giving it the cryptonym "Action Reinhard." From many towns and villages of the General Government, as well as from Ostland (the Wilno, Nowogrodek and Polesie districts), freight-cars full of people set off under the pretext of displacement. They went to the extermination camps in Belzec, Sobibor, Treblinka, Majdanek and Oswiecim (Auschwitz). On July 22, 1942 the Germans began liquidating the Warsaw ghetto, the biggest in Poland. Special troops of the SS and the German police commanded by SS-Sturmbannfuhrer Herman Hoefe, and aided by Ukrainian, Lithuanian and Latvian collaborator units, as well as by the ghetto police—the Jewish Disciplinary Service—sent to the gas chambers in Treblinka, or murdered on the spot, 310,000 inhabitants of the Jewish quarter in Warsaw. This action went on until October 3, 1942. A group of Jewish activists—Zionists and communists, members of the Bund— aware of the exterminations, considered the chances of resisting the German action.

"Unfortunately, the entirety of public opinion was against us," Marek Edelman reported after the war. "All the members of the community thought such a move provocative and argued that if the Jews would quietly provide the wanted contingent, the rest of the people in the ghetto would not be affected. The instinct of self-preservation gradually directed people's psyche to ways of saving their own skins even at the cost of other people's lives. Indeed, few of them believed that displacement meant death. But the Germans had already managed to divide the Jewish population into two groups—those doomed to death and those hoping to survive. And slowly, with time, the Germans played one group off against the other, and as a result Jews led other Jews to death so that they could save their own lives."[13]

In this latter group one has to include, above all, Jewish policemen, about whom Emanuel Ringelblum wrote:

The Jewish police had a very bad reputation even before the evacuations. Unlike the Polish police, who did not take part in the round-ups from which people were sent to labor camps, the Jewish police were involved in this hideous job. They distinguished themselves by terrible corruption and lack of morals. However, they truly reached their nadir during the evacuations. They did not raise one word in protest against their horrible role of leading their own brothers to death. The police were psychologically prepared to do that dirty job, and they did it eagerly. Nowadays one tries hard to figure it all out: How did it happen that Jews (...) lent their hand to the extermination of their brothers? How was it possible that Jews dragged women and children, the old and the sick, onto wagons, knowing that all these people were going to their deaths?[14]

The first Jewish secret associations were already established in Warsaw by the beginning of 1940. Several days after the Germans had begun the massive extermination action in the Warsaw ghetto, the Zionist Combat Organization was born; and at the end of October the Jewish National Committee was established, uniting almost the entire Jewish underground, both Zionist and socialist, except the Bund. Later, at the end of November 1942, as a result of agreements between the various clandestine groups, the Coordinating Commission of the Jewish National Committee and the Bund was created, becoming at that point the sole representative of the entire Jewish underground. On December 2, 1942 the Jewish Combat Organization (ZOB) was established, consisting mainly of Halatz and Zionist groups (which contributed to the organization of the July Combat Organization), as well as groups from the Bund and from the Bund youth organization: the Cukunft and the military groups of the Polish Workers' Party, the People's Guard. The commander of this organization was Mordechaj Anielewicz of Haszomer-Hacair; and its officers were Hersz Berlinski of Poalej Syjon-Left, Marek Edelman of the Bund, Icchak Cukierman of Hechaluc, and Michal Rojzenfeld of the Polish Workers' Party.

The attitude of the ZOB was clearly expressed by Arie Wilner, the liaison to the Polish side, when he said to Henryk Wolinski in their first conversation: "We do not want to save our lives. None of us will survive. We want to save our human dignity."[15]

The Jewish Self-Defense Organization in the Bialystok ghetto, which came into being through a union of Haszomer-Hacair, Dror, the Bund and the communists, held a similar view. Part of its proclamation read: "Besides our honor we have nothing to lose! Let the enemy pay a high price for our lives!"[16]

The Warsaw ghetto was preparing for the fight which it was to take up soon. On the morning of January 13, 1943, Colonel Ferdinand von Sammern-Frankenegg's police troops marched into the ghetto.

> Meeting resistance, the German police responded with shots and grenades, killing several hundred people; they were afraid, however, of entering the defended buildings. That is why on Monday and Tuesday only about 5,000 people were evacuated, even though the wagons had space for twice that number. The organized points of resistance were carrying on a defense throughout Monday and Tuesday. They only withdrew on Wednesday after two SS companies entered the ghetto with machine guns, howitzers and ambulances, ready for action. Then began a massacre of the inhabitants, who, inspired by the incidents of the previous days, offered a strong resistance using the most primitive weapons like poles, crow-bars and stones.[17]

The January resistance in the Warsaw ghetto was not able to protect 6,500 people from being transported. Nevertheless, further actions of "displacement" were halted. The moral breakthrough which came about in the Warsaw ghetto inhabitants at the sight of retreating Germans was more important than any actual military success; people now confidently started joining combat organizations.

Two months later, on April 19, 1943, at six o'clock in the morning, 16 officers and 850 Waffen SS soldiers marched into the Warsaw ghetto in order to finally liquidate it. The Jews received them with shots. Only on May 15, 1943 could SS General Jurgen Stroop, who was commanding the liquidation of the ghetto, inform General Kruger in Cracow:

> The Jewish quarter in Warsaw no longer exists. The great operation was completed at 20.15 by blowing up the Warsaw synagogue. [...] The total number of Jews captured and those whose death can be ascertained is 56,065.[18]

Ashes were all that was left of the Warsaw ghetto. Under the ruins of the Warsaw synagogue lay the nation and the culture of the Polish Jews.

* * *

At the outbreak of the Second World War, nearly a million out of the 3.5 million Polish Jews were children. During the first few months of the occupation Jewish children suffered in the same way as all the children of conquered Poland. They were killed under the ruins of falling houses, or they buried their parents there; they were killed in the roads crowded with refugees or waited in vain for their dead mothers to awaken. They froze in railway cars transporting them from Greater Poland to the General Government. For the first time they learned the taste of hunger and all the horrors of war. On December 1, 1939, the Star of David bands, the wearing of which had been ordered by Governor General Hans Frank, was made obligatory for children over ten. For the younger children the bands on the sleeves of their parents, elder brothers and sisters, and relatives would function as identification. They would serve as a symbol of the common Jewish fate prepared for the Jewish nation by Hitler in the name of racial purity.[19]

Behind the ghetto walls were many cold and hungry Jewish children. Their parents did not have anything with which to buy bread or coal—that is, if their parents were still alive. The Jewish Social Welfare Department was only able to feed and warm a few of them. Crying, dirty and dressed in rags, Jewish children were dying in the streets.

Only rarely was a cry from a child dying of hunger heard and noted down:

> Freezing children are the most terrible thing; children with bare feet, naked knees, in ragged clothes, who stand silent and weep. Today, on November 14 [1941—E.K.] in the evening, I heard the crying of a three or four-year-old child. In the morning his frozen corpse will probably be found.[20]

With the transports to Chelmno, Belzec, Sobibor and Treblinka, Jewish children were again leading the way in this terrible procession. In the haggling over who would have the right of survival they lost again—there was no hope for them. They were the first to fill the freight-cars. The children from the orphanages in Dzika Street in Warsaw and from Janusz Korczak's orphanage, the children given away by Rumkowski in Lodz and those caught by the Jewish police, were the easiest addition to the daily "head count." Jewish children were sentenced to death, irrespective of their age and without exception. They were the roots from which the Jewish nation could be reborn in the future. They were small and helpless, and it was easiest to put them to death. They were too little to work for the Third Reich, so they did not even have the right to a temporary "permit" to live.

The fate of Jewish children in Nazi-occupied Poland cannot be compared with the fate of children of any other nation conquered by the Germans.

CHAPTER II

ATTITUDES TOWARD THE TRAGEDY

THE PRACTICE OF SAVING JEWS in Poland during World War II is extremely difficult to analyze. The difficulty lies primarily in the lack of reliable sources and, as time passes, an ever smaller hope for a full reconstruction of the facts. We do not have accurate figures on the number of people who were rescued, nor the number of people who were the rescuers. Similarly, we do not know in how many cases the attempts to save Jews ended tragically both for the Jews and the Poles involved. Estimates of the number of Jews saved by Poles in Poland range from 40-50,000 (Philip Friedman) to 100-200,000 (Joseph Kermisz),[1] and any discussion on which of these numbers is more accurate has no support in sufficient source data.

In considering the saving of Jews by Poles, one must surely not overlook the psychological, social and religious complexities, as well as the political conditions, that shaped the attitudes of the Polish and Jewish nations toward the Nazi occupation.

A handful of the Warsaw ghetto insurgents did not want to save their lives, but rather wanted to die with what they understood as dignity (that is, to die fighting) and overcome the Jews' passiveness toward the death being inflicted on them. The ideals that were the guiding principles for the Warsaw ghetto insurgents prove without a doubt that in Jewish society passiveness was the dominating attitude towards the Nazi occupation. Only a small number rose up in arms. The question must then be asked, what were the reasons for this passive attitude? There are several possible answers.

27

Through the ages of diaspora, in almost every country in which they lived, Jews were subjected to and suffered repressions of varying severity. Gradually, from generation to generation, they became accustomed to inevitable persecutions, and survival became the most important goal—survival of the whole, and if this was not possible, then of at least a part of the Jewish nation. What befell them, however, from the hands of Nazi Germany was beyond the limits of human imagination. They could imagine waves of pogroms, war, death, hunger—but not gas chambers. They could not comprehend that a death sentence had been passed on a whole nation.

Such a seeming impossibility must have influenced the attitude of Polish Jews. Did it paralyze them? Did it fan the hope in each person, in smaller or bigger groups, that it would be just they who would survive? Did it make passiveness a mode for survival? Likewise significant was the language used by the Germans in relation to Jews. They concealed the operation of the planned murder of millions of people under the term "displacement." This word has a different meaning for us today when we know what happened to the Jews, but it had another meaning for Jews during World War II, and was preceded by a whole series of genuine displacements: from hamlet to village, from village to town, from one street to another. During each of these displacements people experienced a shock, and then, amid greater poverty and hunger, they had to organize their lives and wait for the end of the war. If we add to this the collective experience of the Jewish nation through the generations—Jews were time and again displaced or thrown out of different countries—the passive attitude of Jews toward "displacement" will be understandable. For most of them this word meant exactly that and nothing more.

Moreover, the Jews were a special nation, a nation which for ages had been deprived of its own land and state. They had persisted among strangers, and in order to survive they had worked out their own system of political neutrality. It is hard to imagine that any ethnic group, living in dispersion, could survive while waging wars or getting involved in the local conflicts in the countries where they lived.

Then there was the issue of the Jewish religion. For Jews their religion is the fundamental link and norm of social life. From the most ancient times the Jews lived according to the 613 commandments issuing from the Old Testament. Three of these are special commandments, and a pious Jew would rather die than violate any of them. They concern: 1) idolatry, 2) indecency, adultery, lechery, 3) murder. A Jew who would rather suffer death than break one of these commandments attains *Kiddush ha-Shem* (sanctification, purification of God's name) or, in other words, the gates of Paradise. However, if he does not fulfill the duty to sacrifice himself rather than violate a special commandment, he is guilty of *Hillul ha-Shem* (defamation of God's name). Since the 2nd century, when the Council of Rabbis formulated the law of martyrdom, dying for the sanctification of God's name has been considered a martyr's death. Since that time the notion of martyrdom as the ideal model of behavior was inculcated in Jewish children from their earliest days. *Kiddush ha-Shem*, despite the discussions carried on for centuries, was a living commandment, and it was also obligatory for the Polish Jews during the Second World War. There was also a tradition, ensuing from *Kiddush ha-Shem*, of making a sacrifice of the lives of some Jews in order to save the rest of the Jewish community.[2]

It certainly can be disputed to what degree *Kiddush ha-Shem* was the motivation for the passive attitude of Jews, just as the piousness of Polish Jews can be disputed. However, it seems likely that the idea of martyrdom contained in *Kiddush ha-Shem* was one of the more important explanations of the Jewish attitude during World War II.[3]

Jewish insurgents made an attempt to overcome this passive attitude and unite Jews to fight against the Germans by calling upon the example set by Bar Kochba and ancient Jewish history. Unfortunately, a tradition of passiveness, difficult to overcome, had already blurred that history, and it was difficult to organize the Jewish defense. To take an active role towards the Nazi occupation meant overcoming the psychological and social predispositions to passiveness that had been shaped a long time ago.

It would be a fundamental mistake, however, to say that only armed Jewish insurgents took an "active" stance towards the Germans. Because of the character of the German occupation and the way the war was waged, all people who in any way resisted German plans should be included among those who took an active position. I have in mind mainly those who left the ghettos and sought refuge on the so-called "Aryan side." By seeking rescue in

the outside world, a Jew challenged German orders by refusing to
be a mere passive victim.

*   *   *

What was the attitude of the Polish people toward the task of
saving Jews? This is an extremely complex question arousing strong
public feelings on both sides. The most frequent complaint leveled
against the Poles was that among them there were *szmalcowniks*
(people who threatened to denounce a Jew if he did not pay a
ransom). Unfortunately, these ordinary collaborators and criminals
are identified with the entire Polish society, even though this same
society sentenced these collaborators to death at underground
courts of justice. Wladyslaw Bartoszewski writes:

> At the same time that we were saving Jews, we were trying to
> prosecute Polish and Jewish collaborators who blackmailed the
> families hiding Jews and the Jews themselves. In some cases our
> colleagues working in the appropriate sections of the underground
> had to pass death sentences. They had to execute them. There was
> no other way out: those blackmailers were a deadly threat in that
> situation—both for Jews and for Poles.

Denunciations caused a lot of tragedies. But this has nothing to
do with Poles or Jews. This has to do with human nature. If today
one wants to talk about peace between the two groups, one must
also consider this fundamental fact. One must think about man and
the evil that marks its stamp on him.[4]

The Polish nation was not able to save the Polish Jews from the
holocaust. During World War II about three million Polish Jews and
three million Poles were killed.[5] The Polish nation had no political
or military power to save the lives of either Jews or Poles. In a
situation of terror and constant threat to their own lives, Poles could
only struggle for the lives of individual Jews, and the whole
question of rescuing—considering the above-mentioned military
and political impossibilities—was reduced to the moral plane of the
duty of one man toward another.

Polish society certainly faced an exceedingly difficult situation in
the autumn of 1941. Persecuted itself, with a deeply-rooted
anti-Semitism fanned by the news about the reaction of Jewish
communists to the Soviet occupation of the eastern territories of
Poland and with a complete lack of understanding of the attitude
of Jews toward the Nazis, it had to cope with the human urge and

Christian duty to save the lives of those who were even more endangered. Was the society as a whole equal to the task?

On October 15, 1941 Hans Frank issued the decree which stated that Jews escaping from the ghettos were to be punished with death along with the Poles hiding them. Poland became the only country in occupied Europe in which one risked his own life and the lives of his loved ones when saving the life of a Jew.[6] Despite this, Jews found refuge in Polish homes. Here are the instructions sent to the commander of the SS and police in the Radom in September, 1942:

> This concerns Poles who harbor fugitive Jews. The experiences of recent weeks have shown that it was precisely from the small Jewish residential quarters that Jews escaped to avoid evacuation. Those Jews must have been received by Poles.[7]

As a result of this report, hand bills were posted in the district which read:

> Announcement. It has been found repeatedly that fugitive Jews are hiding in Polish homes. In reference to the 3rd order of October 15, 1941 (...) I instruct those concerned that whoever gives shelter or food to fugitive Jews, or sells them food, will be punished by death. This instruction is final. Ostrowiec, September 28, 1942, Town Commissioner.[8]

Similar announcements appeared in all the districts of the General Government. In the entire country punishment by death threatened any Pole who hid a Jew.

The introduction of the death penalty and applying it to all those who helped Jews worsened an already psychologically difficult situation, both for those rescuing and those being rescued. In order to save a Jew, one had to overcome the fear for one's own life and for the lives of one's loved ones, while to agree to being saved meant reconciling oneself to the thought that someone is risking their life for one's own. No one can describe the thousands of inner struggles that the hemmed-in Jews and Poles must have gone through, or to count how many Poles managed to overcome their fear and reach out to help a Jew in a variety of ways, from offering a plate of soup to hiding him, or how many Poles refused assistance to any Jew. No one knows how many Poles paid with their lives for helping Jews, and finally, how many Jews refused to be saved only because they did not want to endanger the lives of others.

Another difficulty was the great number of Polish Jews. Nearly one out of ten Polish citizens was a Jew. How could this great mass of people, who mostly did not speak Polish, be absorbed? Poles did not speak the language of the Polish Jews, and to undertake common actions in order to save the more endangered Jewish nation, it was first necessary to have a means of communication in order to establish mutual contacts. Communication was only possible with those Jews who were polonized and spoke Polish. Wladyslaw Bartoszewski writes:

> In the case of most Polish citizens of Jewish nationality the slight degree of their nationalization, a glaring dissimilarity of customs, and at times an inadequate knowledge of Polish language and society created serious difficulties in trying to save them.[9]

Ringelblum adds:

> There were Jews with a first rate Aryan appearance who did not speak Polish well or who had a noticeable accent, people who could not even pronounce their Aryan name correctly.[10]

It is worth mentioning several equally fundamental issues in regard to saving Jews in Poland. Until the Second World War the imagination of the Polish people did not go so far as gas chambers—Poles were as unaware of the planned extermination of Jews as the Jews themselves. For some Poles, saving Jews took second place to working for the underground. The necessity of fighting for one's country was more clearly understood; young men had been brought up with this ideal from childhood. This group sympathized with Jews, and if they faced an individual Jew, they often helped; but they saved their energy for fighting Germans. Furthermore, the necessity of fighting for Jewish lives was a new experience for Poles, and there was little or no time to educate the Polish populace toward such an effort on a general scale and particularly for a people who were, for the most part, strangers to them in terms of culture and language. Therefore, Poles primarily risked their lives to save Jews on an individual basis. For this they had to have a sympathetic understanding of the misfortune of another man—and courage.[11] And a lot of courage was necessary. Not for a single action, like secreting a briefcase of underground publications for a while, but for an action that would necessitate persistent courage from the day of admitting a Jew until the last day of the war.

For Poles to fight the Germans in the ranks of the underground army, in clandestine activities or in partisan squads, was a sort of ennoblement. It was dangerous. If someone was caught by the Germans, he could be sentenced to death. Yet there was always a chance of survival. One could be taken to prison or a concentration camp, and, once there, escape or survive. But if a Pole was caught helping a Jew, death was certain.

Moreover, in the mentality of the average Pole the Jews' passiveness toward their German murderers was simply inconceivable. Why do they not run away? Why do they not defend themselves? These questions pervaded the whole of Polish society in occupied Poland. Poles whose knowledge of Jews was limited to general stereotypes could not understand the Jewish attitude. And generally it is easier to help those who defend themselves, who fight, who run away.

The particular political reality of occupied Poland, the terror and fear that accompanied the rescue of Jews, was the basic reason why only those Jews who took an active attitude, in the broadest sense of the word, toward the Nazi invaders had a chance of survival—that is, those Jews who resisted by fighting or running away or seeking help. Certainly, the better one's knowledge of the Polish language and the greater the number of Polish acquaintances one had, the greater the chances of hiding and of survival. The active attitude of Jews was a fundamental condition for their survival.

There is no doubt that Polish Jews had the hope and the strong will to live. But there is another problem here. One which is difficult and which requires separate study: why so few Polish Jews placed their hopes for salvation in Polish society. Surely, the above-mentioned awareness that someone would have to risk his life was a factor. Surely, the traditionally bad opinion of Poles, fanned by stories told in the ghetto (some true, others false) was of consequence. But of greatest consequence was the isolation of Jews from the rest of Polish society, an isolation that could only increase the fear of Jews about leaving their own communities.

*   *   *

According to the estimates of the Remembrance Institute of Yad Vashem in Jerusalem, of the nearly one million Jewish children in Poland, only five thousand survived the Holocaust. Even if these estimates are incorrect, it is certain that tragically few were saved, both in absolute numbers and when compared to the number of adult Jews who survived in Poland. Saving Jews in Poland was a very difficult thing, but the scale of difficulty grew immeasurably in the case of Jewish children. To all the usual difficulties which adults had, a fundamental one was added: the decision that Jewish parents had to make to part with their child. It took a lot of strength to give one's own child a chance of survival by making such a decision. Of course not everybody was able to make such a decision, just as many parents would not be able to make that decision under any circumstances. This is why Jewish parents and their children often died together.

There is no doubt that Jewish children, whether they were aware of the realities around them, had an enormous amount of will to live. But they were too young to determine their fate. The world of adults and the laws that ruled it decided if Jewish children were to be saved.

The attitudes of Jewish adults to the question of saving children is a complex problem—perhaps the most difficult one.

In the summer of 1942, when Hitler's plans for the Jewish nation became obvious and the worst forebodings among Jews became a real threat, discussions were carried on in many Jewish circles, as well as in Warsaw circles, on the subject of saving children. Emanuel Ringelblum wrote of one such discussion:

> The following problem was discussed: What should be done if it was possible to send somebody out to the world? Everybody agreed that at all costs the world must be informed about the extermination going on, without wondering if this would aggravate our situation, for we had nothing to lose. [...] Then the question was discussed if a list should be sent abroad of eminent persons, so that they could receive passports and leave the country and in this way save their lives. Some said that the elite should remain with the people and die with them. Others referred to examples from Jewish history and to the traditions that require saving even a single Jew. Finally it was decided that every social group should make efforts to help their eminent individuals, and not the whole nation as such....[12]

When a ship is sinking the first places in lifeboats are reserved for children. This is obvious and simple, and looking for an answer as to why this is so exceeds the scope of this book. Undoubtedly the Warsaw ghetto in the summer of 1942 can be compared to a sinking ship. And there was not much room in the "life-boats." The participants in the discussion did not reserve any space in these imaginary lifeboats for their children. They did not include them in that group which should receive from Jewish society special help and protection. Why? I cannot find an answer to this "why." Another "why," rooted deeply in the first one, arises at the moment when the need to save, above all, Jewish children was perceived by the Polish side and an offer of help was made to the Jewish society in Warsaw—a small offer when compared to how many "life-boats" were actually needed—and the representatives of that society rejected the offer. To fully understand this issue I must quote the whole of what Emanuel Ringelblum wrote on this subject in December 14, 1942:

> The priests want to save Jewish children. In certain circles the issue has been put on the agenda recently of saving a certain number of Jewish children (several hundred) by putting them in convents in all the corners of the country.
>
> What made the clergy do it? Three reasons. Firstly: hunting for souls. The Catholic clergy has always made use of hard times in the life of Jews (pogroms, deportations, etc.) for winning both adults and children. This point undoubtedly plays the most important role, although the priests assure us that they have no intention of baptizing the Jewish children they will receive in the convents. Secondly: the material factor. For each Jewish child, 600 zloty monthly will have to be paid for one year in advance. This is a rather good deal for the convents. Food is very cheap there, for they have their own fields and farms. For the poor children whose parents will not be able to cover the costs, parents of well-to-do children will pay a double sum. And thirdly: the factor of prestige. The Polish clergy has done very little as yet to save Jews from slaughter, from displacement. As the whole world is protesting the mass murders of Polish Jews, saving several hundred children will serve as a proof that in these hard times the Polish clergy did not remain inactive, that they did everything to save Jews, and especially Jewish children.
>
> I took part in a discussion in which several intellectuals talked about this problem. One of them declared categorically that he was against sending Jewish children to convents. He felt that although it had been established that children from the age of 10 to 14 would be received at the convents (according to wishes of Jews), they would still be influenced by the priests, and sooner or later they would agree to be baptized. The priests' promise that they would

not be baptized would not matter. Time and education would do their work. He thought we should follow in the footsteps of our ancestors and die in the name of our faith. We should not consent to baptizing our children. The community, as such, should not deal with such things. Let everybody decide for themselves. What meaning does saving several hundred children have in the face of the murder of over 300,000 Jews in Warsaw? Let them be killed or spared, but together with all the others.

Others said: We have to think about the future. After the extermination of the Jewish population in Europe, each Jew will be a great treasure and must be saved. After the war the clergy will not be influential; there might not be any clergy at all. If so, we needn't be afraid that the children will be under the influence of the clergy. A thorough knowledge of our history teaches us that we did not die in the name of the faith, but that, on the contrary, we accepted Christianity to save ourselves. Jews have always accustomed themselves to even the hardest conditions; they could always survive the hardest times. Taking a handful of Jewish children (to the other side) will save a new generation of Jews. We must not take the right to live away from this new generation.

It is necessary to emphasize very strongly the difference between being baptized and marrionism. The priests themselves declare that they will not baptize the children, and that the children will have to behave like Christians only because of their surroundings. It is true that there is a danger that if this lasts for a long period of time some of the children will be influenced by the clergy. But if we reject the clergy's help in saving the children, then after a certain time no one will be left; even those few that we might have saved will die.

Some participants in the discussion claimed that saving the greatest number of Jews was one of the most important tasks at the moment. We must save as many Jews as we can at all costs, and this is why we must accept the proposal for putting the children in convents.

Others maintained that this must be done, even if it was without the approval of the representatives of the Jewish society. People save themselves in various ways; let the convents' action have an individual character.[13]

Ringelblum returned to the offer made to the Jewish children again when he wrote the following:

For the sake of history it is worth mentioning the plan to put several hundred Jewish children in convents on the following conditions: children ten- years-old or older will be admitted, and the payment for one year in advance will be 8,000 zloty; the children will be card-indexed and their distribution will be recorded so that they can be taken back after the war. This plan was discussed in Jewish circles and was met with opposition both from orthodox circles and from certain national spheres. Objections were put forward saying that the children would be baptized and lost to the Jewish nation forever. It was argued that future generations would blame us for not rising to the occasion and not teaching our children Kiddush ha-Shem (martyrdom for the faith), in the name of which our ancestors died at the stakes of the Spanish Inquisition. A conference of social activists on this problem did not reach in an agreement; no resolution was passed, and this gave Jewish parents the freedom to decide about their own children.[14]

The outcome of the conference is very difficult to understand. How was it possible to miss the opportunity to find organized help for the children and just leave the decision to the parents? It was obvious, after all, that the united capabilities of Jewish organizations and an organized group of the clergy were far greater than the capabilities that average parents in the Warsaw ghetto had, particularly when one realizes that the clergy had little chance of contacting these Jewish parents directly. But this was and is the Polish way of thinking. The Jews had their own national and religious reasons, and though from an individual point of view, in this case of a real Jewish child, they might appear unjust, from the point of view of the Jewish religion and nation, they were not to be questioned.

The outcome of the conference in the Warsaw ghetto was determined by Jewish national and religious leaders, and from their point of view, the Jewish social activists did not have much choice. They could accept the proposal concerning organized help for Jewish children in Polish convents, and thereby expose them to a Polish-Catholic influence and possible denationalization; or, protecting them from these possibilities, they could send them to a certain death. They could organize help for Jewish children in convents and expose them to the sin of defamation of God's name, Hillul ha-Shem; or protecting them from that sin, they could secure for them the gates of the "Jewish Paradise" through a martyr's death. Jewish children in other ghettos in Poland were in a situation similar to that of the children in the Warsaw ghetto. There is evidence that many rabbis, when Jewish parents asked them for advice on the question if they might hide their children in a convent if they had a chance to do so, answered they might not, explaining their decision with serious religious reasons.[15]

One thing is certain: a portion of the rabbis and Jewish activists who took part in the conference, the elite of the Warsaw ghetto, subordinated the value of the lives of Jewish children to religious and national considerations. In this sense, for important groups in Jewish society saving the lives of Jewish children was not a matter of the highest importance and significance. Apart from other duties, Jewish children had a duty of *Kiddush ha-Shem*, and they were "taught" it by being sent to death, even though this was not demanded of all Jews. In the aforementioned plans of saving the Jewish elites, the obligation for some Jews to die offered no contradiction, just as it was no contradiction for the rabbis to save their own lives.

CHAPTER III

JEWISH CHILDREN IN CONVENTS

BEFORE THE OUTBREAK OF THE SECOND WORLD WAR the Roman Catholic Church in Poland comprised nearly 23 million believers out of over 35 million inhabitants. Its five Church provinces—Gniezno-Poznan, Warsaw, Cracow, Lwow and Wilno—formed 21 dioceses and archdioceses comprising 458 deaneries and 5,200 parishes, in which 10,375 diocesan priests and 1,779 monastic ones worked; over 2,000 young men were in seminaries learning to become priests. Men's orders had 6,430 monks and 350 houses; and women's convents had more than 20,000 nuns and nearly 2,300 houses.[1]

As a consequence of Nazi Germany's invasion of Poland and the occupation of her eastern territories by the Soviet Union, as well as Hitler's decrees of October 1939 incorporating Poland's western territories into the Third Reich and establishing the General Government on the remaining Polish territories, Poland had two new borders: one between the Third Reich and the General Government, and the other between the General Government and the Soviet Union. Those borders cut through the units of the territorial organization of the Catholic Church in Poland. The whole of the Gniezno and Poznan archdioceses, as well as the Chelmno, Wloclawek, Katowice and Gdansk (Danzig) dioceses, were incorporated into the Reich, and seven other archdioceses and dioceses were incorporated partially: almost all of the Plock diocese, a considerable part of the Lodz diocese, two thirds of the Czestochowa diocese, a part of the Cracow archdiocese, a small part of the Warsaw one, a part of the Lomza diocese, and a fragment of the Kielce diocese. Before the war there were about 2,000 parishes and over 4,000 priests in this territory.

Almost all of the Warsaw archdiocese, a small part of the Plock diocese, about one fifth of the Lodz diocese, all of the Sandomierz and Lublin dioceses, all of the diocese of Podlasie, whose bishop resided in Siedlce, the Cracow archdiocese (except the Chrzanow, Wadowice and Zywiec districts), the Kielce diocese (except the Olkusz district), a part of the Czestochowa diocese, a fragment of the Lomza diocese (the Ostrow Mazowiecka district)—found themselves in the General Government. Together with the territories of the Lwow archdiocese and the Przemysl diocese, incorporated into the General Government in the summer of 1941, they had about 2,000 parishes and about 4,000 priests.

The Wilno and Lwow archdioceses, the Pinsk and Luck dioceses, and parts of the Przemysl and Lomza dioceses, lay in the territories occupied by the Soviet Union. From the summer of 1941, when after the outbreak of the German-Soviet war the border was moved to the east, these territories were divided between different German administrative units. The incorporated territories included the remaining part of the Lomza diocese, a part of the Wilno archdiocese and a part of the Pinsk diocese, with more than 600 parishes and over 1000 priests. All of the Luck diocese and greater part of the Pinsk diocese were included into the Reich Commissariat of Ukraine, and the remaining part of the Pinsk diocese and a major part of the Wilno archdiocese (over 300 parishes and nearly 500 priests) into the Eastern Reich Commissariat.

The situation of the Roman Catholic Church in Poland was unique among the European countries occupied by Germany. The new borders that divided the territory of the Polish state were at the same time the borders between various attitudes both toward the subjected nation and toward the Church. The territories incorporated into the Reich were to be subjected to a complete and ruthless germanization. This is why, besides repressions aimed at the Polish and Jewish people, the Church was also subjected to particularly severe repressions.

The Catholic Church in Silesia suffered relatively the least, although here, too, from the very first months of the occupation priests who had been engaged in social and political work were arrested or expelled to the General Government. Of the 489 priests in the Katowice diocese, 140 were removed from the list of working priests as early as September 1939. In the same year the Germans closed down the Silesian Theological Seminary, and in May 1940 they introduced German as the only language permissible in services, sermons and catechization. All the Church associations were dissolved, and about sixty monasteries conducting educational work were abolished. In 1941 both the Katowice bishops, the Ordinary Stanislaw Adamski and the Suffragan Juliusz Bieniek, together with eleven other priests, were expelled to the General Government. After the bishops had been expelled the diocese was run by two German priests. Forty-six Silesian priests were killed in prisons and concentration camps for their sympathies to Poland.

The results of the German policy toward the Church in Pomerania (the Gdansk district—West Prussia) were apparent already in the first months of the war. In Gdansk ten out of the twelve Polish priests were arrested, and in the Chelmno diocese 380 priests were arrested or detained in the first few months, more than fifty percent of the total number of priests working there before the war. The arrested bishop suffragan of the diocese, Konstanty Dominik, stayed under house arrest from October 1939 and was expelled to Gdansk in January 1940. The ordinary of the Chelmno diocese, Bishop Stanislaw Okoniewski, was abroad, so the Apostolic See put the Gdansk (Danzig) bishop, Carlmaria Splett, in charge of the diocese; Splett was known for his anti-Polish policy. According to German data, in September 1939 there were 649 Catholic priests in the whole territory of District Gdansk—West Prussia. In October 1942, only 210 were left, including the priests brought from Germany. The Germans closed down the theological seminaries, dissolved all the religious associations, and abolished monasteries. Up to 1941 in Pomerania, only those nuns of the Sisters of Charity and St. Elizabeth could stay who were German or who had signed the Deutsche Volksliste. The Germans expelled the others to the General Government, put them into camps and prisons, or murdered them. The churches in Pomerania were turned into warehouses, cinemas or garages, and of the ones which still served their original purpose, all elements were removed which testified to the fact that those territories had been Polish—even tombstones with Polish inscriptions were destroyed. The use of Polish was strictly forbidden, even in confessions.[2]

The situation of the Church in the territories incorporated into East Prussia (part of the Plock and Lomza dioceses) was equally difficult. The Germans arrested and then imprisoned in the camp in Dzialdowo Archbishop Antoni Julian Nowowiejski, the ordinary of the Plock diocese; he was ultimately murdered in the camp in May or June 1941. Bishop Leon Wetmanski, the Plock suffragan cast his lot with him—he was arrested and murdered by the Germans in October 1941. In prisons and concentration camps 116 priests died, which decreased the number of priests in this diocese by about 40%. The German governor of the largest administrative unit in the Polish territories incorporated into the Third Reich—the Wartheland, with an area of 44,000 km and nearly 5 million inhabitants—was Arthur Greiser. He pursued an experimental radical policy toward the Church in his territory, a policy which the Germans intended to enforce throughout the Reich after the war. Before the war there were more than a thousand parishes in this area, while during the occupation only sixty churches fulfilled their function. Of the 1,800 or so diocesan priests who had worked in the territory which later was to become the Wartheland, only 73 were left in October 1941. Of the 389 priests in the Gniezno archdiocese the Germans imposed repressions on 261; 139 of these were murdered. In the Poznan archdiocese only 34 priests, both diocesan and monastic, survived out of about 800. Of the 432 priests in the Wloclawek diocese, 224 died in concentration camps and prisons, or were executed. Of the seven bishops in the Wartheland, two stayed abroad (the Primate of Poland and the Wloclawek ordinary); the Wloclawek suffragan, Michal Kozal, was arrested and murdered in Dachau; both the Lodz bishops were expelled to the General Government, and the suffragan of the Poznan archdiocese remained under house arrest. Vicar General Edward van Blericq, who had the capacity to act as the ordinary of the Gniezno archdiocese when the curia was closed down and he was expelled to Inowroclaw, tried to run the archdiocese from there. In the Wartheland the Germans closed down all the theological seminaries, dissolved all the social, cultural and charitable Catholic organizations and institutions, closed down all the convents, and either expelled the nuns to the General Government, imprisoned them, or placed them in the labor camp at Bojanowo. At this camp 615 nuns from 25 orders were imprisoned; eleven of them were murdered there.[3]

The fate of the Bialystok district, incorporated into the Reich in 1941, was similar. Of the priests arrested there, more than a hundred died in prisons and concentration camps, about 10% of the pre-war number. The Germans' attitude towards the Church in the General Government was influenced by their intention to use it for achieving certain political and economical aims. Among other things, they tried to use the Church for encouraging the people to pay their taxes, to go to work in Germany or to actively join anti-Communist actions. Officially, Church administration was managed in the General Government by the plenipotentiary for the Church affairs in the Hans Frank government. In actual fact, however, the local police and party authorities were not without influence.

Terrorist actions against priests, friars and nuns, as well as against bishops, were undertaken in the General Government from the very first weeks of the occupation. Admittedly, they never assumed the same range and character as the actions taken against the Church on the Polish territories incorporated into the Reich, but they still made a significant impact on the work the Church could do in the General Government. On October 3, 1939 the Gestapo imprisoned about 300 Catholic priests in Warsaw and several dozen in the Warsaw district. Some of these priests were released after several weeks, while others were sent to concentration camps; several were murdered. At the end of the war the losses of diocesan priests in the Warsaw archdiocese amounted to 11.5% of the pre-war number.

In the Lublin diocese many of the professors of the Catholic University of Lublin arrested in November 1939 were sent to concentration camps; two of them were shot in December of that year. Also both the Lublin bishops, the Ordinary Marian Leon Fulman and the Suffragan Wladyslaw Goral, were arrested and sent to the concentration camp in Oranienburg. After the intervention by the bishops of the General Government and the Apostolic See, Bishop Fulman was released and placed under house arrest outside his diocese; bishop Goral died in Oranienburg. The vicar general of the Lublin curia died in Auschwitz in 1941. The losses in the clergy of the Lublin diocese reached nearly 11%. A similar situation occurred in the Cracow diocese, where, up to the end of 1939, 87 priests and 37 friars of that diocese found themselves in concentration camps. These actions anticipated the words Hans Frank uttered during a conference in Cracow on December 19, 1940:

> I state emphatically that I will wage war on the clerics; I will use whatever means at my disposal and will not back down. I will even have the bishops arrested immediately should anything happen.[4]

The still incomplete data shows that in the Polish territories during the Second World War six Polish bishops, 1,923 diocesan priests (18.5%), 63 seminarists, 580 friars and 289 nuns died at German hands. In some dioceses the losses reached even 50% of the pre-war number.[5] In Poland neither consecration nor the cassock or the monk's frock protected one from persecutions, concentration camps, prison and death. On the contrary, knowing the important role the Church played in Poland, the Germans tried to lessen its power by using special oppressive measures.

The main factor creating the special situation in which the Roman Catholic Church in Poland had to work during the years of World War II was the disintegration of the administrative structure and hierarchy that existed before the war. The Primate of Poland, Cardinal August Hlond, left the country together with the government and for the whole period of the occupation had practically no contact with the Church in Poland.[6] In this situation the role of the leader—in the moral and not official sense—fell on Archbishop Adam Sapieha, the Cracow metropolitan. Deprived in a practical sense of the basic keystones—that is, the administrative structure and the hierarchy—the Catholic Church in Poland faced the necessity to work and survive the years of struggle and terror on the lowest' administrative-hierarchic levels.

Disintegrated, decimated, deprived of authoritative recommendations and counsels, the Catholic Church in Poland never stopped fulfilling its religious, national and charitable functions in the difficult years of the Nazi occupation. With the perspective of time, one cannot overestimate the importance and value of the various actions taken by the Polish clergy. Besides pastoral work, both legal and illegal, the clergy took an active part in the life of the underground in Poland by co-operating, above all, with the authorities and institutions of the underground in its efforts to save the existence and the future of the nation. Under the auspices of legal charitable work, they actively participated in the illegal action of saving those who were most endangered: soldiers, underground activists hiding from the Germans, and Polish Jews and their children.

*　　*　　*

On the eve of World War II, there were 74 active convents and 11 contemplative ones in Poland, in which over 20,000 nuns lived.[7] The five largest orders, comprising nearly one third of all the Polish nuns, were the Sisters of Charity, the Sisters Servants of Mary Immaculate (Stara Wies), the Franciscan Missionary Sisters of Mary, the Sisters Servants of the Immaculate Virgin Mary and the Sisters of St. Elizabeth.

The network of the convents covered the entire territory of pre-war Poland, although, as in the case of the whole Church structure, certain areas were more populated with nuns than others. In the eastern territories of Poland there were relatively few nuns—these were the territories formerly belonging to the Russia-occupied sector of partitioned Poland before World War I—while the greatest concentration of convents was found in the Cracow archdiocese.

The nuns belonging to the active orders in Poland worked among and for the Polish people. They satisfied Polish society's great needs concerning child care through their work in orphanages, nurseries, kindergartens, primary and secondary schools, and boarding-schools; they took care of the poor, the sick, the homeless, as well as outcasts; they constituted the bulk of the junior medical staff in hospitals all over Poland; they taught religion and helped with the work of numerous Catholic parishes. The outbreak of World War II interrupted these activities or necessitated a change in their operation.

The living and working conditions of Polish nuns were no different from those in which the Polish Church and Polish society found themselves after September 1, 1939. The nuns working in the Polish territories incorporated into the Reich were in the most difficult situation. With few exceptions, the Germans defrocked them and either expelled them to the General Government or sent them to labor camps; their houses were taken over by the German administration and organizations.[8] A handful of nuns worked in hospitals, usually as lay persons. A very few managed to maintain, in secrecy, their convent communities and to carry on forbidden activities, like clandestine teaching or catechization. On a practical level, however, the nuns were only able to act with relative freedom in the General Government, and—from 1941—in the eastern territories of Poland, although there, in light of the Ukrainian-organized massacres in smaller villages, they were confined to the bigger towns.

Before the war, child care in Poland was to a considerable degree the nuns' domain. And it was children who were particularly affected by the war and by the misfortunes it brought. Every week of the war brought more orphans, children with nobody to take care of them when their parents were arrested, children lost, homeless, and living in poverty. This is why Polish nuns, whenever possible, not only tried to continue the activities they had been engaged in before the war, but, as the needs grew, to expand them by increasing the number of children in certain houses and establishing new institutions for child care. Those nuns expelled by the Germans from the territories incorporated into the Reich and deprived of the convents' houses and property were trying to get to the General Government, and there they either looked for sponsors or on their own initiative established institutions that were most necessary for Polish society: orphanages, nurseries and soup kitchens giving out cheap or free meals. Convents which before the war were active in Eastern Poland, after liquidation or temporary loss of their houses, resumed their activity again from mid-1941. These nuns were returning to their old places. They collected their stolen bedclothes, mattresses and beds, and hastened to help the most desperate children. The nuns in the General Government did the same. Since the number of educational-protective institutions proved inadequate to meet the enormous needs caused by the war, particularly as the Germans made it impossible for some of them to function, the nuns were looking for new houses into which they could move, and they organized—usually in spartan conditions—new homes for children. All the children living within Poland's borders were endangered by the war. This is why side by side with Polish children were Jewish, Ukrainian and Gypsy children, and at the end of the war also the enemy's children, Germans. Certainly, Jewish children were the most imperilled. The Polish nun's attitude toward the persecution and killing of Jews—and particularly toward the persecution of Jewish children—was unequivocal from the very first days of the occupation. It was perhaps best expressed by the behavior of a nun of the Sisters of the Resurrection, Sister Alicja Kotowska. In November 1939 three-hundred prisoners sentenced to death set out from Wejherowo to Piasnica. Among them was a group of Jewish children and Sister Alicja. According to an eyewitness, Sister Alicja came up to the Jewish children, took them by the hand and entered first into the lorry with them to accompany them on their last journey.[9] Unable to save their lives and her own, Sister Alicja offered them a merciful gesture of reaching out her hand in compassion and understanding, a gesture that was repeated toward other Jewish children by many nuns in the convents of occupied Poland.

* * *

The decision to admit a Jewish child into one's home was not an easy one to make for any Pole during World War II. For Polish nuns this decision was twice as hard. This was so because it involved jeopardizing the lives of all the inhabitants of the convent—both the nuns and the children being raised there, usually a considerable number.

Both before and during the war every convent in Poland operated independently. It had its general authorities—in Rome, in Poland, or somewhere else—it had its aims and its spirituality, its frocks or its lay clothes; and finally, it was ruled according to its own constitution. There was no superior power which could co-ordinate the work of the convents throughout all of Poland and plan particular actions. Each of the convents had different material and personnel possibilities, just as they differed in the geographical range of their work and their fate during the occupation. This is why saving Jewish children, like all of the actions undertaken by the nuns during the occupation, resulted from decisions taken by the authorities of individual convents, and more often by mother superiors of particular houses or simply from decisions by individual nuns.

In several convents the action of saving Jewish children was directed by the nuns in charge. This was the case with the Franciscan Missionary Sisters of Mary, where saving Jews and Jewish children was directed by Mother General Ludwika Lisowna and Mother Provincial Matylda Getter. This was the case with Grey Ursulines, whose house in Wislana Street in Warsaw, the seat of Mother General Pia Lesniewska, operated as a center for helping Jewish children. In the houses of the Grey Ursulines and the Franciscan

Missionary Sisters of Mary, the mother superiors decided in favor of admitting Jewish children, and the nuns under their charge took a position similar to that of their leaders. If the circumstances and the democratic traditions of the order allowed, the decision concerning the action of saving Jewish children was taken jointly by all the nuns. Indeed, such a decision was taken by the Sisters of the Immaculate Conception of the Blessed Virgin Mary in Warsaw at the end of 1942. This was possible only because most houses of this order found themselves in the General Government, and they were able to keep in touch with each other during the whole period of the occupation, and also because Sister Wanda Garczynska, the superior of the Warsaw house, thought that each of the nuns should know about and agree to the action—and to consent to a possible death sentence. The decision was taken during a conference presided over by Sister Wanda Garczynska. Several years later the conference was recollected by Sister Maria Ena, a very young nun at the time:

> I will never forget the conference called by Sister Wanda Garczynska. It was 1942-43. Our school on Kazimierzowska Street had been closed. The SS was based in a huge block opposite our house, where the social welfare kitchen was open and functioning almost without a break. The people, too, came in a constant stream—children, young people, adults with canisters for soup. Only for soup? For everything. Kazimierzowska pulsated with life—from the nursery to the university. Amongst this hive of activity there were also Jewesses. [...] It was well-known that concealing a Jew meant the death sentence.
> Sister Wanda knew that other orders had already been warned and searched. So she hid nothing, withheld nothing. She called us together. She began the conference by reading a fragment of the Gospel of St. John 15:13-17. She explained that she did not wish to jeopardize the house, the sisters, the community. She knew what could be awaiting us. There was no thought of self. She knew: You should love one another as I have loved you. How? He gave His life.
> I lowered my head. I did not dare look at the other sisters. We had to decide. If we said one word, if we openly and honestly admitted fearing for our own skins, our own lives, the lives of so many sisters, the community.... Was it prudent to risk it for a few Jewesses? It was our decision whether or not they would have to leave.
> Silence.

No one stirred. Not a single breath. We were ready. We would not give up the Jewish children. We would rather die, all of us. The silence was overwhelming—we did not look at each other. Sister Wanda was sitting with closed eyes, her hands folded over the Gospel. She was no doubt praying. We got up. We did not even pray together as we normally do. We went to the chapel. We felt light and joyful, though we realized the gravity of the situation. We were ready.[10]

They were ready. In Slonim two nuns of the Sisters of the Immaculate Conception of the Blessed Virgin Mary, Sister Marta Wolowska and Mother Superior Ewa Noyszewska, were shot by Germans for hiding adult Jews and one Jewish child. The former sister died for helping them directly, and the latter as the one responsible for all the nuns, and therefore, according to the German authorities, equally responsible for hiding Jews.

The regional convent authorities could make the decision of admitting Jewish children only for a few orders. The borders, geography and reality created by the war made it difficult or simply impossible to contact the central authorities, and the specific character of actions requiring quick decisions impelled particular convents to act autonomously—and not only in regard to rescuing Jewish children. Moreover, I think that in many orders the admission of Jewish children was intentionally left as an open question, for the nuns involved were liable to get the death sentence, and normal convent duty had never dealt with such an issue.

Among the accounts of nuns we find numerous situations in which a mother superior, asking a nun to do something connected with hiding Jewish children, added that she could refuse, as complying with the request might, in effect, cause her death; or situations in which a nun who was asked to help a Jewish child approached the mother superior for a decision and heard that it was up to her to decide, for she, the mother superior, could not forbid or order anything in a situation where a nun's life was endangered.

Yet the rescue of Jewish children was chiefly a result of decisions made by mother superiors of particular convents. This is the situation most often found in nuns' accounts. They say that admitting Jewish children was mother superior's business. But it also happened that individual sisters—courageous, intelligent, with unusually strong personalities—engaged in the action of rescuing Jewish children on their own initiative, and with time they involved their superiors in it or at least gained their kindly approval and help. This was certainly the case with Sister Syksta of the Sisters Servants of Mary Immaculate (Pleszew) and with Sister Ludwika Malkiewicz of the Sisters of St. Elizabeth. When Rachela came to the gate of the Sisters of St. Joseph's convent in Trzesowka, the mother superior was away; waiting for her return would mean death for the child, so the kitchen sister decided to admit Rachela. The first group of Jewish children that found themselves in the care of Polish nuns during the occupation years were those who had already been placed in convent orphanages before the war. As has been mentioned, it was nuns who ran a decided majority of orphanages in Poland before the war, both in the houses belonging to their own convents and on behalf of state institutions. Jewish children were also admitted into these orphanages. Most often they were orphans or children abandoned by their parents, illegitimate children sent there by hospitals, and children from the margins of society. They were not numerous, as Jewish society had its own system of orphanages. But this small group of children grew somewhat in the first months of the occupation. Confusion brought about by the military operations, the first repressions and displacements resulted in children of all ethnic groups, including Jewish children, being lost by their parents and becoming homeless. In December 1939, for example, the Germans closed down a sanatorium for tubercular children in Zakopane. Turned out into the street, the children, including two Jewish ones, were admitted by the Grey Ursulines.

As a result of the persecution of Jews, an influx of Jewish children to the educational-protective institutions run by Polish nuns could be seen at the turn of 1940-41. At that time children most often came to the convents for a short period of time and then disappeared. The nuns often did not consider them their permanent wards. These short stays of Jewish children at a time when ghettos were being closed shows that convents served as types of "repositories" until the Jewish parents could find a place to live on the "Aryan side," or decide if they were to share the fate of the people in the ghettos.

Nevertheless, some children who arrived during that period stayed with the nuns until the end of the occupation. In those days the nuns did not risk much, for—as must be remembered—the Germans issued the decree saying that Poles would be punished by death for helping and hiding Jews only on October 15, 1941.

The first wave of Jewish children coming to the convents coincided with another German decree, namely, the one issued at the turn of 1940-41, which said that the nuns had to send all the Jewish children staying with them to the ghettos being established at that time—even if the children had arrived at their convents before the war. The nuns treated this decree like many others and tried to find ways of keeping the children in the orphanages. They destroyed the documents which showed a child's Jewish origin, they bribed the employees of the Social Care Department and other offices in order to conceal a child's personal data. Unfortunately, they did not manage to keep all the children. Sometimes it was impossible to secure a child's stay in the convent or in an institution, and sometimes the nuns—not knowing that all the inhabitants of ghettos were doomed to die—did not try hard enough, the more so that Judenrats, searching for the children on their own account, required them to be sent there. It was one thing not to comply with German orders and another to wage "war" with the Judenrats. The two above-mentioned children from the Zakopane sanatorium did not find themselves in the ghetto in Nowy Targ only because the nun who was transporting them, seeing what was happening to Jews, deceived the Judenrat representatives and ran away with the children to Warsaw. One child, at his parents' request, was sent to the Warsaw ghetto, where he died on August 15, 1942, and the other, also according to his parents' wish, stayed with the nuns and saw the end of the war. The second and greatest wave of Jewish children coming to the educational and protective institutions run by Polish nuns is undoubtedly linked to the systematic action of the total liquidation of the ghettos in the cities, towns and villages of the General Government and in the territories of Eastern Poland, begun by the Germans in the spring and summer of 1942. From that time to the first half of 1943, one can see a constant increase in the number of Jewish children in convents. In the accounts of both the nuns and the saved children we most often find the following phrases describing the time of the children's arrival in the convents: "when the greatest campaign against Jews began," "when the greatest persecutions and transportations of Jews were started," "when the Germans were liquidating the ghetto." Jewish children came to Polish convents by a variety of ways and means. As the nuns of the Sisters of the Resurrection report, one day a young female Jewish doctor came to their Lwow convent in tears and gave her two sons over to the nuns' care. She could not leave them on the street—and she was not able to take them with her.

Similar scenes took place in many other convents. Jewish parents came to the nuns on their own initiative. Without knowing them, without any connections, straight from the street and counting on their pity. Those Jewish parents who had connections within Polish circles asked their Polish acquaintances to act as their intermediaries. The Poles, whether they knew the nuns or not, turned to them for help.

The nuns had a duty to keep records of the children they admitted—files and registration cards which they had to present to any German authority. This is why it was best to pretend that the child was a foundling, and in this manner evade the whole procedure of the formal admission of the child. And this is why the nuns, when asked by Jews and Poles what they should do to save a child who came from the ghetto, told them most often to simply leave the child at the threshold of the convent.

Priests also fulfilled the role of intermediaries between Jews and convents, and they extricated children from the ghettos. Children were led out of the Warsaw ghetto by, among others, Rev. Prelate Marceli Godlewski, the pastor of the Church of All Saints, and by Rev. Piotr Tomaszewski, the chaplain of the Father Boduen Home, who, for example, brought three-year-old Monika to the Sisters of Charity during playtime. Monsignor Antoni Godziszewski had contacts with the Czestochowa ghetto, from which he smuggled children to suitable institutions in that town. A similar role was played in Kielce by Rev. Jan Jaroszewicz, the future bishop of the Kielce diocese.

A whole series of similar cases can be quoted. However, the sources do not support the conclusion that there were any organized groups or teams of priests that took part in the action of rescuing Jewish children.[11]

We may assume that most Jewish children found themselves in convents as genuine foundlings. In the Boduen Home in Warsaw children were found "in gateways, on the stairs, in the church porches, or in waiting-rooms; often in front of the Boduen gate. [...] The greatest influx of children occurred between the beginning of 1943 and the final liquidation of the ghetto. Within these three months, 57 girls and 66 boys arrived in this way."[12]

The same Sisters of Charity were compelled to organize in Kielce in 1942 a nursery beside their small hospital, as children, probably Jewish ones, were often abandoned on the premises of the hospital.

From the autumn of 1941 Poles had the death penalty hanging over them for hiding or helping Jews. The Polish people soon found out that this was no mere threat on the part of the Germans. Especially from 1942, when the Holocaust was begun, this terrible law was ruthlessly enforced upon Poles. At the same time it was a period when individual Jews—including children—managed to escape from the ghettos where exterminations were going on. The children found themselves on the street. Some of them could not find shelter and sooner or later were caught by the Germans, and some of them were hidden by Poles. Sometimes Poles who unexpectedly met a Jewish child in the street did not have the courage to give him or her shelter. But it also went against their conscience to condemn the child to death, and so they pointed to the nearest convents as places where they could be rescued, expecting that the nuns would be more courageous and would not refuse help. Frania A., who now lives in Israel, was walking out of Warsaw and crying. Hungry, homeless, in a summer dress although it was winter—she drew the attention of a woman passing by. The woman pointed to a convent visible on the horizon and advised her to go there. The nuns did not refuse her help.

Younger children, found in the most tragic circumstances, were brought by Poles personally. A streetcar conductor brought to the Cracow Ursulines a several-year-old boy who had been riding in the streetcar all day, a slice of bread in his hand; a pre-war Polish policeman brought to the Albertine Sisters a baby in a basket found in an empty Jewish house; and a ferryman brought the nuns a Jewish child fished out of the Vistula in Cracow. There are numerous similar examples.

Through a feeling of human solidarity or of pity, or for material profits, Poles often decided on hiding a Jewish child. However, as time went by, and as the Holocaust intensified, along with the repressions against entire Polish families for hiding Jews, Poles hiding Jewish children became seized with fear. Some of them, unable to overcome it, sent the children to the nuns. Some Jewish children found their way to the nuns thanks to the contacts the convents had with the underground. Maria Ruminska stated:

> In the years of the Nazi occupation, as a member of the Home
> Army, I took care, to the best of my ability and means, of people

abandoned and miserable (...) especially the old and children. During that period I came into contact with the Warsaw ghetto. I helped those miserable people by supplying them with food and medicines, but I took special care of the children. The nuns were helping me with self-sacrifice and self-denial; among them Sisters Servants of Mary Immaculate (Pleszew) in Czersk on the Vistula, where some children from the Warsaw ghetto found shelter and tender care.[13]

And finally, the nuns themselves collected Jewish children they met by chance in the streets and on the roads. One such child came out of the sewer in Nowolipki Street in Warsaw and was taken by a nun who had just been passing by, and wound up in an institution in Ignacow.

The most noteworthy page in the history of rescuing Jewish children in Poland during World War II was written by the Franciscan Missionary Sisters of Mary. This poor order, numbering somewhat less than 200 nuns, took the most open attitude toward all children: Polish, Jewish and Ukrainian. The nuns had been expelled from Labunie to Radecznica in the middle of June 1941, and, as one of them reports, "Children started pouring in day and night."[14] And there were a lot of children who needed help in the Zamosc region. Polish children thrown out of their own homes and separated from their parents, or those who escaped from transports or from a transition camp, were soon joined by Jewish children who escaped from burning ghettos.[15] Nobody in the Radecznica convent or in the ones in Zamosc asked them about their birth certificates, their origin or knowledge of religion. They needed help, so the convent gates were open for them. To accommodate the greatest possible number, the nuns turned the chapel into a children's bedroom, and they listened to the Holy Mass in the corridor. When they could not find enough room for the children even there, they gave them, if it was possible, to Polish families, so as to admit the next groups to the vacated space.

The first attempts at organized help for Jewish children were undertaken by the employees of the Social Welfare Department of the Municipal Government of Warsaw, the RGO (Rada Glowna Opiekuncza/Central Welfare Council), and some underground organizations. The Children's Welfare Section in the Social Welfare Department of Warsaw had the duty of directing Polish homeless children to tutelary institutions. Social welfare workers, since they could not officially take care of Jewish children, wrote false interviews, and each of them, on their own initiative, directed Jewish children to the institutions they were familiar with. As time went by and the needs grew, this proved too dangerous; so they turned to Jan Dobraczynski, the director of the Department at that time, and he chose the institutions he knew—only those run by convents—and in consultation with their mother superiors sent Jewish children there.

A letter with Jan Dobraczynski's signature was a recognition signal. "This way of doing things proved to be exceptionally efficient," said Jadwiga Piotrowska, a social welfare worker. "Of the several hundred children placed in the tutelary institutions only two boys were murdered. The institutions, run mainly by convents, admitted every Jewish child without reservations, being quite conscious of the imminent danger."[16] The Children's Welfare Section took care of both the children whom its workers managed to extricate from the ghetto and the ones who sneaked out of the ghetto to the "Aryan side" by themselves. A similar action was undertaken by the RGO, where the Children's Section was headed by Aleksandra Dargielowa. In the summer of 1942, when the extermination of Jews in Poland slowly stopped being a secret both for the Jews themselves and for the Poles, a plan was worked out in the Bureau of Information and Propaganda of the Home Army

Headquarters to create a special clandestine institution for helping Jews that would be subsidized by the Polish Underground State authorities. Earlier still, to the best of its modest possibilities, a small social-pedagogical organization, the Front for Poland's Revival (FOP), administered by Zofia Kossak, undertook to help ghetto refugees. The FOP derived funds for helping Jews from contributions from the gentry and intelligentsia; and Zofia Kossak's personal contacts with the pre-war army circles and convents made it possible to supply the refugees with forged documents and place the women and children in convents. It was owing to Zofia Kossak's efforts that on September 27, 1942 a committee was established, initially called the Social Committee for Aid to the Jewish People, and for clandestine aims—the Konrad Zegota Committee—which later, on December 4 of the same year, evolved into the Council for Aid to Jews (Rada Pomocy Zydom). Even before that, in November 1942, the representatives of "Zegota" had a meeting with Irena Sendlerowa, who represented the employees of the Social Welfare

Department of the City of Warsaw, and with Aleksandra Dargielowa representing the RGO (Rada Glowna Opiekuncza).[17]

Since its inception, the Council for Aid to Jews considered the problem of Jewish children as one of the highest importance, requiring special attention. However, since help for children had already been organized in both the Social Welfare Department and in the RGO, the Council for Aid to Jews concentrated its efforts on facilitating contacts with the ghetto, and also, as far as it was possible, on financial assistance.

The rescue of Jewish children took place under clandestine circumstances. That is why—when taken with the passage of time—the history of the co-operation between the nuns and the Social Welfare Department, the RGO, or the Council for Aid to Jews, can only be loosely reconstructed for Warsaw and its surroundings; and in the case of convents situated farther from the capital, it is possible only when their contacts with Warsaw were obvious, as in the case with Lomna and Turkowice. It is unlikely, however, that the circumstances of admitting Jewish children into convents were very different in other places in Poland. Among others, the nuns of Przemysl, Czestochowa and Drohobycz mention the Social Welfare Department sending Jewish children to their convents. Various sources indicate that Jewish children sent by the Social Welfare Department, the RGO, or the Council for Aid to Jews were admitted by the nuns of at least the following 15 orders: the Sisters of St. Elizabeth, the Albertine Sisters, the Felician Sisters, the Franciscan Missionary Sisters of Mary, the Oblate Sisters, the Sisters of Divine Providence, the Samaritan Sisters, the Seraphites, the Sacred Heart Sisters, the Sisters Servants of Mary Immaculate (Stara Wies), the Sisters of Charity, the Grey Ursulines, the Sisters of the Holy Family of Nazareth, the Ursulines of the Union of Rome, and the Sisters of the Resurrection.

Besides those Jewish children admitted by nuns who were aware of their ancestry, there were many children in Polish convents—not only foundlings—whose Jewish descent was not known to the nuns at the time of admission. Later, some of them, in various situations, informed the nuns that they were Jews. The nuns learned about others after the war when their parents turned up to collect them. They still don't know the true identity of many even to this day. Surely there were cases where nuns refused to admit a Jewish child, but I have so far been able to uncover only one such instance. The

Sisters Servants of Mary Immaculate (Pleszew) refused to take in a Jewish boy to their orphanage in Czersk, and eventually the boy, after a short stay there, was moved to the orphanage run by the Sisters Servants of Mary Immaculate (Stara Wies) in Turkowice. Unfortunately, the mother superior of the Czersk convent died a long time ago, and thus she cannot explain the reasons for the refusal which she undoubtedly gave herself.

Sister Syksta, who was heavily involved in helping Jewish children during that time, has never heard of such a situation. Perhaps we can find an answer for the refusal by examining the situation in which the Czersk orphanage found itself. It was a so-called war orphanage, that is, one established during the war in response to the increasing need for child care. The number of children in the orphanage never exceeded thirty-five. Among them were seven or eight Jewish children. Therefore, every fifth child was Jewish. The children from the Warsaw ghetto came to Czersk by the usual way—via the Home Army. So the mother superior probably reserved the beds in the orphanage for children arriving in that fashion. What should be remembered, though, is that the boy in question had protectors. He did not find himself out on the street. He found shelter in another convent.

The fundamental rules of clandestine activities, rules which had to be kept in order to succeed in saving the children, dictated the number of Jewish children admitted to one convent. An orphanage or a boarding-school could not house only Jewish children. To cover the presence of these children the nuns had to have a definite number of Polish children. The nuns made the decision about the maximum number of Jewish children they could allow in a particular convent depending on the geographical position of the convent and on their appraisal of the general situation. However, it was not always so—sometimes life itself dictated the number of children. When at the request of her foster-mother, Nina E. was admitted into the convent in Staniatki, the Felician sisters running it were glad that the girl would be a cover for the five Jewish children already staying there. To their surprise Nina disclosed that she was the sixth Jewish girl among the eighteen girls in the convent... The nuns expressed their grievance to the foster-mother in rather sharp words, but the child stayed in the convent until the end of the occupation. There could have been other, though no less important reasons for refusing to admit a Jewish child into an orphanage. The nuns had to be especially cautious when a stranger came to the convent straight from the street asking them to admit a Jewish child. It was very easy to meet with a ruse, and such a ruse could be the work of both Germans and *szmalcowniks*—both were well aware of the fact that convents offered refuge to Jewish children. And the nuns also knew that among the *szmalcowniks* and Gestapo agents there were Jews. This is why the Semitic features of a person asking to admit a child were not sufficient.

The possible consequences of a successful provocation were not difficult to imagine. It is also easy to imagine the nuns' terrible perplexity. Left to their own intuition, they had to decide about the life or death of a child in whose name the request was made and, at the same time, possibly put the lives of all the nuns living in the convent in jeopardy. If there was slightest doubt, the safety of the children already there and of the whole convent community prevailed. The result was that, giving the most ingenious reasons, the nuns could refuse to admit the child. Certainly, their intuition must have failed the nuns once in a while, resulting in the most sincere people, who really needed immediate help for their children, being turned away on occasion. There could also have been far more prosaic reasons for refusing to admit a Jewish child into an orphanage. When asked if she had not been scared when she had been risking her life for Jewish children, Sister Jadwiga Skalec, a Sister Servant of Mary Immaculate (Stara Wieś), answered: "So many people were dying. It is obvious that one must die for something. It might as well be for Jewish children."[18]

These simple words of Sister Jadwiga contain the deep truth about unconditional love toward another person. A great majority of Polish nuns remained faithful to this, the deepest of Christian truths. But surely there were also ones among them who had too little strength and courage to stand by that truth during that great ordeal which was the Nazi occupation. There were probably also nuns who thought that it was not worth dying for Jewish children.

CHAPTER IV

HIDING CONDITIONS

IN ORDER FOR A JEWISH CHILD to be admitted into a convent two things had to occur: the child had to safely reach the convent gate and obtain the approval of the nuns. This does not mean, however, that the nuns concerned themselves with children only when they were within the walls of a convent. The duty to take the child from an appointed place in the outside world to the convent often fell upon them also.

The children were transported to convents in various ways. Over short distances, which did not take long to cover, the nuns usually preferred to take one child at a time, so as not to raise suspicions. However, when the distance was long, the nuns took the risk and transported several at once. Needless to say, such journeys were dangerous. The children, usually just out of the ghetto, were frightened and not used to the "Aryan side." Moreover, despite their disguises, they drew everyone's attention, especially when changing trains, which was necessary when the journeys were long. Sisters Irena Monaszczuk and Hermana Romansewicz frequently experienced moments of terror and fear for the safety of the children and themselves in the train station in Rejowiec. Sister Hermana recollects those journeys:

> When you were transporting children from Warsaw and there were Jewish ones among them, people on the train were scared.
> "It's not a good thing that you are going with us," they said. "These are Jewish children!"
> I did not enter upon a conversation on the subject with them, but briefly answered that I had not inquired about their descent,

and the only thing I knew was that they were orphans and had to be taken care of.

Jewish children stood out a mile. When they started eating they crossed themselves three times.

"Do not cross yourselves so often or else people will think that you are Jews," I explained to them, but that did not help much.

In Rejowiec we had to wait all night for our train. The waiting-room was so crowded that the children had to stand. One German was decent and made room for the children to lie down. Then the Jewish children knelt down and started to pray aloud: "Our Father who are in heaven," which they did with a Jewish accent, to which the people, frightened, said again that they were Jewish. The children must have heard those words, for they stopped praying and put their heads to sleep. But the fear did not pass, for it happened that a Jewish child cried out something in Yiddish while asleep. To save the situation, I had to wake him up. I was so worried the entire time. I was constantly on the lookout for Germans who might seize the suspicious children.[1]

The nuns running the orphanage in Lomna near Przemysl were also transporting children—some from as far away as Warsaw. They remember with gratitude the Polish conductors who, knowing the situation full well, assured the safety of the nuns and children by closing their compartment and drawing the curtains to protect them from the unnecessary comments of their fellow passengers and the watchful eyes of Germans.

Those children who were admitted through the influence of a third party or their parents, or via the above-mentioned institutions or underground organizations, were clean and well-dressed when they entered the convent. Usually they had already been in the so-called "protective readiness distribution points," which generally were the apartments of those involved in the action of saving Jewish children. There they were washed and, if necessary, clothed properly and disguised with make-up.

The sanitary state of the children coming to convents straight from the streets or from the ghetto was deplorable. As the nuns recollect, the newly-arrived children needed, most of all, a bath and a clean change of clothes. Many had survived a long time after their parents had died—some were just ten years old or even younger. They were all distrustful, scared, sad, numbed and made much older by their experiences.

"Six-year-old Irka was brought to Wrzosow by her father," relates

Sister Maria Ena. "She was screaming, stamping her feet, crying, and hysterically asking: 'Daddy, take me from here, or else these "deaths" will kill me!' She associated our white frocks with death. Her father promised her that he would come a week later, and if she were unhappy he would take her with him. He did come, but Irka had already changed her mind."[2]

Once a child arrived at a convent, it was necessary to legalize his or her stay. Those children who were sent by underground organizations or who had Jewish or Polish guardians created the least trouble. They arrived in the convents with birth certificates, usually false ones, and already knew their new names and lineage. Legalization of the other children's stays was more difficult—the nuns had to arrange for it themselves. They had to find proper certificates in the neighboring parishes or, in the case of abandoned children, take care of all the formalities connected with admitting the child. In this respect, several convents constituted an exception: there, the nuns made it a rule of not complying with all the formalities, both in the case of Polish and Jewish children. This was probably possible because the kind of institutions they ran could not be called orphanages in the strict sense of the word. Rather, they were shelters or refuges for homeless children, where any child could come and stay.

Legalization, therefore, which for convents with traditional orphanages was the basic hurdle connected with admitting Jewish children, was not an issue in other convents. There, the child was simply given a name and a surname which he had to remember, and then he just stayed. These were the rules according to which several convents in the eastern territories of Poland worked. The situation there was made even more complicated by the displacement of the Polish population from the Zamosc region and by a growing wave of massacres by Ukrainian nationalists, which resulted in a great number of Polish orphans, as well. Probably in all that confusion the German authorities were not able to ensure that the convents keep proper files, and there was always the explanation that Polish children were barely able to save their own lives from the so-called "pacifications" of the Germans and Ukrainian massacres, and could not even think about saving any documentation of birth and baptism. Sometimes if a child's legal stay in a convent was impossible the nuns took the child's name off the books, and from then on the child's stay in the convent was illegal.

Once a Jewish child was within the convent walls, whether or not its stay was legalized, he or she was still not out of danger. A constant struggle for the lives of the children and the nuns had begun and would continue until the end of the occupation. As for all the Jews in Poland, the most important key to survival for the children was assimilation into the surrounding world. First, there had to be a physical assimilation. The nuns, trying to conceal a child's Semitic features, used various methods. For girls sometimes it was enough to cut or bleach the hair, or change the hair-do. Boys usually were in a terrible position. They had short hair and it was difficult to do anything with it, apart from a change in its color. So the nuns used bandages and various caps. As a last resort they gave the boys skirts to wear, or they isolated them altogether from the outside world.

Most children, especially the older ones, were perfectly conscious of the fact that their survival depended on their abililty to act in a manner identical to their Polish peers. They had to collectively recite prayers, behave properly in church and also possess an "appropriate" past—one which would not reveal their real prior identities or any facts which could testify to their Jewish origin.

Hiding oneself and one's past is difficult for anyone, regardless of his or her age, since it requires continuous self-control over one's behavior and utterances. Often the children, even those trying very hard to play their roles correctly, made slips, especially during conversations with their peers. In the orphanage run by the Sisters of the Holy Family of Nazareth in Czestochowa a few girls came running to the nun-tutor one evening with the news that "little Czesia is a Jew because she said that her aunt got a stocking full of money for her from her mom." After calming down the children, the nun took Czesia to her bedroom. After a conference with the mother superior of the convent, it was decided that for reasons of safety the girl would have to be moved to another convent immediately. In the morning Czesia's bed was empty.[3]

These "slips" were sometimes unintentional and sometimes an expression of a Jewish child's protest against the situation in which the child found itself. As long as the children could remember, the adult world had taught them that lying was a terrible thing and that they must not lie under any circumstances. Now, suddenly, the world was turned upside-down, especially for those children who had not learned the lessons of the ghetto. Mom and Dad were lying, all the adults were lying, and now they, the children, were told to lie too! Then came the separation from their parents, travels with strangers and stays in unknown people's homes—all which was perceived by still-naive children as a silly masquerade. When Doctor K.'s son, Oles, was brought to the orphanage in Laszczow near Sokal, Sister Bernarda presented him to the other children and said that he had been brought by his aunt. After adding several other details, she went to have supper. At that point Oles began to correct the nun's lies: "Listen, children, that is all a lie! I am a Jew's son, and that woman who brought me here is not my aunt at all!" After several speeches of this kind, the nuns had to send Oles to another convent.[4]

There were cases when the behavior of Jewish children was extremely rude and arrogant. A Jewish boy, a little older than the other children, who was staying in the Przemysl orphanage run by the Sacred Heart Sisters, reacted to the nuns' remarks with the filthiest invectives and threats. He even threatened them by saying that his father was a policeman and would shoot everybody. In spite of this, he survived the war with the nuns. A "slip," or revealing the secret of his origin to his peers, usually meant that for that child's own protection, as well as that of the other children and the nuns, the child had to leave the orphanage. In such cases the nuns sent the child to another home, run by the same order, or to another order or another safe place. Sometimes, if the child had parents or a guardian, the task of finding a new hiding place fell to them. However, those children who had neither parents nor guardians, no matter if they made any "slips," stayed under the nuns' protection.

Those children with an especially "wrong" appearance, even if they made no slips, were doomed to a life of constantly changing their hiding places. When Jasia, entrusted to the Sisters of the Immaculate Conception of the Blessed Virgin Mary, was once again brought to Kazimerzowka Street in Warsaw after having changed her hiding place several times, Sister Wanda Garczynska said, according to the child's aunt, that irrespective of the danger involved she would keep the girl with her and that "the Germans will take Jasia over my dead body."[5] Sister Wanda was not the only nun who decided that no matter what, a Jewish child would stay with her.

Generally, the nuns of all the orders took care to keep the true identity of Jewish children a secret from non-Jewish children—a difficult task at times. But a child's world has its own rules. One day, after Sister Paulina brought several children to Lomna, a little boy came up to Mother Superior Tekla and said: "Mother Superior, Sister Paulina has brought some children from Warsaw, all of them Jews."[6] In the Boduen Home children played a game where Jewish children would hide under tables and beds while the Polish children would cover up their hiding places.[7] Such incidents indicate that children could be especially attuned to any differences in ethnicity.

There is only one incident I know of where Jewish children were introduced to each other by the nuns and their interaction and mutual assistance encouraged. Despite this, the nuns claim that in all the convents the Jewish children were joined by a particular bond and that in a most extraordinary way they recognized and protected each other. Even those Jewish children who did not admit their origin to the nuns were recognized by their Jewish peers. To this day the nuns wonder how the Jewish children recognized each other. This riddle has turned out to be very simple and was explained by the children, now adults, themselves. Most often this recognition was possible owing to some words or behavior typical of Jews only.

The nuns did not recognize them because they did not pay special attention to them, and if they did, they did not understand them and thought them mere childish eccentricities. But the Jewish children knew that a particular word or gesture proved beyond doubt that their mate was a Jew. Nina, who stayed with the Felician nuns, says that during the weekly change of the underclothes a friend of hers, upon receiving an undershirt, said: "This *lejbik* has so many holes in it!" Nina knew then and there what to think of her, for *lejbik* is a typically Jewish word. When pressed by Nina, the owner of the *lejbik* with holes in it eventually admitted she was Jewish.[8]

Nuns and children weren't the only residents of the convents. Many orders did not have their own doctors, teachers, cooks, charwomen and caretakers, and had to employ lay ones from the community. Usually this co-operation between the nuns and the medical staff of the homes went well. Sometimes it was even difficult to tell who was more committed to rescuing Jewish children, the doctors or the nuns. There were exceptions, however, to this rule, and it happened sometimes that the nuns were afraid of a doctor's indiscretion or betrayal, and did not let the Jewish children be examined by him. Time has proven that, in the case of doctors, these misgivings were unjustified—there was not a single case reported in Poland of a doctor contributing to the death of even one Jewish child hiding in a convent.

It was the same with other lay personnel employed in the convents. Despite the nuns' discretion, everybody knew about the Jewish children. In Czersk, for example, the cook working in the convent, the shoemaker mending the children's shoes, and a teacher from a nearby school were all very well-informed about the Jewish children hiding in the convent. Of the convents I am familiar with, only in the Czestochowa orphanage run by the Albertine Sisters was there a case of betrayal; the traitor was the cook, who informed the Gestapo about the Jewish women and children living there. The nuns had to continually take care of the disguises of the Jewish children, teach them correct religious behavior, conceal their real origin from the other children and sometimes from the lay personnel, but if any of these duties was not done the consequences were not as ominous as an unfavorable outcome of a German "visit." In case of a German search every convent had its own pre-arranged plan: bandagings, going out for walks, promptly organized games, hiding-places. In Przemysl, Marysia received from Sister Bernarda the key to the nearby church, and in case Germans made a search, she was to go to a hiding place inside the altar.

The nuns attempted to learn in advance about these planned visits or searches. Sometimes the local inhabitants warned them; sometimes the searches ended as they did in the home run by the Sisters of Divine Providence in Miedrzyrzec Podlaski, where the mayor, realizing what the Gestapo from Lublin came for, got his "guests" drunk so that they did not do their duty with respect to the convent rigorously enough.

The Germans knew very well, however, that if they would find any Jews at all, it would be in the convents. This is why they tried to arrive at the convents unexpectedly, before any Jews could have time to hide. They also came to the convents to get food. Each of those visits was a mortal danger for the children and the nuns. This is why there is not a single convent in Poland that, when hiding Jewish children, did not experience moments when the lives of the nuns and children hung by a thread, when only the nuns' quick wits, nerve, tremendous courage and, sometimes, plain luck saved them from tragedy.

"One day the Gestapo burst into the convent so unexpectedly," recollects Zofia Szymanski, "that the nuns had no other choice but to hide the Jews immediately. Without losing her composure even for a second, Sister Wanda placed the girls with the most Semitic features in long frocks inside the wardrobe. After many years Jasia told me the story of how they were standing dressed in long white frocks and the Germans were riddling the clothes with bayonets, looking for the hidden children. They did not hurt any of them, and two little girls laughed afterward and thought the adventure quite amusing."[9]

Lea B. of Israel, upon visiting the convent in Brwinow after almost forty years, told the following story:

> I never really understood why they were hiding me. They did not explain it to me; they only said that there was danger. I remember one more thing. The Germans used to come to the convent and take eggs, or sometimes pigs. There was a garden there, fruit and vegetables were growing—and the Germans came and took them. One day, there was a large basket full of eggs and straw. Perhaps there were hens in the convent? I do not remember.
>
> The Germans came in so suddenly that I was left inside the room and could not be taken out through any door. Sister Helen—she was tall and slim, her face was like that of the Madonna; she was beautiful—took those eggs out so quickly! She put me inside the basket and covered me with the eggs and straw. A German came in, kicked the basket and asked what was in it. She calmly answered that there were eggs in the basket. The German said he was taking the eggs. The sister started begging him, saying there was a seriously ill nun in the convent who had to have those eggs. The German persisted, but then started paying her compliments, for she was very beautiful. Finally he left the basket where it was and went away.[10]

Blackmailers, people who during the Second World War made a profit from tracking down Jews and the Poles hiding them, people for whom there was nothing in the world more important than money, did not respect the sanctity of the convents. In such cases help sometimes came from an energetic priest, sometimes from the nuns' contacts with the underground. But once in a while there was not time for intervention, and the nuns had to find some money quickly and pay the demanded ransom.

The Nazi occupation, more than any other war, brought about a quick pauperization of the whole Polish society. Women's religious orders did not escape this. Only a few of them managed to maintain living conditions similar to those of the pre-war period. In this category should be included the convents which had paid boarding schools, such as some of the homes run by the Sisters of the Immaculate Conception of the Blessed Virgin Mary, the Sisters of the Holy Family of Nazareth, the Grey Ursulines, the Ursulines of the Union of Rome, the Franciscan Sisters of the Family of Mary, and the Disrobed Sacred Heart Sisters.

The orphanages, including the ones run by the above orders, were in a far worse situation. Because they had been supported before the war by subsidies from the state, they were left without the means of subsistence once the war began. With time, they received ration cards from the Germans, and they were helped by the social welfare departments. However, the social welfare departments were institutions that were working officially, so they were strictly controlled by the German authorities, which decided both the budget and its distribution among particular groups of the Polish population. It need not be added that caring for the children of Poland was not a priority of the Germans. This is why the budget assigned to orphanages was a fraction of the actual need, and why the assistance the nuns received for the children from the above-mentioned institutions should be called a supplement rather than an adequate material basis for their work. Thus, the burden of securing proper living conditions for the children fell on the nuns. Luckily, many convent orphanages were situated in places, like the suburbs or villages, where there was a garden and some livestock. During the war every piece of land was used for growing vegetables and fruit, and as far as possible the amount of livestock was increased. But we have seen, the food produced by the nuns was sometimes a tasty morsel for the Germans. Whenever they felt like it, at any time of day or night, they could rob the cellars and larders filled by the nuns with so much trouble.

Despite great difficulties, the living conditions in those orphanages which remained in their own buildings throughout the war were not the worst. Their own furniture, utensils and bedclothes, even if patched and mended, managed to suffice for those five long years—but barely so, for all the orphanages were overcrowded. Designed for a specific number of children, they had to house two or three times as many during the war.

In the worst position were those orphanages that had been displaced from the Polish territories incorporated into the Reich or those in the General Government whose buildings had been seized by the Germans or bombarded or burnt as a result of military actions. Without any financial support, the nuns running those orphanages were placed, together with the children, into buildings unsuitable for dwelling, sometimes even into barns. They faced the necessity of securing not only food, clothing and fuel, but also basic utensils: cutlery, pots, plates, wash-bowls, bedclothes and beds; and in orphanages of this sort, there were on average about ten children to one nun. How could one manage to take care of such a group?

The occupation years for these nuns were extremely difficult and filled with hard work. In order to secure the means necessary to support the children, they turned their hands to many different jobs. The ones who had been trained as nurses went to the neighboring villages giving injections and dressing wounds. They earned money by knitting, spinning wool, sewing, ebroidering or working in the fields for the farmers in the neighborhood. They learned to collect contributions or simply to beg. After many years they still recollect their burning shame when for the first time they had to wander from one home to another asking for groats, flour and potatoes for the hungry children.

When the Franciscan Missionary Sisters of Mary had to cover greater and greater distances, as the farmers in the neighborhood had nothing more to give them, it became necessary to use a vehicle, for the nuns were not strong enough to carry the heavy bags for so many miles. They did not have horses, for the Germans had taken them away. So they struck upon the idea of organizing a team of dogs to pull a cart, upon which they loaded whatever goods they could get. As a last resort, when there was nothing to eat and the children were threatened by hunger, as was the case in the orphanage run by the Passionist Sisters in Janow, the situation was saved by stealing from nearby fields. Since the nuns had contacts with the underground, the partisans helped them, sharing with the orphanages the food they had taken from the Germans. The nuns in these convents and the children under their care frequently lived on the verge of hunger, and maintaining the proper hygienic conditions exceeded the physical abilities of the nuns, who otherwise felt so strongly about that aspect of human life. Maria Klein, saved by the Sacred Heart Sisters in an orphanage established during the war, writes: "Hunger reigned in the convent, for the war was on. There was no electricity; various diseases caused by malnutrition were prevalent; and we were all verminous. Medicines for fighting lice were lacking. The infected children conveyed the lice to the others. Those children from Volhynia [the Polish orphans who had lost their parents in the Ukrainian massacres—E.K.] were in no better condition. Furthermore, their parents were murdered by the Ukrainians right in front of their eyes, and one of the girls, Tekla, was wounded in her belly with a knife and was very weak."[11]

Despite the difficult conditions, the nuns never tried to get rid of a single Jewish child. How unfair and unfounded then are the accusations brought against the nuns by some parents and some of the saved children.

Ewa Goldberg, who had been hidden by the Disrobed Sacred Heart Sisters, wrote after the war:

> The conditions in which we were living were not in the least pleasant. The underclothes were in an outrageous state; my impression is that even a washcloth made of them would be too weak and would have too many holes in it. Our dresses and aprons were in a regrettable condition. Worn-out or patched-up, outgrown in the extreme, they presented quite an unesthetic sight.
>
> It is true that we had new navy-blue scouts' uniforms and white sailor blouses and very nice navy-blue dresses, but they were resting quietly in the wardrobe and were worn only on feast-days. [...] Our food was awful. Sometimes we remarked sarcastically that we were given pigs' food by mistake. And this statement was not exaggerated at all, for often, when we were served leftovers of our earlier meals, even the pig ate them without her usual voracity.[12]

I doubt that the homes run by the Disrobed Sacred Heart Sisters had the worst living conditions of all the institutions run by nuns. Some Jewish children in those homes simply came from very rich Jewish families, families whose wealth could not be diminished by the poverty and hunger in the ghetto. These children were used to wearing smart clothes and eating good food—even during the war. Forced to hide in the conditions of poverty that the Polish people found themselves in because of the war, both these children and

their parents must have considered such poverty shameful.[13] Ewa
Goldberg's account, despite the author's clear intention to present
the nuns in the worst possible light, actually portrays them
favorably. If in those hard times the teenage Ewa's greatest problem
was old underclothes, patched dresses and tasteless soups, it means
that the nuns gave her everything. They took away from her the
threat of death, the fear and the tragedies of war to such an extent
that she could concentrate her energy on matters more normal for
one her age. It proves that those "awful nuns" (as Ewa called them
in another part of her account) took all the risks connected with the
protection of the child's life upon themselves.

Ewa Goldberg's parents probably paid for their daughter's stay
in the convent, since the home was a boarding school, where each
child's stay was paid by parents or guardians. There were cases,
however, where due to the circumstances brought about by the war,
there was no one to pay for a Jewish child in such a school, and
then Polish parents paid a double charge. In the orphanages, on the
other hand, the financial situation of the Jewish children did not
differ from that of the non-Jewish ones. Most often no one paid for
the children, and the nuns supported them in the ways described
above. In individual cases the nuns received financial support from
the Council for Aid to Jews. On sporadic occasions Jewish parents,
leaving their child with the nuns, offered sums of money, but as one
father of a saved girl states, money played no role here. It was not
a question of money but a question of saving a child's life. Some
parents, even many years after the war ended, offered lavish
contributions as an expression of their gratitude for what the nuns
had done to save their children.

As has already been mentioned, the nuns in the orphanages
worked hard during the war. Sometimes the children in their
institutions, whether Polish, Jewish, Ukrainian, Gypsy or German,
worked equally hard. In many homes the number of nuns was
insufficient, and the older children had to do the work on the fields
and farms. The older girls helped the nuns to spin wool, knit and
embroider. They also shared some of the duties connected with
taking care of the younger children. All of the children—as much
as their age allowed— helped in cleaning the rooms, and they
washed by themselves under the supervision of the nuns.

Undernourished and overworked, the children and the nuns were
equally attacked by various diseases. A lack of medicines was

certainly the greatest problem all over Poland during the war and caused a great number of deaths. Jewish children's, and especially Jewish boys', diseases were a problem for several reasons. Treatment of their illnesses by an unsympathetic doctor could lead to exposure, so as long as it was possible a trusted doctor came to the orphanage. The situation changed radically when a child had to be sent to the hospital. Here the cause was helped by the fact that the junior medical staff in Polish hospitals consisted mainly of nuns. Hence, even if they were of a different order, an understanding was reached, and I do not know a single case where a Jewish child taken to a hospital was discovered by the Germans. It would be wrong, however, to think that the lives of Jewish children and of the nuns who were hiding them passed only amid diseases, work, poverty, "slips," searches and blackmailers' threats. To be sure, all of these things were there; the nuns had to be aware of them each and every day of the occupation. The children unanimously say that if it was not for this attention to various details, all the details, they do not know how they would have survived the war. But the atmosphere in the convent homes, and the nuns' strong will to create for the children conditions as close to normal as possible, made the war recede into the distance. A monotonous and systematized routine of learning, prayers, work, games and sleep was of great help in this respect. What also helped was the isolation from the outside world, often intensified by the geographic areas where the convents were located. This is how the timetable in the orphanage run by the Sisters Servants of Mary Immaculate (Pleszew) looked for a winter day during the war:[14]

7:00-8:00	wake up, washing, straightening the rooms and gymnastics
8:00-9:00	prayer and breakfast
9:00-12:00	learning at school or at home
12:00-13:00	lunch, washing the dishes, cleaning up
13:00-14:00	games
14:00-15:30	manual work
15.30-18:30	doing assigned duties, supper
18.30-19:00	recreation
19:00	evening prayers and going to bed

In the other children's homes the days were probably similar.

There were special feast-days and other celebrations that children liked so much: the end of the school year, the harvest festival, the nuns' name-days, for which the children prepared surprises like recitations, dances or performances. The nuns on their part tried to add a measure of splendor to those occasions by serving dainties they had obtained in various ways. Jewish children even today remember the rhymes written for a nun's name-day; some have kept with reverence for over forty years the presents they received for their own name-days, and still tell about Santa Claus passing through the gate and bringing sweets for the children.

The convent orphanages were undoubtedly an oasis of peace and safety for Jewish children exhausted with wandering or with the hell of the ghetto. They were places where they could finally stop thinking about the war, where they had the luxury of being children again and where their child needs were attended. At first the children were distrustful: they stood aloof and preferred to be alone. But after a while they began to drop their suspicions and join in with the activities of the other children. Even today the nuns recollect that this Jewish child was very good at recitations or dancing, or that that one distinguished herself in organizing shows.

Sister Syksta recollects that when the school in Czersk invited the children from her orphanage for a Christmas celebration, all the children went, so that the Jewish children—who had not been seen anywhere yet—would not be deprived of the fun afforded the others. Taking Jewish children outside could, of course, be considered an act of folly. But the nuns decided that is was better to take the risk than to deepen their feelings of inferiority. That is why little Lea could say in Brwinow: "Now I have come back to my childhood, and it was not a bad one at that! All in all, my war experiences were not tragic. I think that if during the war it was possible for me to be on a bed of roses, then the bed was prepared for me here. And that is why the war is not so terrible for me."[15]

The principle of not singling out Jewish children reigned in the convents and not only as a means of hiding their real identities. The same rules—and the same punishments—applied to all children. Certainly, the nature of some of these punishments may raise a lot of objections. No more, however, than the punishments administered by parents in homes that are considered normal. In some orphanages corporal punishment was given: whippings on the bare bottom, kneeling on peas, etc. Punishments were administered to all the children equally. This, I believe, was crucial. Jewish children needed such equalizing in duties, prizes, as well as punishments. It added self-confidence, allowing them to forget about their being different and the dangers resulting from their difference. Individual children hidden in convents that did not run foster homes or orphanages were treated by the nuns as if they were part of a normal family. Rachela, saved in Trzesowka, says that the nuns treated her like any other country child: she did chores, the shopping and many other things, and even liked it.[16]

Burdened with their tragic experiences, Jewish children needed more love than their Polish mates did. After many years, Sister Eliza says about Janeczka:

> She clung to me so deperately; she almost did not talk to the children, and used to say to me: "I very much want everyone to love me!" I always assured her that we all loved her. On Sundays I took the children to church. Janeczka used to sit next to me and look at me with so much trust....[17]

And this is what Maria, who stayed with the Sacred Heart Sisters, said:

> The nuns' attitude toward Jewish children was more indulgent and full of understanding and patience. If they got some dainty for supper, they often shared it with me in secret.[18]

And Lea from Israel said:

> I always felt that somebody loved me, and this was very important.[19]

Undoubtedly, a feeling that someone loves them is most important for children, and Lea could not have given the nuns a better endorsement. She was kept together with a large group of children who—as the sisters themselves say—were treated in the same way. Nevertheless, she—Lea—felt that she was surrounded with a love meant only for her.

CHAPTER V

PSYCHOLOGICAL AND RELIGIOUS EXPERIENCES

JEWISH CHILDREN NEEDED MORE LOVE AND CARE than their convent peers because the problems with which the German occupation burdened them was by far greater, in terms of both weight and value. Nowhere in the world is there a single Jew on whom the years of holocaust did not leave their mark, but the experiences of children differed fundamentally from those of adults. The difference in the psychological and religious experiences of children resulted from their age, which made it impossible for them to properly evaluate reality, from their ancestry, from the vicissitudes of the war and the conditions in which each of them endured the German occupation. All these elements, together with the individual personality features of each child, determined the value and intensity of their experiences.

The fragmentary character of the source material hinders us from knowing the social background of all the Jewish children saved in Polish convents; we may only draw indirect conclusions. It is easiest to find out about the background of those children who found refuge in boarding schools run by nuns. Boarding schools, it should be added, with high educational standards. These were private schools and tuition had to be paid. According to the nuns, they had Polish and Jewish children from the intelligentsia, from the families of businessmen, manufacturers, scientists, lawyers, and doctors. The other children, the ones from orphanages, nurseries, or those who were staying in small groups or even individually in private homes, can be reasonably divided according to their age, that is, divided into those children that spoke and those that still did not speak.

It is well known that a good command of the Polish language was the first and basic condition of survival for older children, as well as for adult Jews. Among the cases I know about, only a little girl saved by the nuns of St. Teresa in Luboml learned Polish in the convent, having spoken only Yiddish beforehand. In various accounts we also come across, though very rarely, expressions or phrases which suggest that not all the Jewish children spoke Polish well enough, or that a child's command of it did not allow a safe use of it among people from outside the circle of the convent home. In Lwow "one of the girls with a typically Semitic face was hidden by the nuns under a barrel when a German inspector came. If discovered she was to pretend that she was mute."[1]

Pretending to be mute was often the only way, for Jewish children as well as for adult Jews, to conceal an insufficient command of Polish. Almost all the children who could speak when they were admitted to convents spoke perfect Polish. This meant that they came from homes where Polish was commonly used, that is, from assimilated Jewish families. According to the accounts written by the nuns and by those who had been saved, a majority of Jewish children in the orphanages came from families belonging to the intelligentsia. Only rarely did the nuns have reliable information on this subject when the children were admitted, for the children came with forged documents, after all; but their backgrounds were revealed by the children's subsequent confidences, as well as by linguistic troubles of a different kind. The good vocabulary and high intellectual development of the Jewish children in various age groups caused them to stand apart from their Polish peers, who usually came from diverse social groups and frequently from the margins of society. Of course, in the orphanages there were also some Jewish children from craftsmen's and small shopkeepers' families, but these constituted a decided minority.

In the other group of children, the ones who did not yet speak, the chances of survival were equal. It was difficult to ascertain, even approximately, the social background of these children. They could not say anything about their parents, and, moreover, in this group a majority of children were abandoned in front of the convent, or brought to the nuns by Poles who had found them.

One would think that because of the religious character of the homes run by the nuns the majority of the hidden children should come from Catholic families of Jewish descent. The sources do not confirm this assumption. The troubles the nuns had with baptismal certificates and with the legalization of Jewish children's stays in convents indicate that a great majority of them had false certificates or that the nuns had to fabricate such certificates for them. Therefore, the children had not been baptized. But the children's behavior, their confidences during the war and accounts after the war, show that only in sporadic cases had they been brought up in religious Jewish families. Mostly, therefore, these were children from families that were assimilated, from the intelligentsia, and in large part non-religious. Long before most of the Jewish children entered the convents the war had made them realize that all the misfortunes affecting them were the result of their being Jewish, that to be a Jew meant to be hungry, cold, beaten; it required them to escape from the Germans and to hide in the most remote corners accessible to them. Their war experiences instilled in their psyche the conviction that to be a Jew meant to be denied the right to live, and this negative association was for Jewish children their first experience of war. Adults knew that this was true only of this particular war. Jewish children, on the other hand, who were growing and developing their consciousness during the war, took these conditions as normal. Many Jewish parents watched with horror as their children played games during which they pretended that they were proud, well-fed and strong Germans, and declared that when they grew up they would be Germans. The war also changed the natural relationship, or more precisely, accelerated and warped the natural evolution of the relationship between Jewish children and their parents. For every child, up to a certain moment in his life, the adult world is concentrated around his parents. It is just mother and father who, in the child's understanding, can do everything. Under normal conditions this "omnipotence" gradually loses its attributes, until the child notices one day that his parents' abilities are limited by their place in society. The war disturbed this natural evolution. Under the conditions of war, the "omnipotent" father and mother lost their attributes of omnipotence overnight. Jewish children suddenly noticed that in this world the Germans were stronger than their parents, that their parents were afraid of the Germans and as defenseless against them as the children themselves. Jewish children sensed that their parents could not secure safety for them, their own children, and they felt deceived. The first bitterness and anger at the parents appeared.

The possibilities of hiding Jewish children and their parents together in one place were virtually nil. While Jewish parents were looking for ways of saving their children, they did not hide from them the fact that if they found people willing to hide the children, the family would be separated and such a separation would give parents and child a better chance of survival. Jewish children often understood their parents' plans and attempts unequivocally: Mommy and Daddy do not love me, they want to get rid of me for I am an obstacle in saving their lives; they want to get rid of me at all costs; this is why they are eager to give me, their own child, up.

The fact that even today some of these people—now grown adults, usually with children of their own—are still convinced this was the case is evidence of how strongly those childish accusations were believed. Because of the particularly personal nature of this perceived rejection and because of the cherished memory of their parents, these survivors all speak about this with the same tragic feeling of unloved children in their voices. They hold grudges against their parents, even if their parents were killed during the war or committed suicide because they could not see any chance of survival for themselves. Some still cannot be persuaded that only in rare cases was their separation a result of a lack of love. In the eyes of the children there are no reasons or justifications good enough for parting with one's parents. They felt abandoned, especially in those instances when they were left to be found by strangers.

Jewish children, therefore, entered convents with a double burden: their status as a Jew, which took away their basic rights, and their feeling of being unloved and abandoned by their own parents. They entered convents with anxieties about the unfamiliar "Aryan side," fearing the life that awaited them there and uncertain whether they could play the role of someone else convincingly enough.

Quite a different attitude toward parents can be observed in older children, those around ten years old and older, who to a great extent rescued themselves. They escaped from the ghettos that were being destroyed because their parents told them to do so and because they feared death—and they took various roads leading them to convents. But mother, father, sisters and brothers were left behind.

The children knew, or they were convinced, that their families were dead. An irrational feeling of guilt grew in them and the conviction, haunting some even to this day, that if they had stayed, maybe they would have been able to save those near and dear to them. Likewise, a feeling that they had betrayed their families grew in these children. If they could not have prevented the deaths of their family members, they reproached themselves for not having died with them.

Once in the convents and orphanages, Jewish children's perceptions of the life which had befallen them was conditioned by their earlier experiences. If their parents had been able to maintain the peace, warmth and living conditions of a normal home until the very moment of parting, the child could not understand the loss of these comforts and had difficulty adapting. A life in a group setting, with a strictly defined and monotonous existence, sometimes under strict discipline and usually under difficult living conditions, became the cause of a great deal of stress, rebellion and protestation. The period of assimilation was very long in such cases; sometimes it was never completed. A vast majority of the children, however, had already lived through the typical, tragic experiences of the ghetto: the death of loved ones, hunger, homelessness, and an uncertain future. When they came to the convents they were numbed, frightened, and expected the worst. But nothing happened. Day after day went by, and each day they got up in the morning, had breakfast, said their prayers, played, learned and worked. Slowly their numbness passed, and in a short time the convent home became to them an oasis of peace in which they could feel safe.

The feeling of peace and safety reigning in the convent made the war recede into the background, outside the convent walls. Little by little their lives became concentrated on what was happening in their own worlds, on their friends' problems, and on carrying out the duties assigned to them. An atmosphere developed in which emotional bonds could be established. Friendships were born between mates, and bonds arose between children and their favorite nuns. Never, or only very rarely, do the children, now adults, speak in the same way about all the nuns in a given home. Most of them are described as "awful" or "not too bad," but usually there is one, a special one, who was "wonderful."

Obviously Jewish children, like all children, were extremely critical of adults—in this case the nuns—and it must be conceded that these feelings were often justified. Not all the nuns could or wanted to act toward the children in a way which would be considered pedagogical. Even the best mothers happen on occasion to do something wrong in regard to their children, and the best Polish nuns were no exception. Children forgive their mothers everything—but they do not forgive nuns. This is why some of the children have remembered the injustices and wrongs done to them in the convents to this very day. It is significant, however, that despite even the sharpest criticism, each of the children seems to have known at least one nun about whom he or she says today: "She was different." And this is usually followed by descriptions of the kindness, righteousness, and "wonderfulness" of that nun who was chosen by the child and who accepted the child in a special way.

The convent community typically consisted of a dozen or so overworked nuns, and a group of children. The nuns made a point of treating all the children in the same way, but the children could not treat all the nuns in the same way. The Jewish ones were orphaned, lonely and unhappy, and a "ration" of warmth and kindness was not enough for them. At least from their favorite nun they received more, and, in turn, they gave more. They became more open with their favorite nun and confided to her past experiences and everyday problems. Life was easier when there was someone before whom one did not have to play a role, whom one could tell about his or her Jewish family and the nightmares witnessed in the ghetto. Those children who were told by their parents or guardians to hide their identity from everyone, even from the nuns, were in the worst situation. The nuns, not knowing about the children's background, were not able to secure them such protection as their situation required, and throughout the time of the occupation the children were alone with their tragedy.[2]

A Jewish child's survival in a convent was dependent on a complete assimilation into the surrounding Polish environment. When Germans visited convent orphanages to look for Jewish children, they not only checked their documents, but they also checked their religiousness by telling them to pray or to repeat the catechism. It was not enough to have a baptismal certificate with a new name and surname, or a new hairstyle or a bandage hiding Semitic features. Equally important was a new manner and the knowledge of proper religious behavior. Jewish children realized the rules of this game, even many of the youngest. At times they gave expression to this in a simple-minded way by saying, for example: "I am not Icek, I am Jacek," or "My name has to be Wroblewski, or else the Germans will kill me." Then they usually added a Catholic prayer, or quickly crossed themselves.

Making the sign of the cross, keeping a rosary in the pocket, and wearing a holy medal on the neck constituted a sort of set of magic charms protecting the child from German hatred. They provided a zone of safety which strengthened the attachment to these, the simplest outer signs of Catholicism. The children most often had learned a few things about Catholicism from their parents or guardians. In the convent observation of their peers, taking part in daily prayers and receiving religious instruction made the religious education of Jewish children progress very quickly, and in a short time the initial imitation and mimicking of prayers evolved, unnoticeably even for the children themselves, toward an authentic religious involvement. Several factors facilitated this evolution, among them—as previously mentioned—the fact that a decided majority of the Jewish children saved in Polish convents came from non-religious families. They were the children who had received no notion of God in their homes, who had received no model of religious thinking and religious traditions which could constitute an efficient barrier, or some other reference, in regard to the religion learned in the convents. For most of them the Catholic religion was the first religion in their lives, and an authentic religious involvement did not require them to give up anything or experience guilt for the betrayal of their own religion and tradition. In the case of older children, even if they did not know the Jewish religion but were conscious that it existed, another, equally important factor influenced their attitude toward Catholicism. To a certain degree they were affected by the problem of feeling that the Jewish God had abandoned His nation. This was expressed in questions and statements like: "Where is God?" "God has left the Jews" and "There is no God." That is why some children, even before they actually got to know the Christian God, sometimes, in especially tragic circumstances, took a pledge of faith to Christ. One of the saved girls, now living in Israel, came from a religious family and when she was abandoned by the whole world, she knelt in a field and for the first time started praying to Christ, promising Him that if He saved her it would mean that He is God and she would never leave Him. That same day she came upon a convent and was admitted.

A more profound knowledge of the Catholic religion brought a different meaning to their religious experiences. The children from the suffering ghettos found themselves in the convent chapel where they met Christ-the-Jew, the Redeemer of the world, suffering on the cross. With Him their carefully hidden Jewish nationality acquired a different meaning, it lost the character of a brand—for, after all, Christ was also a Jew. Therefore, at least in front of Him, the Jewish children stood without barriers. In the Christian consciousness Christ was never a Jew. But for tormented Polish Jews and their children, who in their suffering during the war turned to Christianity, their first thoughts were likely of a tortured, crucified Christ-Jew whose suffering and death was not unlike their own. When seen through Christ's Passion and Death, the suffering and death of Jews acquired a new dimension.

Orphaned, lonely Jewish children who had been deprived of both their families and their childhood in one stroke, who had lost their mothers or were convinced that they had lost their love and had been abandoned by them, also met in the chapel of a Catholic convent Christ's Mother, a Jewess, who cried over Her Son's suffering and over the suffering of all Her children on the earth. The nuns, as well as the priests from the pulpit, said that all people are Christ's brothers and that they, Jewish children, are also Mary's children. The children understood that owing to Her, Mother-Jewess, who loves and protects all children, they had found refuge in the convent; that it was She who told the nuns to rescue Rachela, Icek, Marysia and others; that it was for Her and through Her that the nuns were so good to them. The strength of the religious feelings connected with the Mother of God was increased in the Jewish children by the cult of Mary, which was greatly developed in Polish Catholicism and which expressed itself by the great number of Church holidays and their rich liturgy, and also by the children's longing for their own mothers. To this day rosaries, as well as pictures and holy medals depicting the Madonna, constitute a great majority of the mementos kept by the Jewish children saved in convents. Inset in albums or secured among objects of highest value, they are a relic or a remembrance of the Mother during the war.

The absurd accusation that Jews as a nation are guilty of Christ's death, common in the liturgy and in the Catholic teaching of that time, was a source of yet another burden for Jewish children. The children, already deeply believing and loving their God-Christ, when they heard that they, as a tiny part of the Jewish nation, were saddled with the blame of crucifying Him, felt the need for expiation for a crime they had not committed. Perhaps this is why they spent solitary hours thinking, praying, lying prostrate with their arms outstretched in an empty chapel, or showing other signs of religious zeal which differentiated Jewish children from others. In the nuns' accounts we often come across the claim that this or that Jewish child was baptized at his or her own request or even demand. On the surface such statements should not be taken too seriously, for how can one take the demands of young children seriously? But the war created children who were different, and comparing them with the children who lived in peaceful times serves no purpose. Jewish children knew that they were being persecuted because they were "different," and that the difference stemmed from their being unbaptized. And they did not want to be different! They wanted to have the right to live like all the other children; they wanted to get rid of their difference by being baptized. And sometimes they were not satisfied with private baptism, for they wanted to be baptized in the truest way, at church and by a priest. Only such a baptism made them real Catholics to whom Germans— as the children understood it—had no claim.

Certainly, the children's desire to be baptized also arose from their own religious zeal. Constantly threatened with death, they wanted to be baptized so that—in case they were caught by the Germans and died—they could, according to the Catholic teaching, go "straight to the angels, to heaven." The need to constantly appear to be Poles and scrupulously conceal their Jewish traits, coupled with a religiousness that grew with time and was eventually crowned with baptism, created a situation in which Jewish children began to pretend less and less, for they identified themselves increasingly with Catholicism and with the Polish character. The more assimilated the child's family was, the faster this identification took place. This new identification, together with the nuns' ceaseless care, made the Jewish children feel safe in the convents. "I wanted to be alive!" says one of them. "I wanted very much to be alive! And at a certain moment I reached a tremendous feeling of safety. I was absolutely convinced that I would survive that way. I was sure of it...."[3]

This new internal identification seemed to guarantee them life and safety, which, consequently, forced the children to view their Jewishness as something only of the past. They reasoned: "For me Christianity equalled heaven and life, while being a Jew equalled hell and death." Identification with Polish nationality and Catholicism (which meant for Jewish children "life") together with the negative attitude to Jewishness ("death") became one of the primary reasons why a negation arose in their psyche toward Jews and Jewishness as alternatives to their own national and religious identification. Then there were the experiences of the ghetto—experiences which returned with redoubled strength after the first period of numbness had passed. The children remembered that in the ghetto one had to be afraid, above all, of the Jewish policemen, and many of them could repeat each of Icchak Kacenelson's words:

I am the one who saw it, who watched it at close range,
As children, wives and husbands, and my grey-headed old men
Were tossed like stones and wood onto wagons by butchers
Who beat them mercilessly and abused them with inhuman words.

I was looking at it through the window; I saw gangs of murderers—
O God, I saw the beating and the beaten on their way to death;
I wrung my hands in shame—shame and disgrace—
Jewish hands were inflicting death on Jews—defenseless Jews!

Shiny-booted traitors running furiously in the empty street
With a swastika on their caps—and the shield of David,
With their piercing foreign words, proud and savage ones
Who threw us downstairs and dragged us out of our homes,

Who tore doors out of their frames and forced their way inside,
With clubs raised to deal a blow in our homes full of fear;
They beat us, they drove the old ones, rushed our youngest
Somewhere to the terrified streets. And they spat straight in God's face.

They found us in wardrobes and dragged us from under beds,
And cursed: 'Damn you, get to the umschlag where your place is!'

They dragged us from our apartments and went through them for a while
To take the last clothes, a piece of bread and some groats.

And in the street—madness! Look and be shocked,
Here's a dead street, with one cry it's become a nightmare;
Empty from end to end, but full as never before—
Wagons! Wagons heavy with despair and screams...

There are Jews in them! Tearing their hair, wringing their hands.
Some are silent, and their silence is an even louder scream.
They look—they see—can it be? Or is it a bad dream and nothing more?
Beside them are Jewish police—cruel and savage cut-throats![4]

In the scene described by the poet, or in incidents where they had been betrayed by Jews, the parents and siblings of the children hiding in the convents died. And the children who went through such an ordeal in this way expanded the negative view of the Jewish police to the Jewish nation as a whole.

Polish war experiences seen by the Jewish children from the perspective of the convent also had a share in creating and strengthening the negative image of Jewishness in their minds; these experiences induced them to make comparisons. Jewish children, coming from assimilated families, identifying themselves with Polishness, and knowing only the Polish concept of a dignified death, could not and did not understand, like many adult assimilated Jews and all Poles, the Jewish dignity of dying. This is why Rachela, saved by the nuns co-operating with the partisans, said: "In the convent I felt safe, although I also saw Poles die. But this was a different sort of dying! A different sort of dying!"[5] Certainly, the negative attitude of Jewish children toward Jewishness was also deepened by the Christianity they were learning about, in which the words of Gospel, speaking about the circumstances in which Christ was sentenced to death, were the source of a centuries-old tradition of accusations directed against Jews as the people guilty of His death. Such accusations were never brought directly against the Jewish children, but, as Sister Bernarda recollects:

In our orphanage there were various children, a real medley. Once I had a reading from the Bible from which it followed that Jews crucified Christ. Oles, an intelligent boy, took me aside and said, not in the presence of the other children: "Sister, so the Jews were worse than the Germans!" That child felt. He felt everything! I should have paid special attention to that child, that Jewish child, because Oles... well, but this is how it was.[6]

It is tragic that these Jewish children, who suffered so much during the occupation, were not spared in this regard by Christianity, and that to their thousand torments was added misplaced guilt for the death of Christ; and, consequently, the torment of a negative attitude toward their own heritage. The years of the German occupation of Poland and the years of the holocaust became for Jewish children hiding in convents a difficult time for self-definition, which eventually resulted in a national-religious identification with Polishness and Catholicism that gave them a feeling of safety. Reaching the "safe side" and this Polish-Catholic identification involved the denial of their pre-convent Jewish status and led to a negation of their Jewishness.

CHAPTER VI

WHY THEY SAVED THEM

AS AN EMPLOYEE OF THE SOCIAL WELFARE DEPARTMENT of the capital city of Warsaw and a Zegota activist, Jadwiga Piotrowska contributed to saving at least fifty Jewish children. When asked what she thought her gains were from those years, she answered:

> The awareness that I behaved in a decent manner and with dignity. And also, a deep wound in my heart which is there even today. ... When Poland was liberated in 1945 a Jewish Community was established, and Janek Dobraczynski and I went over to it to give them the lists of the saved children. They were not even full lists but the best we were able to reconstruct. We did not count on any gratitude, but we did not even think someone could accuse us....
>
> During the conversation we were told that we had committed a crime by stealing hundreds of children from the Jewish community, baptizing them, and tearing them away from Jewish culture. We were also told we were worse than the Germans. The Germans only took the body; we took the soul, condemning the children to damnation. Our arguments that we were fighting for their lives were put off right away: "It would have been better if those children had died...."
>
> We left completely broken. ... Over forty years have passed, and I am still grappling with this in my conscience. Would it really have been better if we had sent those children to their deaths? I sometimes even pray for a wise rabbi to take this burden off my shoulders.[1]

The accusations brought against Jan Dobraczynski and Jadwiga Piotrowska by representatives of the Jewish nation were also leveled at Polish nuns. This argument was the same one that led the Warsaw ghetto activists to reject an offer by the Warsaw clergy to shelter several hundred Jewish children in convents, and it was the same argument used by some rabbis to discourage Jewish parents from individually putting their children in convents. The conference of the Jewish social activists of the Warsaw ghetto took place in 1942, more or less at the same time rabbis, facing the extermination of Jews, gave their advice to Jewish parents. Since it was just at this time that Jewish children began appearing in Catholic convents, and the isolation of the ghettos made it impossible for the Jewish religious leaders to get reliable information on the treatment of children in these institutions, their negative judgment was made before Polish nuns were able to demonstrate their good intentions. It appears, then, that the accusations made by these leaders did not result from negative experiences or appraisals of the conditions in the convents, but were deeply rooted in the religious, national and cultural tradition of their society, as well as in the principles of co-existence with the Christian world.

To Jews a Polish nun might have seemed like a Christian soldier whose task it was to convert the infidels. And not only were nuns perceived in this way. Wladyslaw Bartoszewski, who during the war hid Moryc Gelber-Artymowicz in his apartment, recollects:

> Artymowicz asked for something to read, as he was terribly bored; and then he wanted to work for the underground. I refused to help him, explaining that he could not work in the underground for he could not walk the streets or else he would be arrested in a matter of a few hours. He was hurt by this response and insisted that he still wanted something to do. So I said that if he wanted I could bring him underground newspapers to fold and cut—as a bookseller he knew the job....
>
> Artymowicz was very eager to do this, for he was bored, so we brought whole loads of the papers from the printing-house (it was a Catholic press), and he cut, folded and packed it, and then the parcels were taken away by the girls who brought him food. Thus he became, in a sense, a collaborator with a Catholic organization.
>
> One day when I visited him he said he would like to do something for me. And what can you do for me? Perhaps some day, after the war; but now it is not important.
>
> "Perhaps, perhaps you would like me to be baptized?"
> Surprised, I assured him that it did not matter to me.
> "But perhaps you care about it?"

I left almost with tears in my eyes. For, please understand, this rather simple man, reading the Catholic papers because he was bored, came to the conclusion that since I had connections with such an organization, he would repay me by accepting baptism.[2]

Actual evidence that Jewish children were being baptized in convents was not necessary to formulate accusations against the nuns. The stereotype of Christian missionaries prevalent in Jewish circles was sufficient to alarm the community, the more so that from the point of view of the Jewish religion this was a problem of the highest rank.

Jewish tradition allows for a temporary, ostensible conversion to another religion if this would save a Jew's life. The Marranos, the Portuguese and Spanish Jews are examples of such a situation; in the Middle Ages they accepted baptism in order to avoid religious persecutions, while secretly remaining with their own faith. Hence during World War II there were no obstacles for adult Jews to save their lives by accepting baptism and becoming confessors of Christ. The consciousness of adult Jews was already shaped, and there was no fear that if they survived, they would be prevented from returning to the Jewish religion.

This was not the case for the children, especially the youngest ones. The reality of the exterminations going on made religious Jews assume the worst, including the possibility that no one would survive who could reclaim Jewish children from the convents and restore them to their own religion. In such a situation the children, unaware of the fact that they belonged to the Jewish faith, would remain Christian, and in this way break a fundamental Jewish commandment forbidding idolatry. They would be guilty of *Hillul ha-Shem* (defamation of God's name) and doomed to damnation.[3]

Jadwiga Piotrowska and all the nuns taking part in rescuing Jewish children should not bear a grudge against those who made accusations against them, charges difficult for Christians to understand, for they resulted not so much from a negative appraisal of their actions, as from a desire to prevent Jewish children from breaking the rules of the Jewish religion. The accusations brought forward by Jewish national leaders seem to be equally difficult to understand and absolutely unjustified. They were also levelled during the war and were clearly characterized by anit-Polonism, while ignoring the value of human life. According to those accusations the people rescuing the children were guided by the desire to deprive them of their true nationality, and the lives of those children only had meaning and value when they lived for and in the Jewish nation. Jewish children, however, wanted to live.

According to the rules of their own religion Polish nuns, unaware of the fact that they did so against Jewish national-religious objections, rescued those Jewish children who stood before them crying and unhappy, hunted and terrified. And one should underline the fact that whether uttered by a child, parent or a good samaritan, there was always a request for this help. So the nuns always faced the problem of either saving a child or dooming it. In accordance with the dictates of their own religion and vocation, they admitted Jewish children in their convents and rescued them as best they could under the conditions imposed by the occupying Germans.

Asked why she risked her life saving Jewish children, Sister Syksta replied:

> I was guided by the thought of bringing relief to a child who was especially persecuted. I was conscious of my vocation. Looking from the perspective of many years, I am aware that I was exposing myself to a great danger, but at that time saving the life of that little helpless creature was all that mattered.[4]

Nuns, who gave up the worldly life to serve God by helping other people, strove to realize Christian ideals, which included putting aside hatred, resentment—and in the case of Jewish children perhaps anti-Semitism. It is no accident that among the orders active in Poland we find ones with names like "sluzebniczki," "sluzki" (Servants), "samarytanki" (Samaritans), "siostry milosierdzia" (Sisters of Charity), etc. They were obliged to serve those in need, and many of them saw that need in Jewish children. They risked their lives because this, too, was a Christian ideal.[5] As Christ said, "Greater love has no man than this, that a man lay down his life for his fellow man." (John 15: 13) Jan Dobraczynski, director of the Children's Welfare Department of the Warsaw Council during the war and involved in the action of rescuing Jewish children, recollects:

> There was an additional issue: Should those children be baptized? I thought that there could be no other solution. A Jewish child could not stay among Christian children without participating in their group prayers or without receiving the sacraments. Otherwise, this would cause a sensation which would

echo beyond the walls of the convent. [...] In the convent baptizing the children was an obvious thing. But objections arose from the Jewish side. One day I was given a message saying that a secret representative of the Jewish authorities—described only as a "doctor"—would like to see me about this problem. During our conversation the man asked: "And what will happen to those baptized children when the war is over?" I must admit that I just shrugged my shoulders. This did not seem to me a problem worth considering when we both could die at any moment. But I replied:

"I am a Christian, but my reasoning is like this: parents are responsible for their children and also for their religion. So, if after the war the parents, or the grandparents or close relatives, reclaim the child, they will have the right to restore it to the religion they confess."

"And if it will not be the parents? If it will be just some Jews?" the man asked.

"Then, I think, we shall have to wait until the children grow up and decide for themselves what religion they choose."[6]

Jan Dobraczynski was wrong in saying that for the nuns baptizing Jewish children was an obvious matter of course. He could not have known the opinions of all the sisters who were rescuing Jewish children. As the sources prove, he did not even know the opinions of the nuns he closely co-operated with.[7] To the Jewish representative he only expressed his views on the matter. In fact, some nuns did baptize the children, while others did not, and a majority of them accepted without question the false baptismal certificates presented to them. Some of the children were baptized in the convents because of a request by their parents. One such scene occurred when a Jewish father or grandfather threw a baby to a nun of the Franciscan Sisters of the Family of Mary in Ostrowiec Swietokrzyski, crying: "Bring him up! He's yours now!" And we will never know what Ania's mother felt and thought when she was leading the girl to the home of the Grey Ursulines in Radosc. The child had a chamber-pot and some clothes in her hand, and on her neck there was a card saying, "Baptize her and bring her up; her name is Ania."[8]

We cannot know what Jewish parents went through when, unable to save their own lives, they tried to save their children. Not infrequently, parents or relatives, upon giving a child to the nuns, made it clear that in case they should die the nuns should baptize the child and bring it up as a Catholic. Baptism and Catholicism for some Jews in Poland became a sort of magical charm that guaranteed one's life. Ania's mother probably believed that baptism would protect her daughter from death.

Certainly Jewish children were not always baptized at their parents' request. Sometimes the request was made by the children themselves. If we want to understand thier decision we would also have to take up the entire problem of adult Jews receiving baptism during or after the war, for the children who asked to be baptized were children in name only. "Teresa," Mother Tekla relates, "came to us when she was eleven. Certainly, she had a certificate. As it turned out later, she had not been baptized. However, she was receiving the sacraments all the time. She was a rather pious, practicing Catholic. Only after the Warsaw uprising in 1944—she had probably taken some oath—did she turn to an old nun and ask to be baptized. We baptized her in secret, so that nobody knew."[9]

In Teresa's case the decision to receive baptism was probably preceded by a long period of indecision. Obviously, if not for the fact that she got to know Christianity in the convent, she would most probably never have been baptized. But, on the other hand, if not for the convent, would Teresa have survived the occupation?

Sometimes the decision to baptize a child was made by the nuns, amongst other reasons because of a religious conflict arising as result of the contact of Jewish children with Catholicism. Receiving the Holy Communion without previously being baptized is a sacrilege—a sacrilege Jewish children were forced to commit. The nuns sometimes knew about it, more often they guessed. But the children themselves, having learned the rules of Catholicism, were unable to reconcile this, which sometimes led to situations like the one in the convent of the Sisters of the Immaculate Conception of the Blessed Virgin Mary in Szymanow:

> A group of children were preparing to take their first confession. One of the girls, brought to the sacristy which contained the confessional, suddenly burst out crying. The child admitted to the priest, who tried to comfort her as best as he could, that when her father had left her and her younger brother on the Aryan side, hoping that they would be saved, he forbade her under oath to reveal to anybody that they both had not been baptized. The conflict between the oath and the awareness that in going to Holy Communion she would commit sacrilege proved too much for the conscience of a nine-year-old. The nuns, when they were informed

of the incident by the priest, had the girl secretly baptized, and she was able to join the other children at first communion.[10]

The girl had to go to communion for her own safety, so that no suspicions would be raised. In this case the nuns had a choice between consciously allowing the child's sacrilegious communion or baptizing her in defiance of her Mosaic religion—a dilemma beyond human measure.

In some convents—perhaps in all of them—the colloquial term "Zyd" (Jew) was used. It meant someone who had not been baptized, though not necessarily a real Jew.

"We had a girl named Bozenka," Mother Tekla relates. "The children, as children are wont to do, teased her, saying, 'You are a Jew!' And she would reply: 'Weren't you a Jew before they baptized you? You were also a Jew!'"[11] Jewish children were probably frequently reminded by their mates about their descent, and in this case it could have been the nuns who suggested this form of "defense," which in a playful way eliminated the "difference" between Jewish and non-Jewish children. Because if everyone is born a Jew—Bozenka did not have to feel inferior.

The nuns, using this mental scheme of Jew—unbaptized, non-Jew—baptized, would probably have preferred that the Jews in their convents were baptized. Concerning one of the Jewish girls kept with the Sisters of the Good Shepherd in Lublin:

"The Germans remarked," Sister Michaela relates, "that she was a Jewess. As she had already been baptized and had a certificate, this could be resolutely denied. The child was saved."[12]

The child was saved. Maybe just because the nuns denied the Germans' suppositions with such resoluteness and earnestness? Who knows—if the child "had still been a Jewess," perhaps the denial would have sounded less certain? Perhaps the nuns, especially sensitive to lies, would not have been able to lie in such a way that would have sounded convincing? In this case, the girl's baptism exempted them from lying and the nuns could, with full conviction, even take an oath in front of the altar that the girl was not a Jew—for the day before she had been baptized!

Lying did not come naturally to the nuns. It was not an easy thing. A lie was always a lie. But they knew that they had to rescue the children, and in order to do that they had to lie. Yet it must have frequently happened that they raised their eyes to the sky whispering, as one Sister of Charity in the Boduen house did, "God, forgive me!"[13]

When considering the question of baptizing Jewish children, one must not overlook other important aspects of the problem. First of all, nuns were women who consciously and intentionally, by their vows, transferred all their maternal love to children who needed love and were deprived of it. They loved the children not because they were Polish, Ukrainian, Gypsy or Jewish—they loved them because every child needs love. And Jewish children, burdened with the heavy burden of their experiences and exceptionally endangered, required their special care and a double amount of love. The natural result of this was the formation of unusually strong emotional bonds between the Jewish children and the nuns.

"She always reached out with her trembling little hands," Sister Gregoria recollects, "and this moved everybody very much. It was like a symbol of a request, of a plea."[14]

When a man brought a little, beautiful Jewish girl to the Carmelites of the Child Jesus, and asked them to take care of the child, "the carriage was put in the room near the telephone and every nun wanted to do the girl a good turn. Tela had already learned to babble," the nuns noted down; "once, when she saw our Mother Superior she started calling 'mother,' but the Mother was in a hurry. Then, without any prompting and out of the longing for a mother, she cried: 'mommy!' Once a trusted person brought in a little girl, a beautiful black-haired Jewess. The miserable, infested child looked at Sister Anuncjata and said: 'mommy!' And this little Zosia, nursed back to good health and cleaned, walked around the convent making the life of the adults happier."[15]

Sometimes the word "mommy" was uttered in desperation, as in the case in Sambor, where a Jewish girl who had miraculously escaped a German bullet, several minutes after her parents had been murdered, rushed into the convent yard: "She threw her arms round the Mother Superior's neck and said: 'Germans have just killed my Mommy and my Daddy; Sister, please be my mother!'"[16]

Polish nuns were mothers for those children even if the word "mommy" was not commonly used. Therefore, they baptized Jewish children, doing what all Christian mothers do to protect their children. It seemed to them that in such cases baptism was something like a "pass" to paradise. Then too, there were nuns who baptized the children because they thought that only their religion would give redemption, and they wanted everybody to be redeemed. Little Janeczka Kapral, who was hiding with the Sisters of the Holy Family of Nazareth, used to say to Sister Eliza: "I want everybody to love me so much!"

"I always assured her," Sister Eliza recollects, "that we all loved her. Unfortunately, I was not able to defend her. One day a car drove up to our little house in Olsztyn; some Germans got out of it. I saw this and ran. Janeczka was standing against the wall, it seemed that her fingers were hooked into it. I rushed to the verandah. There were two Germans. One was holding the child with one hand and, with the other hand, a machine gun. I explained that it was a mistake. I wanted to baptize her—all in vain. They took her to the car. Even today I can see the poor dear resisting; her little feet sinking in the sand..."

"Janeczka's parents were arrested," another nun adds, "and they disclosed where their child was staying; and as it was in Olsztyn, the Gestapo came here and took her away. I regretted very much I did not baptize her. We wanted to do it but the Gestapo forbade us."[17]

Today Sister Eliza and Sister Rozmaria live in different places, and gave their accounts independently of each other, but both remember Janeczka very well; they loved her. Sister Eliza knew she was Jewish, yet she had not baptized her earlier. Since love proved insufficient to save the child's life, the nuns wanted to baptize her for her way to death. That was the last assistance they could offer. After forty years they recollect bitterly that they failed. The nuns instinctively behaved like Christian mothers. If Janeczka had been their own child, the despair after her loss would likewise have been deeper if she had died without being baptized.

The nuns also baptized abandoned children, and of this group the rate of baptism seems to be the highest. This stands to reason, as only with respect to circumcised boys was there no doubt that they were Jewish. This certainly does not mean that baptizing Jewish foundlings was a rule in all orders—there were no rules in this respect, regardless of the children's age and the circumstances of their admittance. In the same order we can come across children who were baptized immediately after they had been taken into the convent, and children whose lack of baptism did not really bother the nuns. Chris N.N., who was hidden throughout the war, had arrived at the Albertine Sisters' home in Cracow as a baby before the war. "When he was eighteen," one of the nuns relates, "he needed his birth certificate. He came to us to get it, and then he learned that he had not been baptized—so he received baptism."[18]

Janek B. stayed with the Passionist Sisters from his infancy. When the war broke out he was eleven.

"He somehow preserved his faith, hiding it before others, and prayed in his own way," a nun recollects. "He was baptized only in November 1943."[19]

Maria Klein from Israel, saved by the Sacred Heart Sisters in Przemysl together with twelve other Jewish children, wrote:

> I did not get baptized in the convent, even though I wished to. During the bombardment of Przemysl I asked a priest who was with us in the shelter to baptize me but he refused.
>
> When I came to the convent I did not even know how to cross myself. I took Sister Ligoria's advice and knelt at the very back of the chapel and mimicked praying. Sister Ligoria said I should do it in order not to differ from the others, but she also said that each of us had our own faith; the war would end someday, and if my parents survived I would remain Jewish, but one's faith is not a pendulum and one cannot change it. So when I became twenty-one, I would have the right to do what I wanted.
>
> The nuns in no way tried to influence me to receive baptism. Somehow a Hebrew prayer-book found its way to the convent. Keeping something like that jeopardized one's life, just like hiding us did. I could even differentiate and read some letters when Sister Bernarda asked me what they were. So she locked me in her room every other day so that I would not forget how to read those few letters that I knew. She said: 'Pray to the Jewish God, and we will pray to Lord Jesus. If we all pray, then perhaps we will survive the war.'[20]

One of the main reasons Jewish children were baptized in the convents is that the nuns were ill-prepared to work with Jews. Many of the nuns did not realize that it was against the Judaic religion for Jewish children to be baptized, and they had no guidance on the issue from Catholic authorities. This is why we see such a variety of responses. Some Jewish children were baptized immediately, while others were supported in their Jewish traits and customs and required to exhibit Catholicism only in external form to save their own lives.

In 1960 Tadeusz Berenstein and Adam Rutkowski wrote: "A number of Jewish children found refuge in convents, not only for purely humanitarian reasons, but—it must be said for the sake of historical truth—for missionary ones."[21]

The sources at our disposal do not allow for such a statement about a "historical truth." The whole complexity of the issue of baptizing Jewish children in Polish convents still cannot be grasped. But it is certain that the authors quoted above have formulated their rather audacious opinions without proper foundations, without even an attempt at understanding the complexity of the issue, while applying only one criterion: baptism. According to them, there were two types of nuns: those who baptized Jewish children (that is, those who rescued them for missionary reasons), and those who did not baptize the children (that is, those who rescued them for humanitarian reasons).

The issue of baptizing Jewish children is certainly immensely important in understanding the psychological-religious reasons why Jewish children were rescued in Polish convents. However, this cannot constitute the only, or even the most important, factor in evaluating the motivations which guided the nuns. What had the strongest impact on saving Jews in Poland, including Jewish children, what weighed heaviest on making the decision to rescue them, was the death penalty with which Polish rescuers were threatened.

In order to try to save a Jewish child's life, a Polish nun had to overcome her fear of death and be prepared for the highest sacrifice, that of her life. It is very unlikely that Polish nuns, even those in the missionary orders, would make such a decision solely based on the hope—and not even the certainty—of adding one more member to Catholicism. Such a decision can only be taken in the name of the highest ideals. For Polish nuns the ideal was Jesus Christ, and they had to follow His example in their lives. When a Jewish child stood at the convent gate, begging for help, the nuns had to ask themselves this one question: What would Christ do in such a situation? The Jewish child standing at the convent gate was a human being, a human being whose life should be saved, even if one had to sacrifice one's own life. Of the missionary orders, only the Franciscan Missionary Sisters of Mary rescued Jewish children during the war. Their convents in Zamosc and in Labun-Radecznica were open to all the children from the Zamosc region, and in those convents nobody asked where the children were from or what their religion was. This was in agreement with paragraph 112 of the convent constitution, which says: "Let them take special care of poor and abandoned children, remembering that the Lord Jesus loved the little ones of this earth above all."[22]

CHAPTER VII

THE EXTENT AND TERRITORIAL RANGE OF THE ACTION

ACCORDING TO HISTORIAN SZYMON DATNER, one should distinguish between temporary and sustained actions in the rescue of Jews in Poland during the Second World War. The temporary actions consisted in "a single, short, and passing contact; in giving the pursued one what he needed most at the moment: a piece of bread, some soup, old shoes or clothes, a moment of rest in a warm recess, or a night's lodging." Rescuing in the proper sense of the word consisted in continuous or systematic contact with the one who was being rescued; and according to the same author, when more than one person was rescued, this was collective rescuing; and when more than ten were saved, it was mass rescuing.[1]

Of the active women's religious orders working in German-occupied Poland, I was able to find documents, participants or witnesses for thirty-seven convents which took part in the action of permanently rescuing Jewish children by hiding and educating them. For another six convents there is only an oral tradition passed on to the young nuns by the nuns who had taken part in the action and who have passed away.[2] In still another six, the nuns rescued only adult Jews. Altogether forty-nine—that is, two-thirds of the seventy-four active women's religious orders in Poland—took part in rescuing Jews.[3] As far as the contemplative orders are concerned (on the eve of World War II there were eleven of them) I have been able to find evidence of sheltering Jews only in four: in Wilno, with the Dominican Sisters; in Lowicz, with the Bernardines: in Lwow, with the Clarists of Perpetual Adoration and the Benedictines. On the basis of the collected sources it can be said that of the above-mentioned 37 convents, five saved one child each, while fifteen convents rescued between two and ten children, and seventeen sheltered more than ten young Jews.

It should be remembered that the sources collected or reconstructed forty years after the war do not give a complete picture of the nuns' work during the war. Because the number of saved children is based upon what is known (most often the smallest possible number), we may assume that the number of Jewish children saved in convents is actually greater; only in a few cases is it probable that nuns were not hiding more Jewish children than we know about. The following orders saved one Jewish child each: the Antonine Sisters, the Sisters of Charity of St. Charles Borromeo, the Passionist Sisters, the Sisters Servants of the Cross and the Notre Dame Sisters. The following convents saved from two to ten Jewish children: the Daughters of Mary Immaculate, the Dominican Sisters, the Sisters of St. Michael the Archangel, the Elizabethan Sisters, the Disrobed Sisters of the Holy Name of Jesus, the Canonical Sisters of the Holy Spirit, the Carmelite Sisters of the Infant Jesus, the Oblate Sisters, the Sisters of Divine Providence, the Sisters of the Good Shepherd, the Sisters Servants of the Sacred Heart, the Seraphite Sisters, the Servants of Jesus, the Disrobed Sisters Servants of the Blessed Virgin Mary and the Sisters of St. Teresa. And the following orders saved more than ten Jewish children: the Albertine Sisters, the Disrobed Sacred Heart Sisters, the Felician Sisters, the Franciscan Missionary Sisters of Mary, the Sisters of St. Joseph, the Magdalene Sisters, the Sisters of the Holy Family of Nazareth, the Sisters of the Immaculate Conception of the Blessed Virgin Mary, the Franciscan Sisters of the Family of Mary, the Samaritan Sisters, the Sacred Heart Sisters, the Sisters Servants of Mary Immaculate (Pleszew), the Sisters Servants of Mary Immaculate (Stara Wies), the Sisters of Charity, the Grey Ursulines, the Ursulines of the Union of Rome and the Sisters of the Resurrection.[4]

Finding the exact or even approximate number of Jewish children saved in Polish convents is—and this should be stressed—impossible for many reasons. First of all Jews and Jewish children in Poland were rescued in deep secrecy. No reasonable nun kept a separate record of the Jewish children that were admitted to her institution, for such a record could cause the death of both the children and the nuns. Where records still exist, the Jewish children usually cannot be distinguished because they were often given Polish names. Moreover, the mothers superior were often the only nuns who knew all the Jewish children admitted to their convents, and these women were, as a rule, older, more experienced nuns, of whom only a few are still alive. Most have not left any memoirs, and if they have, there is no mention made of saving Jewish children—an action they viewed as their Christian duty, not an extraordinary accomplishment. For this same reason, they did not supplement the registration books or other official records with proper notes after the war. Asked why they had not done it, the nuns answered that they thought no one would be interested in such things. The only primary source of information about the number of rescued children is the nuns who are still alive, and who, during the war, were usually young tutoresses. Unfortunately, they only know about those children directly under their care. Such a nun can fully account for the number of Jewish children in her own group, but what if there were more groups in the orphanage, and what if the nuns in those groups are deceased? Estimating the number of children seems unreasonable in such a case, for one group might have been the only one with Jewish children or the one with the fewest Jewish children. The nuns' accounts reveal that during the war convents involved in various forms of illegal activity abided by the old conspiratorial rule: the less one knows the better. Each sister knew only what was indispensable for the work she was doing. Nuns who were friends did not ask each other about the Jewish children in their groups—it was safer not to know. But what about after the war, when they could have talked about everything? Nuns in active orders are often transferred from one home to another, especially the younger ones. The period after the war especially favored these peregrinations because of repatriation and the reconstruction of convent life within Poland's new borders. This is why the tutoresses, scattered in various parts of Poland, did not have the time, nor the opportunity, to exchange their war experiences concerning hiding Jewish children.

The four most active organizations concerned with caring for Jewish children in Warsaw prepared a report in March 1979 summing up the number of children saved by the Council for Aid to Jews. It stated that through the mediation of Warsaw's social welfare departments about five hundred children were admitted into the homes run by convents. Another two hundred were admitted into the Boduen Home, in which the Sisters of Charity were working. Moreover, about five hundred children were placed in social welfare institutes, some of which were also run by nuns from various orders.[5]

Becasue full lists of Jewish children saved by the Council for Aid to Jews did not survive the war, the above numbers are the only ones that can be considered more or less reliable. The same lack of documentation exists for the convents which did not have any institutions for children and just sheltered one or two Jewish children. It is impossible to find out the precise number of children in all the other homes. It would be impossible to do it even if full lists of the children transferred to particular convents by the Council for Aid to Jews had been preserved, for Jewish children found their way to the convents by other means also. Besides the children sent by the Council for Aid to Jews and institutions co-operating with it, the nuns also hid children that were found abandoned at the convent's threshold or sent by acquaintances, children who, of course, were not included in any lists. Therefore, if we accept the Warsaw report as reliable, the Council for Jewish Aid and the institutions co-operating with it sent more than seven hundred children, and if we add another several hundred children who found themselves in convents by some other means, we can reasonably state that the number of Jewish children saved in Polish convents was roughly 1,200.

How many more Jewish children were saved will probably always remain a secret. If we use the number of children saved as the criterion by which we judge the orders, then the Franciscan Sisters of the Family of Mary and the Sisters of Charity, the two orders with the greatest number of institutions in Poland during the war, made the greatest contribution. These orders also had the greatest number of nuns, and for each, the care of children was an important priority. Additionally, most of the homes of these orders found themselves in the General Government, and in the case of the Franciscan Sisters of Mary, the authorities of the order were involved in the action of rescuing Jewish children from the very beginning. The number of Jewish children saved by the Sisters of Charity runs into hundreds.[6] Sister Teresa Fracek has estimated the number of children saved in the convents run by the Franciscan Sisters of the Family of Mary at more than five hundred.[7] For several reasons girls constituted a decided majority of Jewish children saved by Polish nuns. The most fundamental one was that nuns did not run boarding schools for boys. Most of the orphanages run by nuns were for girls, too. Eventually, because of the needs created by the war, many of these orphanages also admitted boys, including Jewish ones. Infants' nurseries were as a rule for both sexes, and so there is not much difference between the number of very young boys and girls who were saved. Boarding schools and some orphanages for boys were run by priests and monks, and the story of rescuing Jewish boys in these institutions is left for others to tell. Another, important reason why more girls were saved, was the fact that it was easier to disguise their appearance. With boys, however, even if their appearance was "not bad" and their documents were perfect, the fact that they were circumcised was irrefutable proof of their descent.

"The circumcision of Jewish boys," wrote Emanuel Ringelbaum, "is a great obstacle in arranging their stay on the Aryan side. The number of Jewish children who are not circumcised is very small. The pressure of pious parents and relatives, and legal objections on the part of the Jewish community, were so great that very few parents, even very progressive ones, were able to refrain from having their male children circumcised."[8]

Records indicate 189 convents located within Poland's pre-war borders were active in sheltering children.

As stands to reason, these primarily large homes which saved ten or more children have more people who are still alive, both the Jewish children, now adults, who survived and the nuns who worked at the various institutions. Both groups help ensure the reliability of the statistics.

Inaccuracies arise when we examine the smaller homes where a few nuns saved one or two Jewish children. The death of the nuns, as well as a lack of contact with the saved children, makes it impossible to add such a home to the register of convents involved in saving Jewish children. Taking into consideration the above facts, we can safely say that the number of the convents rescuing Jewish children was probably slightly greater, approaching two hundred.

Some two hundred convents hiding Jewish children in Poland during the war—was this a substantial contribution or not? There are two answers to this question. Two hundred rescuing convents and more than 1,200 saved Jewish children is tragically few when compared with the extermination of tens of thousands of Jewish children in Poland. Yet when it is taken into account that the rescuers were twenty thousand Polish nuns struggling against similar difficulties and subjected to the same inhuman occupation, the number becomes more significant.

On the eve of World War II, women's religious orders were carrying on their activities in 2289 homes located throughout Poland. There has been no comprehensive study of the fate of each of these homes, but several years ago Professor Jerzy Kloczowski began researching women's religious orders during the wartime period, and his research has so far resulted in four volumes dealing with six orders: the Sisters Servants of Mary Immaculate (Pleszew), the Sisters Servants of Mary Immaculate (Stara Wies), the Sisters Servants of Mary Immaculate (Debica), the Sisters of St. Joseph, the Felician Sisters and the Sisters Servants of the Cross.[9] These studies reveal a marked decrease in the number of Polish convent homes working during the war when compared with the number before the outbreak of the war.[10]

Name of Order	Homes on Eve of War	Homes Where War Stopped Work
Sisters Servants of Mary Immaculate (Pleszew)	68	58
Sisters Servants of Mary Immaculate (Debica)	110	48
Sisters of St. Joseph	45	34
Sisters Servants of Mary Immaculate (Stara Wies)	339	158
Felician Sisters	78	40
Sisters Servants of the Cross	3	1
TOTAL	643	339

As we can see, the work of 339 out of the 643 homes of six woman's orders was stopped by the war, a 53% decrease.[11] If the number of convent homes closed down during the war was about 50% of the 2289 homes working before the war, the number of two hundred convents rescuing Jewish children assumes a new significance, allowing us to understand better the scale of the effort involved.

The best conditions for hiding and bringing up Jewish children during the war existed in the boarding schools and orphanages run by nuns—90% of the rescued children were sheltered in such institutions.[12] The six orders for which the data have already been published were running seventy-nine orphanages and boarding-schools at the moment of the outbreak of the war; these constitute 12.5% of the total of 643 convent homes.[13]

Keeping in mind this percentage, if we look at the bigger picture and compare the number of convent orphanages and boarding schools working in Poland in the years of World War II with the number of institutions of this type known to have rescued Jewish children, we can make an estimated guess that about three-fourths of the convent orphanages and boarding schools working on the Polish territories during the Nazi occupation took part in the rescue action.[14]

In compiling a map of places where there were convent homes rescuing Jewish children, I have mainly used convent sources, confirmed in ten cases by the accounts of the saved persons. In two cases, the saved persons' accounts were the sole basis for including the places in the map.[15]

Even at first glance we can see a great disproportion in the location of the 189 rescuing convents in Poland.

The main reason why the territories incorporated into the Reich in 1939 show no convent activity is Germany's particularly repressive policy toward the Polish Church, including the Polish nuns. A large scale displacement of the Polish population and severe restrictions imposed on Poles were accompanied by the ruthless persecutions of priests and nuns, plundering of convents and sacred buildings, closing of churches, raids on churches during services, and desecration of sacred objects.

The effects of this policy toward the Church in Wielkopolska and Pomerania were devastating to women's religious orders. This is best exemplified by the fate of the Sisters Servants of Mary Immaculate (Pleszew), of whose sixty-eight homes sixty were in the territories incorporated into the Reich. By September 1942, of the forty-five homes in the region of Wielkopolska, the nuns were working only in the alms-house and hospital in Szamotuly. They had been displaced from eighteen homes, expelled from another eighteen, and, after prior repressions, they were sent from eleven homes to the labor camp in Bojanowo. In the region of Pomerania, out of the fifteen existing homes, up until October 15, 1941, the nuns were working in only five.[16] Of the five orphanages existing in Wielkopolska and Pomerania before the war, all run by the Sisters Servants of Mary Immaculate (Pleszew), not one was left.[17] The only convent home in the discussed territory which was known to have rescued Jewish children, was the Lodz orphanage on Karolewska Street, run by the Sisters Servants of Mary Immaculate (Stara Wies). They did this until they themselves were expelled from their home and sent to the labor camp in Bojanowo. Anticipating they would be expelled from their home, they wanted to protect the children from getting into the Germans' hands and managed to give the Polish and Jewish children to Polish families.[18]

In the region of Silesia, where the policy toward the Polish Church was only a little more lenient than in Wielkopolska and Pomerania, the nuns managed to save several Jewish children: the Dominican Sisters in Chorzow, the Antonine Sisters in Wielun, and the Carmelites of the Child Jesus in Sosnowiec.[19] Jewish children, therefore, were rescued in the Silesian convents only sporadically. Here, too, a great majority of Polish nuns were expelled from their homes and deprived of the opportunity to undertake any activity. Unlike the Polish territories incorporated into the Reich in 1939, German policy was not the main reason why Poland's eastern territories (the Bialystok district incorporated into the Reich in 1941; the Wilno district and Volhynia, which in 1941 were renamed Reich Commissariat Osten and Reich Commissariat Ukraine; and Galicia, included into the General Government in the same year) constitute another blank on the map.

The beleagered status of the Catholic Church in the Bialystok and Wilno districts and in Volhynia was a result of the more than hundred-year period of partitions when those territories—called "the taken lands"—were incorporated into the Russian Empire. The czars' policy toward the Polish clergy, and especially toward religious orders, consisted of strict repressions. In 1832, after the November Uprising against the Russians, an order was issued to close down about two hundred convents and monasteries (nearly two thirds of the number in that area); the remaining ones were doomed to slowly die out.[20] In the Russian sector of partitioned Poland, opening convents or undertaking attempts at reviving convent life were doomed to fail due to the ever-increasing restrictions aimed at the Polish Church. Only when Poland won independence in 1918 were the necessary conditions created for the development of Polish religious orders. Despite the twenty years between the two World Wars and the dynamic development of new religious homes, on the eve of the outbreak of World War II that part of the country had the fewest convents and monasteries.[21] Galicia found itself in a far better situation before the outbreak of the war. During the period of partition, as part of the Austrian sector, Galicia saw the dynamic development of Polish religious orders in the second half of the 19th century. The low density of the Polish population in eastern Galicia, especially in the Stanislawow and Tarnopol districts, was the reason why there were fewer convent homes there than in western Galicia. Since Galicia's Polish population resided mostly in towns and villages in the west, it was there that active religious orders located their homes, establishing schools, nurseries, orphanages, and other centers which did various charitable works. From the first months of the war, the convent homes in the Bialystok and Wilno districts, in Volhynia and Galicia found themselves in the very difficult conditions imposed by the Soviets, who invaded Poland in September, 1939. The buildings and property of the convents were taken over by the occupying authorities, and the nuns were forced to take off their habits and take up jobs which often involved relocating. This led to the liquidation of some small provincial homes. In many cases Polish nuns shared the fate of the lay people living in Poland's eastern territories, and in several waves were transported to Siberia. The Soviet occupation of Poland's eastern territories fundamentally influenced the functioning of the convent homes in the area, even after it had ended in June, 1941, when Germany attacked the Soviet Union. Many of the homes, deprived of personnel and material goods, never resumed their work. In the remaining homes, shortages of staff and economic ruin—in the case of orphanages a shortage of bed-clothes, beds and dishes—limited their work.

Another important factor limiting the existence and reconstruction of convent homes in German-occupied Galicia and Volhynia was the Ukrainian massacres which began in 1942. These assaults and murders forced the nuns, along with the rest of the Polish population, to find refuge in bigger towns or to flee to central and southern Poland.

Apart from individual convent homes located considerable distances from each other, the only hub or center for rescuing Jewish children in the entire Bialystok, Wilno and Volhynia areas was in Wilno, where rescue action was undertaken at six convent homes. It should be added that the Wilno convents, cut off from their authorities and from material or organizational assistance by the new borders, undertook the action of rescuing Jewish children independently, from beginning to end, and at their own cost. In Galicia, which after the outbreak of the German-Soviet war in 1941 was absorbed into the General Government as its fifth district, thirty-four convents were rescuing Jewish children despite difficulties. As far as the number of rescuing convents is concerned, Lwow was second only to Warsaw: Jewish children were rescued by the nuns in eleven Lwow convents. This by no means trivial result of the rescue action in Galicia was possible mainly because of the above-mentioned broad diffusion of the convent homes throughout the towns of western Galicia, homes which were rooted in that area from as early as the second half of the 19th century and which managed to survive the Soviet occupation or were promptly re-established after it had ended.

Another important reason for the high number of saved Jewish children was the fact that the Lwow ghetto was the second largest ghetto in the General Government and a center of Jewish intelligentsia. Here Jews took a more active role in resisting the Nazis, which included sending their children to convents. Of all the territories in occupied Poland, only those incorporated into the General Government had a margin of freedom which allowed the Church to continue some of its proper functions. This was the area where the nuns managed to keep most of their convent homes; the war merely changed the range of their work, which evolved toward broadening charitable actions. The General Government was the only area in occupied Poland where rescuing Jewish children in convents assumed the character of a massive phenomenon—of the 189 convents rescuing Jewish children in Poland, 173 ones were located in the General Government; however, their distribution was not uniform and depended on many different factors.

The nuns in Warsaw and its surroundings were the most active. In Warsaw itself, twenty-three homes were refuge for Jewish children, along with forty-one more in Warsaw's environs; this constituted more than 37% of all the homes in the General Government known to have rescued Jewish children. There were many reasons why the Warsaw nuns were so active, and one of the most important was probably the atmosphere in Warsaw under the occupation. The author Zofia Kossak, together with members of the Front for Poland's Rebirth, was the first one in Warsaw to see the tragedy of Jewish children. Writing, speaking and acting in their defense, she tried to make Polish society aware of and sympathetic to the most defenseless victims of the war. The Warsaw Social Welfare and the RGO, as the first organizations of their kind, began the largest organized action of rescuing Jewish children in the General Government. And it was in Warsaw that the Council for Aid To Jews (Zegota) was established and worked most actively. All these factors certainly stimulated the Warsaw nuns to be active, forcing them both to respond to the need of the above-mentioned organizations, and to follow their example and undertake rescuing Jewish children on their own. Moreover, the Warsaw ghetto had struggled with the Germans long before the uprising of 1943. The Jews' resistance consisted of smuggling goods, escapes, and the will to maintain contacts with the Polish side. All this multiplied the needs and had a great significance for rescuing Jewish children in general, including rescuing them in convents.

After the above-mentioned Lwow, the third greatest center of convent rescue activity was Cracow, with seven rescuing convents in the city, five homes in nearby Tarnow, and several others in the surrounding villages and small towns.

The remaining convents, nearly seventy in number, were isolated in the various other territories of central and southern Poland included in the General Government. Noteworthy in this respect are Czestochowa and Lublin, with five saving convents in each of these towns, Kielce with four, Radom with three, and Busko Zdroj and Piotrkow Trybunalski with two in each. The question still arises, however, as to whether the Polish convents were used to their fullest potential in rescuing Jewish children. In truth, they were not. There were several reasons for this, but the primary one was that the rescue of Jewish children was never centrally directed or organized on a general scale.

Why did it happen like this? Because the Polish nuns did not have any central authority which could co-ordinate some common action or at least maintain communication between the orders. The conditions during the war made it difficult, or impossible, for convents to communicate, even with convents of of the same order, and likewise ruled out any declaration on the question of saving Jewish children, as in Nazi-occupied Poland such a declaration would be tantamount to death for both nuns and children.

Then there was the attitude in Jewish circles toward an organized action of rescuing their children in convents. Emanuel Ringelbaum concluded his relation of the conference in the Warsaw ghetto with the words: "People save themselves in various ways; let the convents' action have an individual character."[22]

So Polish nuns were rescuing Jewish children without the approval of the religious and national representatives of Jewish society. Their action was a response to the requests of individual Jewish parents and the nuns' own sense of decency.

CHAPTER VIII

RECLAIMING THE CHILDREN

THE WAR WAS OVER. Jewish children no longer needed to hide. The nuns in some convent homes, when they heard about Jewish communities being established, sent their Jewish wards there. But most of the children waited for their loved ones to retrieve them from the convents. Surviving Jewish parents were the first to reclaim their children. Those who were hiding near the convents or had stayed in Poland, came immediately after the military operations ended. Those who were driven farther, came as soon as they were able. When reclaiming their children, parents expressed their deep gratitude to the nuns, then they set out to re-establish the family bonds that had been severed by the war. If the child was baptized in the convent, the nuns informed the parents. The reaction, with few exceptions, was typically parental—the fact that the child was alive was more important than anything else. Baptized or not, the children were still their sons and daughters, and treasures to their parents. Sister Janina recalls:

> When the war was over a man with a Semitic appearance called at the convent and introduced himself as Helenka's father. Asked what proof he could give us that he was her father, he started to explain. He told us the story of her coming to our home, and he even knew that she had been ill with diphtheria and had to have a tube inserted; he told us many other details—all of them true. During the war, he had some people who watched what was happening to the child, and after his return he learned everything from them. With tears in his eyes he thanked us for our care of his daughter, especially when she was dangerously ill. It gave us a lot of satisfaction to have saved the child from death.

Helenka did not want to go to her father and would not accept anything from him. [Helenka was brought to the nuns as a several-month-old baby. E.K.] The father was heartbroken. We told him to come every day so that the child could gradually get used to him. Her mother also came. One cannot describe the moment when she saw her baby so big now and looking so well. She seized Helenka, crying with joy. She cuddled and kissed her, and thanked us. She was completely overwhelmed with joy. The child's heart warmed up, and she changed her attitude. The father, a tailor by trade, had already rented an apartment, so they wanted to take the child home. It was difficult to make her go with them. Finally she went, and all the children saw her off; we all cried; and Helenka said she would visit us every day.

And indeed she did. One day they all returned, and the parents said: "Well, Helenka has really put us through the mill! We had to pray together with her on our knees and cross ourselves, and only then could we go to bed!" We told them that Helenka had been baptized, to which they replied: "Let her be a Catholic; it is good that she is alive!" During their stay in Piotrkow they took her to church every Sunday, and afterward they called on us. In 1946 they left for Palestine.[1]

Few Jewish parents knew the fate of their children. Many did not know if their children had survived the Holocaust, much less, where they were living.

During the war none of the Jews kept records of the children leaving the ghettos or noted under what name the nuns would be hiding them, as the rescue of Jewish children had an individual character and depended exclusively on the efforts of their parents or a lucky coincidence. The moment children left the ghetto, their parents usually lost all contact with them, especially if the children received help from Polish underground organizations, who provided them with forged birth certificates with new names and surnames. The children adopted Polish names, and the nuns knew them only by these new names, with the result that parents searching for their children after the war knew only their real names, and the nuns only knew the names on the forged certificates. Creating more confusion was the fact that some children were transferred from one convent to another, through various parts of the General Government; after two or three years only the older ones remembered their parents and their own real names. The lists compiled by the Council for Jewish Aid employees never included all the children hidden in convents, and only fragments of these records survived the occupation. Therefore, for the first months after the war, anybody who knew a Jewish child's new name could claim to be a mother or father and take the child from the convent. Mother Superior Tekla Budnowska remembers:

> Reclaiming Jewish children started as early as 1945. We were then in Lubliniec Kujawski near Wloclawek. We had children from the institution in Lomna there, especially the little ones. When someone called at the convent, they gave a name and collected a child. But sometimes it was different.
>
> Once during the occupation nuns brought ten children, among them eight Jewish ones. I instructed one of the sisters who had brought them to ask the children their true names so that we could remember them after the war. We were told that all the children had been baptized. We accepted this, though the names on the certificates were certainly false. There was a girl whose name, according to the forged certificate, was Maria Wojtasik. I could tell she was Jewish, so I asked her what her real name was. She said it had always been Wojtasik. Then I asked again, as did the other nun. The girl kept answering that her name had always been Wojtasik. I asked the next girl—I cannot recollect the name she had on her certificate—what her name had been before, and the girl said it had been Jarzabek. And Maria Wojtasik responds: "So mine was Jarzabek too. Why can't I be Jarzabek?"
>
> Late in 1945 a trial took place in Warsaw; there were two fathers for one Jewish child. It just so happened that the child in question was the girl who said during the war that her real name was Jarzabek. I remembered her very well because of Marysia Wojtasik, who had said that her name was also Jarzabek. The trial was speeded up because of my planned departure for Brazil; I was a witness.
>
> The story went like this: There was a professor, a Jew, who managed to get to Israel before the war or, perhaps, at its beginning. Immediately after the war he came to Poland to look for his daughter. He somehow found out that she had been hiding with us, so he came to retrieve her. There was also another Jew who claimed she was his daughter. But the latter man did not know the girl's name was Jarzabek. Reclaiming the child, he gave the name that the girl had on the certificate. Finally the judge asked me which of them is the child's father. I said I thought the professor was, for his name was Jarzabek, and this was the name the girl gave during the occupation. I related the entire story of Jarzabek and Marysia Wojtasik. The girl went with her father to Israel.[2]

A similar case happened with another child. A man, claiming to be her father, came to take a girl who knew very well that her parents were dead. At that point Mother Superior Tekla started suspecting that Jews were taking those children as their own, and then they apparently gave them up to other Jews.[3]

News of cases like the one above reached all the convents. The nuns stopped trusting people coming to collect the children and claiming to be their parents or close relatives. Immediately after the war reclaiming the children from convents was not difficult (anyone who knew a child's name could come and collect it); later, the nuns wanted to know precisely with whom, where, and why a child was leaving. It will never be known, however, how many Jewish children wound up with someone else's parents, and how many Jewish parents searched in vain for their children throughout the convents while others were playing the role of parents.

Another sort of tragedy existed for those children whom the nuns had given up for adoption during the war, but whose parents or close relatives had survived. The nuns' decision to give up a child for adoption lay in the extremely hard living conditions of a convent home, as well as in evaluating the welfare of the child. If there was a family that wanted to take care of a child, the nuns gave it up in order to make room in the home for other children who needed help and to secure for a child a normal family life. It is doubtful that all the adopted Jewish children returned to their own parents, families or even nation. An undetermined number of them are still living among Poles.

The greatest hurdle to reuniting families, however, resulted from the fact that a considerable portion of Jewish children saved in Polish convents had become orphans; they were often the only members of their families to survive the Holocaust. Jan Dobraczynski writes:

> When I returned to Warsaw in 1945, I met some nuns from the establishments I knew. [...] They told me that on Szeroka Street in Praga there was a Jewish organization, the JDC (Joint Distribution Committee), which had brought over a lot of money to Poland. "Let them give something," the nuns asked, "for those few girls you sent to us once....
>
> After due consideration, I went to the JDC office. I was greeted by a young, unappealing clerk. When I told him my name, he nodded. "I know who you are," he said.

"If you know," I said, "then you undoubtedly guess why I am here. In the convent establishments I used to supervise over, there are Jewish children. The convents are in poverty. I am not asking anything for our children, but I think you could give something for yours...."

The young man smiled unpleasantly.

"I heard," he said, "that you once told the 'doctor'(I did not learn his name this time also) that if just any Jews comes to collect the Jewish children and not their parents, then the children would have to decide for themselves who they were: Jews or Poles. So now they are not our children but yours."[4]

After the war these Jewish orphans waited in vain for their parents to return. Those who would not look at them through the prism of national-religious motives and see them just as children were not alive anymore. The nuns' role as protector in those children's lives was technically over. The awareness of the Jewish children's right to leave was always very sharp in the nuns.[5]

Eventually, Jewish organizations in Poland and around the world initiated actions whose aim was to collect Jewish orphans from Polish convents. Among Polish organizations the Jewish Religious Congregation, the Coordination and the Jewish Committee were the first to become active.[6]

The Jewish Religious Congregation had branches in all the bigger cities in Poland and was managed in Warsaw by Rabbi David Kahane, who was also the chief Rabbi of the Polish Army. A Congregation member most involved in the action of collecting children from Polish families and Polish convents was Captain Jezajasz Druker. Connected with the Army Rabinate, he acted for and on behalf of the Congregation. The Congregation was financed by the Joint Distribution Committee (JDC), probably the largest organization of American Jews. The reclaimed children were put in Congregation orphanages in Zabrze and Gieszczepustem in Lower Silesia, and then sent to Jewish families in the United States, Great Britain and other countries. Apart from the money from the JDC, the Jewish Religious Congregation in Poland was supported by the chief Rabbi of England, Dr. Hertz, whose son-in-law, visited Poland twice after the war, returning with about two hundred children to be adopted into the families of English Jews. Among these children were ones who had been saved in convents. The Coordination was an association of Zionist organizations.[7]

In 1946 or 1947 Icchak Grynbaum, an ex-deputy of the Polish

Parliament, came to Poland to organize reclaiming Jewish children from Polish families and Polish convents in cooperation with all the Zionist parties active in Poland. As there were also Zionist parties in the Jewish Religious Congregation, the two organizations started working with each other. However, Icchak Grynbaum did not have sufficient funds at his disposal, so the cooperation did not last.[8] The Coordination had four orphanages of its own in Lodz, where they placed the children they had gathered. To the end of 1947 more than five hundred Jewish children left Poland with the help of the Coordination; they were sent to orphanages located in Germany, Austria and France, and later most of them went to Israel.[9] Independent of the Jewish Religious Congregation and the Coordination, the action of collecting Jewish children from convents was carried on by the Jewish Committee, an organization working in cooperation with and under the auspices of the Polish government. The Committee put the children it collected into its own orphanages located in, among other places, Otwock, Cracow and Bytom, where they were brought up with a goal of assimilation to Polish culture. Independent of all the above-mentioned organizations, the action of reclaiming the Jewish children saved in Poland was carried by Mrs. Lederman, who acted on behalf of the Swiss foundation of Mrs. Sternbuch.[10] Mrs. Lederman sent the children she had collected abroad to be adopted by Jewish families. In 1946 American Jews established an association called Aid to Children. This is what the founder of the association, Herbert Tenzer, wrote in the introduction to the inventory of the association's archival materials transferred to the Archivum of Yeshiva University in New York:

> When the war was over, the main Jewish organization oriented toward the religious rehabilitation of European Jews, the Vaad Hatzala Rescue Committee, faced a drastic shortage of funds, so I, along with a group of my closest friends, established Aid to Children. With the funds raised in America we were able to save many Jewish children wandering post-war Europe, as well as to demand that the children staying in Christian families and convents be returned.
>
> I am proud of having participated in the holy mission of aid which enabled innocent orphans to find the truth and their Jewish identity.[11]

Since Yeshiva University Archives has refused me access to the archival papers on Aid to Children, the only information I have about the activities of the association is from the author of the inventory, the late Lucjan Dobroszycki:

> The children who came under the protection of Aid to Children represented all the countries occupied by the Nazis during the war. A considerable portion came from Poland, a country where the Jewish population had been almost completely exterminated and where, as nowhere else, the children needed help from the outside world. One of the first to devote themselves completely to the orphaned was Dr. Isaac Herzog, the Chief Rabbi of Palestine, who was from Lomza. Provided with funds from the JDC, Rabbi Herzog set out on his journey through liberated Europe in 1946. The aim of his mission was to find and help the children scattered over an area of hundreds of miles, children who were alone in the world and unaware that they were Jews, though they came from very religious families.[12]

When he was leaving Poland, Rabbi Herzog took a considerable number of children with him, who were then given to Jewish orphanages in France. While Aid to Children was established for Jewish children from all of Europe, the main sphere of its operation was in Poland. The association placed the children it had reclaimed in Poland into Jewish orphanages in France, Belgium and Sweden. As Herbert Tenzer wrote, a third of them found their parents, a third were taken by relatives in America, and the remaining ones emigrated to Israel. Unfortunately, the ban on using the archives of Aid to Children does not allow me to establish the number of Jewish children taken out of Poland by the people acting on its behalf, or to find out how many of them were saved in Polish convents.

Collecting Jewish orphans from convents was only one phase of the action in which Jewish organizations participated. It is symptomatic that this retrieval of the children from convents or Christian families is what American Jews refer to as "rescuing," even though the war was over and the children's lives were no longer threatened. Many of the Jewish-American historians whom I have met still use the word "rescuing" when speaking of reclaiming Jewish children—and not only from convents.

It seems that we have come back to the starting point, to the problem of the attitude of Jewish society, or more precisely, of Jewish political and religious establishments, toward the question of saving their children's lives. The representatives of these establishments, faced with the holocaust going on around them, recognized that the only proper choice was the children's death. A small group of Jewish children, however, saved their lives in those terrible years. But in a great majority of cases lives only. And life alone, from the point of view of the Jewish religion and the Jewish idea of the nation, is valuable for people of Jewish stock only when it is a life in the Jewish religion and for the Jewish nation. Ignoring the importance of saving the children's lives during the war, American Jews, after the war, mobilized people and raised funds to energetically begin the proper, as they understood it, rescue action: rescuing the souls and the national spirit of the miraculously-saved Jewish children.[13]

"Saving" the saved—this is, reclaiming them from the convents—was done in a way which disregarded all the rules of pedagogy and the principles of psychology, as well as the welfare of the children as individuals.[14]

For, as David Kahane, the chairman of the Jewish Religious Congregation, told this writer:

> You should know that for the Jewish nation every Jew has something inborn that ties him to his Jewish descent. That is why the Jewish nation takes care that no branch falls off from the Jewish tree. That is why everything must be done to return the child to Abraham's bosom.[15]

The greatest problem for the Jewish organizations reclaiming Jewish children from convents after the war was obtaining information about the location of the convent homes in which there were Jewish children. As I have already mentioned, only incomplete lists of children placed in convent homes by the RGO have survived. Apart from that, there was no one in Poland after the war who knew the quantitative and territorial scale of the action of rescuing Jewish children by Polish nuns. That is why the pleas of Jewish organizations to the bishops for information were fruitless. The bishops did not know precisely what orders were working in their dioceses at that time, let alone how many of them had been rescuing Jewish children.[16] The turmoil of the war lasted six years.

Displacements and repatriation from the east to the west meant that several years passed before the Church administration was able to reorganize itself. The representatives of the Jewish organizations had no other choice but to travel all over the country and inquire in convents and of the local populace about the saved children. On the basis of the convent sources it is difficult to find out which organization reclaimed children from which order. For instance, a nun of the Samaritan Sisters relates the following:

> After the war the children were reclaimed by the Jewish committee—I don't know the particular details because the office took care of this. As a token of their gratitude for keeping the children and adults, the JDC presented us with a considerable amount of food.[17]

Since the JDC (Joint Distribution Committee) had connections with the Jewish Religious Congregation and with Aid to Children, the children were most probably reclaimed from the Samarytanki by representatives of one of these organizations, and not—as the nun says—a Jewish "committee." The nuns, unfamiliar with Jewish organizations, usually use terms like: "Jewish committee," "Jewish common," or simply "the Jews." We cannot be certain that the term "Jewish committee" really corresponds to a committee. It is also difficult to determine which organizations called at convents to reclaim the children officially and which thought that deception was necessary. I have not been able to find any regularities in this respect, as from the same homes some children were taken officially while others by alleged close relatives. One can assume—if we remember the conversation between the "doctor" and Jan Dobraczynski during the war and the stance taken by the JDC representative based on that conversation—that representatives of the organizations connected with the JDC, taking Dobraczynski's attitude as a rule and fearing difficulties in reclaiming the children, used verious forms of camouflage to prove they were a child's parents or closest relatives. Perhaps the only criterion for choosing the way a child was to be reclaimed by a Jewish representative was the child's own attitude toward returning to his own nation; the fact is that in the chaos after the war this caused additional confusion.

The nuns, upon discovering a deception and not knowing the reasons for it, did not understand the behavior of the Jews and suspected them of engaging in a trade of saved children.[18] Those suspicions were strengthened by the fact that the alleged relatives sometimes offered the nuns great sums of money for persuading the child to go with them. The nuns, however, were already familiar with the typical behavior of parents and relatives, who apart from a great gratitude for saving their children, usually had nothing more to give. Sometimes they gave a length of canvas, sometimes some leather for shoes, or a small sum of money saved from several years of wandering. When offered money the nuns said they were not trading children and would not accept it, and as for the child—if it wants to go, then let it go; if it wants to stay, then let it stay.[19]

Very often the children did not want to go. The younger ones, despite their initial defiance, were eventually rather easily persuaded to go, for their aunt or uncle, or grandfather or mother was waiting somewhere for them. The older children who, as they themselves say, "already knew what they wanted"[20] (which was that they did not want any more changes) constituted the greatest problem. The war imprinted upon their psyches a feeling that Jewish children were not safe, and the convent and their new national-religious identification gave them a sense of security. But the war ended at a certain moment and all Jewish children regained the right to life. For adults this fact was obvious and clear. But how were children supposed to know it? The tragic experiences of the war, which caused the deathly fear of admitting their descent, was still in them, and a return to Jewish society was associated with losing the feeling of safety they had miraculously acquired. The chidren's behavior during the war and their more recent statements indicate they understood very well the need to reach and stay on the safe side, which they had found in the convents. Their lack of orientation as to what was happening around them, natural at their age, and the brief period of time which had elapsed since their tragic war experiences were the reasons why the fear of losing this safety was their dominating feeling, which resulted in a bias after the war against or open hostility toward the Jews coming to collect them, even if they were their parents. Jewish children felt abandoned by their own parents and many never forgave them that abandonment. "Abandoned" by their parents, thrown into an alien and hostile world, they passed through their own Way of the Cross alone. Eventually they reached the convents, where, surrounded by love and care, they established new emotional bonds. But the war had come to an end, and they had to go back to their people. The children, however, did not want to breatk off the new bonds they had established. To experience another abandonment was more than they could bear. For the most part, their parents were dead, and they treated the necessity to go to Jews who were strangers to them as another abandonment—this time by the nuns, whom they reproached by saying things like: "You are giving me away!" That is why if a Jewish child was old enough to win the right to stay with the nuns, sometimes even in court, the child stayed and was raised by the nuns to adulthood.

This is what Rachela says about one of the most common reasons for deciding to stay with the nuns:

> I thought it was a miracle that I knew how to pray, that my parents had taught me how to pray before we parted. So I thought that God had managed things in such a way to save me. That is, I thought it was a sign from God that I should remain among Christians, for they had saved me. I felt that I owed it to the Christian religion to stay with it.[21]

Rachela was not the only one who decided that since she had been saved by Christians, her place was among them. Similar decisions were made by adult Jews.

Yet, despite a great deal of trouble and a whole series of misunderstandings accompanying reclaiming Jewish children from convent homes, a great majority of them were saved for their Jewish nation and religion. They started new lives in America and Western Europe, and many built the country of Israel, and there they brought up their own children, a new generation of free Jews, proud of their Jewish heritage.

CONCLUSION

THE SUBJECT OF JEWISH CHILDREN SAVED IN POLISH CONVENTS has been only a small footnote in history books for the past fifty years. More often than not it has been a source of controversy, unsupported by concrete facts, in the unrelenting Polish-Jewish disputes about the war years and the holocaust of Polish Jews. The Polish side most frequently claims that all the convents in Poland were rescuing Jewish children, while the Jewish side claims that rescuing Jewish children by nuns was a minimal phenomenon in relation to the entire country and that its aim was to recruit new believers for Catholicism. If the results of my research make people think about the problem, if the two sides in the dispute, instead of using generalizations and stereotypes, try to understand the tragedy of the rescued children and see the great effort of the Polish nuns, then the aim of my work will have been achieved. Almost all the Polish organizations that provided aid—the RGO, the social welfare, and the Council for Aid to Jews—counted on the nuns, as did the children of several nationalities and the entire Polish society. And the nuns did not fail them. Without any declarations, without orders and decisions from their superiors, nearly all of the orders gave help to the most desperate creatures during the war, the children.

Polish nuns had little doubt as to the value of the lives of the Jewish children they were saving. They risked their own lives for these children and cared for them as best as the circumstances in Poland under the Nazi occupation allowed. Today they speak with equal pride about those few who are Catholics and live in Poland, and those who live in Israel or elsewhere, for whom the only link with Poland and Catholicism for these last decades has been Polish nuns. Those Jewish children saved in Polish convents whom I have interviewed think it is a miracle that they are alive. For them life is a wonderful gift from the Polish nuns. I never had to ask any of them if it would have been better if they had been sent to death. Life itself has answered this question.

WOMEN'S RELIGIOUS ORDERS

Active Religious Orders

Congregation of Sisters Serving the Needy of the Third Order of St. Francis of Assisi. Albertine Sisters (*siostry albertynki*). Polish order established in 1891 in Cracow by Brother Albert (Adam Chmielowski) for the purpose of helping the homeless and caring for the elderly and the chronically ill. At the outbreak of the Second World War, 483 sisters were working in 21 homes. Jewish children were saved in 21 homes: Cracow (3 homes), Bochnia, Tarnow, Lwow, Baworow, Tarnopol, Sambor, Brzezany, Rawa Ruska, Kolomyja, Drohobycz, Przemysl, Busko, Skarzysko-Kamienna, Wolomin, Siedlce, Minkow and Rzaska. Several other homes only saved adult Jews.

Congregation of Sisters for Social Welfare under the Patronage of St. Anthony. Antonine Sisters (*siostry antoninki*). Polish order established in 1934 for the purpose of helping the poor, sick and homeless. At the outbreak of the Second World War, 9 sisters were working in 2 homes. The home in Wielun rescued a twelve-year-old boy, Israel Schtemberg.

Congregation of Sisters of Charity of St. Charles Borromeo (Mikolow). Sisters of Charity of St. Charles Borromeo (*siostry boromeuszki*). French order established in 1652; Polish province created in 1923. In 1939 it had 679 sisters working in 55 homes. The home in Lancut saved one Jewish child.

Congregation of the Daughters of Mary Immaculate. Disrobed Sisters of Mary Immaculate (*siostry niepokalanki niehabitowe*).

Polish order established in 1891 for the purpose of moral renewal in urban centers through acts of charity and educational work. At the outbreak of the Second World War, 271 sisters worked in 29 homes. Jewish children were saved by the sisters in Kielce, Radom, Wilno, Hrubieszow and Rawa Mazowiecka.

Congregation of the Daughters of the Most Pure Heart of the Blessed Virgin Mary. Disrobed Pure Heart of Mary Sisters (*siostry sercanki niehabitowe*). Polish order established in 1885 for the purpose of educating children and young adults. In 1939, 430 sisters worked in 28 institutions. Jewish children were saved by sisters in Warsaw (2 homes), Otwock, Nowe Miasto, Kolno, Sitnik, Skorzec and Wilno.

Congregation of Sisters of St. Dominic. Dominican Sisters (*siostry dominikanki*). Polish order established in 1861 to do charitable work, and the propagation of education and culture among peasants and workers. In 1939, 236 sisters worked in 31 homes. The home in Kielce saved several Jewish children, the one in Chorzow saved Ewa Fajfer.

Congregation of Sisters of St. Michael the Archangel. Sisters of St. Michael the Archangel (*siostry michaelitki*). Polish order established in 1897 for the purpose of aiding and educating abandoned children and young adults. In 1939, 106 sisters worked in 25 homes. In Miejsce Piastowe the sisters saved several Jewish children.

Congregation of Sisters of St. Elizabeth. Sisters of St. Elizabeth (*siostry elzbietanki*). German order established in 1842 for the purpose of providing medical care and charitable aid to the poor and the sick. In 1939 two Polish provinces existed with 123 homes, in which worked 1,080 sisters. Expelled from Torun, the sisters saved several Jewish children in Otwock.

Congregation of Sisters of St. Felix of Cantalice. Felician Sisters (*siostry felicjanki*). Polish order established in 1855 for the purpose of raising moral and religious standards through educational work and upbringing. In 1939, 808 sisters worked in 79 convent homes. Jewish children, and sometimes entire Jewish families, were saved by homes in: Przemysl (2 homes), Sadowa Wisznia, Dobranowice, Lwow, Wawer, Cracow and Staniatki.

Congregation of Franciscan Missionary Sisters of Mary. Franciscan. Missionary Sisters of Mary (*siostry franciszkanki misjonarki Maryi*). International order, active in Poland since 1922. Its purpose is to carry on missionary works in all the countries of the world. In 1939, the Polish province had 5 homes and 194 sisters, most of whom were on missionary duties outside of the country. In Radecznica and Zamosc, the sisters saved children of various nationalities, including Jewish children.

Congregation of Franciscan Sisters Servants of the Cross. Franciscan Sisters Servants of the Cross (Laski) (*siostry franciszkanki z Lasek*). Polish order established in 1918 for the purpose of caring for the blind. In 1939, 106 sisters worked in 18 homes. In Zakopane, Sister Klara Jaroszynska saved a Jewish child.

Congregation of Sisters of the Most Holy Name of Jesus under the Protection of the Blessed Virgin Mary. Help of the Faithful. Disrobed Sisters of the Holy Name of Jesus (*siostry imienia Jezus niehabitowe*). Polish order established in 1887 for the purpose of helping working women. In 1939, 272 sisters worked in 18 homes. Homes in Wilno and Klimontow saved four Jewish girls.

Congregation of Sisters of Charity of St. Joseph. Sisters of St. Joseph (*siostry jozefitki*). Polish order established in 1884 for the purpose of caring for the sick and the needy. In 1939, nearly 300 sisters worked in 45 institutions. Working in hospitals and orphanages, the sisters saved many Jewish families, particularly those with doctors at the head. Jewish children were saved in institutions in Skalat, Trzesowka, Tarnow, Mielec and Laszczow.

Congregation of Canoness Sisters of the Holy Spirit. Sisters of the Holy Spirit (*siostry duchaczki*). Italian order established in 1198; the Polish province existed since 1220. The purpose of the order was hospital work and bringing up abandoned children. In 1939, the Polish province counted 59 sisters working in 8 homes. All homes took part in saving adult Jews. Jewish children were saved in homes in Cracow, Busko, Zablocie, Chmielnik and Lublin.

Congregation of Carmelite Sisters of the Infant Jesus (Sosnowiec). Carmelite Sisters of the Infant Jesus (*siostry karmelitanki*). Polish order established in 1921 for the purpose of caring for the neediest children. In 1939, 35 sisters worked in one home in Sosnowiec, where several Jewish children were saved, along with several Jewish families.

Congregation of Sisters of the Merciful Mother of God. Magdalene Sisters (*siostry magdalenki*). Polish order established in 1862 for the purpose of spreading the faith among criminal women and delinquent girls. In 1939, 328 sisters worked in 14 correctional and rehabilitative institutions. During the war the sisters saved scores of Jewish adults and children in homes in Warsaw (2 homes), Derdy, Walendow, Cracow, Rabka, Czestochowa, Wilno, Radom and Lwow.

Congregation of Sisters of the Holy Family of Nazareth. Sisters of the Holy Family of Nazareth (*siostry nazarentanki*). Polish order established in 1875 for the purpose of educating and rearing girls. In 1939, 523 sisters worked in 22 homes. Jewish children were saved in homes in Warsaw, Czestochowa, Olsztyn and Komancza.

Congregation of Sisters of the Immaculate Conception of the Blessed Virgin Mary. Sisters of the Immaculate Conception of the Blessed Virgin Mary (*siostry niepokalanki*). Polish order established in 1857 for the purpose of rearing girls. In 1939, 338 sisters worked in 13 homes. All those that were active during the war saved adult Jews. Jewish children were saved in homes in Warsaw, Szymanow, Wrzosow, Kozle, Nowy Sacz and Jaroslaw. In Slonim two sisters were shot by the Germans for sheltering Jewish families.

Congregation of School Sisters of Notre Dame. School Sisters of Notre Dame (*siostry de Notre Dame*). French order established in 1833 for the purpose of rearing children. The Polish province existed since the second half of the 19th century. In 1939 it counted 15 homes, in which worked 236 sisters. In Lwow the sisters saved a Jewish girl.

Congregation of Oblate Sisters of the Sacred Heart of Jesus. Disrobed Oblate Sisters of the Sacred Heart of Jesus (*siostry oblatki niehabitowe*). French order established in 1874 for the purpose of charitable aid and rearing children. The Polish province, in existence since 1894, had, in 1939, 127 sisters working in 6 homes. In Czestochowa the sisters saved a dozen or so Jewish children.

Congregation of Sisters of Divine Providence. Sisters of Divine

Providence (*siostry opatrznoscianki*). Polish order established in 1856 for the purpose of rearing needy girls. In 1939, nearly 120 sisters worked in 11 homes. Jewish children, as well as Jewish adults, were saved in homes in Przemysl and Miedzyrzecz Podlaski; homes in Skole and Sterdyn saved adult Jews.

Congregation of Sisters of the Passion of Our Lord Jesus Christ. Passionist Sisters (*siostry pasjonistki*). Polish order established in 1918 for contemplative aims and works of charity and education. In 1939 nearly 100 sisters worked in several homes. In Janow Lubelski the sisters saved a Jewish boy.

Congregation of Sisters Shepherds of Divine Providence. Sisters Shepherds of Divine Providence (*siostry pasterki*). Polish order established in 1894 for the purpose of aiding corrupt girls. In 1939, nearly 100 sisters worked in 10 homes. In Lublin the sisters saved several Jewish teenage girls.

Congregation of Franciscan Sisters of the Family of Mary. Franciscan Sisters of the Family of Mary (*franciszkanki Rodziny Maryi*). Polish order established in 1857 for the purpose of educating and rearing children. In 1939, 1,120 sisters worked in over 100 homes. During the war the sisters saved over 100 adult Jews and several hundred Jewish children, who were hidden in the following places: Warsaw (5 homes), Lwow (3 homes), Anin (3 homes), Brwinow (2 homes), Miedzylesie (3 homes), Bialoleka, Brzezinki, Izabelin, Kolomyja, Krasnystaw, Lomna, Mirzec, Mszana Dolna, Nieborow, Ostrowiec Swietokrzyski, Ostrowek, Pludy, Pustelnik, Podhajce, Sambor, Soplicowo, Turka, Kostowiec and Wola Golkowska.

Congregation of the Most Sacred Heart of Jesus. Sisters of the Sacred Heart (*siostry Sacre Coeur*). French order established in 1800 for the purpose of managing schools. The Polish province, in existence since 1843, counted 158 sisters working in 4 schools in 1939. In Lwow the sisters saved a Jewish family, several young women and two Jewish children.

Congregation of Benedictine Samaritan Sisters of the Holy Cross. Benedictine Samaritan Sisters (*siostry samarytanki*). Polish order established in 1926 for the purpose of charitable aid. At the outbreak of the Second World War, a dozen or so sisters worked in 3 homes (located in Zbikow, Pruszkow and Henrykow) where a dozen or so Jewish children and adults were saved.

Congregation of the Daughters of the Sorrowful Mother of God. Seraphite Sisters (*siostry serafitki*). Polish order established in 1881 for the purpose of providing care for the sick, the needy, and also children and young adults. In 1939, about 400 sisters worked in 50 homes. In Drohobycz the sisters saved several Jewish children.

Congregation of Sisters Servants of the Sacred Heart of Jesus. Sisters Servants of the Sacred Heart (*siostry sercanki*). Polish order established in 1894 for the purpose of caring for domestics, the sick and children. Counting in 1939 over 400 sisters and 44 homes, the order saved 13 Jewish children in Przemysl.

Congregation of Sisters Servants of Jesus. Sisters Servants of Jesus (*slugi Jezusa*). Polish order established in 1884 for the purpose of caring for needy girls and those who worked as servants. At the outbreak of the Second World War, over 300 sisters worked in 16 homes. In Tarnow and Lublin, the sisters saved several Jewish children.

Congregation of Sisters Servants of the Immaculate Conception of the Blessed Virgin Mary (Pleszew). Sisters Servants of Mary Immaculate (Pleszew) (*siostry sluzebniczki pleszewskie*). Polish order established in 1850 for the purpose of raising the standards of villages in Wielkopolska. In 1939, 404 sisters worked in 67 homes. In Piotrkow Trybunalski, Czersk, Przesmyki and Wlodzimierzow, the sisters saved a dozen or so Jewish children.

Congregation of Sisters Servants of the Blessed Virgin Mary Immaculately Concieved (Stara Wies). Sisters Servants of Mary Immaculate (Stara Wies) (*siostry sluzeniczki starowiejskie*). Polish order established in 1850 for the purpose of raising the standards of villages in Galicia. In 1939, 1,520 sisters worked in 339 establishments. In Turkowice, the sisters saved 33 Jewish children; 11 in Chotomow; several in Lublin, Miechow, Czestochowa and Tarnow each; and at least one child in each of the following places: Grodzisko, Rzepince, Szynwald, Brzezany, Piotrkow Trybunalski, Lodz and Lazniew.

Congregation of Sisters Servants of the Blessed Virgin Mary. Disrobed Sisters Servants of the Blessed Virgin Mary (*siostry

sluzki niehabitowe). Polish order established in 1876 for the purpose of providing moral and religious care for the peasant population. At the outbreak of the Second World War, 1,120 sisters worked in scores of institutions. In Lomza the sisters saved several Jewish girls.

Congregation of Sisters of Charity of St. Vincent de Paul, Servants of the Poor. Sisters of Charity of St. Vincent de Paul (*siostry szarytki*). French order established in 1633; in existence in Poland since 1652. In 1939, the Polish province counted 921 sisters working in 105 institutions, mainly hospitals. Aside from saving a great number of adult Jews, the Sisters of Charity saved many Jewish children in the following places: Warsaw (8 homes), Kielce (2 homes), Bialystok, Ignacow, Radom, Wilno, Klarysew and Gora Kalwaria. Eight Sisters of Charity were shot in Warsaw by the Germans for helping Jews.

Congregation of Sisters of St. Teresa of the Child Jesus. Sisters of St. Teresa (*siostry terezjanki*). Polish order established in 1936 for the purpose of charitable and educational work among the Polish population in Volhynia. At the outbreak of the Second World War, about 60 sisters worked in 6 homes. Several Jewish children were saved by the sisters in Luboml and Wlodzimierz Wolynski.

Congregation of Ursuline Sisters of the Heart of the Dying Christ. Grey Ursulines (*siostry urszulanki szare*). Polish order established in 1920 for the purpose of ministration and educational-rearing work among children and young adults. In 1939, the order counted 777 sisters working in Poland, France and Italy. In Poland the nuns worked in 31 homes. The sisters saved a dozen or so Jewish children in Warsaw and Brwinow each, about 10 in Milanowek, at least 5 in Radosc, two in Zakopane and one in Czarna Duza. Aside from this, they hid Jewish adults.

Order of St. Ursula of the Union of Rome. Ursulines of the Union of Rome (*siostry urszulanki*). Italian order established in 1535; in existence in Poland since 1857. The purpose of the order is educational and the rearing of girls, as well as missionary work among women. In 1939 the Polish province counted 485 sisters working in 19 homes. Adult Jews, as well as Jewish children, were saved in homes in Warsaw, Cracow, Kolomyja, Tarnow and Lublin.

Congregation of Sisters of the Resurrection of Our Lord Jesus

Christ. Sisters of the Resurrection (*siostry zmartwychwstanki*). Polish order established in 1891 for evangelization through rearing and education, and caring for the sick. In 1939 the order counted 306 sisters working in 21 homes. Scores of Jewish children and adults were saved in homes in Warsaw (2 homes), Lwow and Stara Wies.

Women's Contemplative Orders

(Because each contemplative convent had its own independent administrative and hierarchal units, there has been no historical research done so far in regard to the number of convents and their inhabitants. Therefore, I have listed only those convents which sources indicate saved Jewish children.)

Dominican Sisters (*siostry dominikanki*). The Order of Dominican Sisters in Grodek, Wilno.

Bernardine Sisters (*siostry bernardynki*). The Third Order of St. Francis of Assisi in Lowicz.

Benedictine Sisters (*siostry benedyktynki*). The Order of Benedictine Sisters in Lwow.

Poor Clares of Perpetual Adoration (*siostry klaryski*). Poor Clares of Perpetual Adoration in Lwow.

APPENDIX II

LOCATIONS OF WOMEN'S RELIGIOUS ORDERS

Anin — Franciscan Sisters of the Family of Mary (3 homes)

Baworow — Albertine Sisters

Bialoleka — Franciscan Sisters of the Family of Mary

Bialystok — Sisters of Charity of St. Vincent de Paul

Bochnia — Albertine Sisters

Brwinow — Franciscan Sisters of the Family of Mary (2 homes), Grey Ursulines

Brzezinki — Franciscan Sisters of the Family of Mary

Brzezany — Albertine Sisters, Sisters Servants of Mary Immaculate (Stara Wies)

Busko — Albertine Sisters, Sisters of the Holy Spirit

Chmielnik — Sisters of the Holy Spirit

Chorzow — Dominican Sisters

Chotomow — Sisters Servants of Mary Immaculate (Stara Wies)

Cracow — Albertine Sisters (3 homes), Ursulines of the Union of Rome, Sisters of the Holy Spirit, Magdalene Sisters, Felician Sisters

Czarna Duza — Grey Ursulines

Czersk — Sisters Servants of Mary Immaculate (Pleszew)

Czestochowa — Albertine Sisters, Magdalene Sisters, Sisters of the

Holy Family of Nazareth, Disrobed Oblate Sisters of the Sacred Heart of Jesus, Sisters Servants of Mary Immaculate (Stara Wies)

Derdy — Magdalene Sisters

Dobranowice — Felician Sisters

Drohobycz — Albertine Sisters, Seraphite Sisters

Gora Kalwaria — Sisters of Charity of St. Vincent de Paul

Grodzisko — Sisters Servants of Mary Immaculate (Stara Wies)

Henrykow — Benedictine Samaritan Sisters

Hrubieszow — Disrobed Sisters of Mary Immaculate

Ignacow — Sisters of Charity of St. Vincent de Paul

Izabalin — Franciscan Sisters of the Family of Mary

Janow Lubelski — Passionist Sisters

Jaroslaw — Sisters of the Immaculate Conception of the Blessed Virgin Mary

Kielce — Sisters of Charity of St. Vincent de Paul (2 homes), Disrobed Sisters of Mary Immaculate, Dominican Sisters

Klarysew — Sisters of Charity of St. Vincent de Paul

Klimontow — Disrobed Sisters of the Holy Name of Jesus

Kolno — Disrobed Pure Heart of Mary Sisters

Kolomyja — Albertine Sisters, Franciscan Sisters of the Family of Mary, Ursulines of the Union of Rome

Komancza — Sisters of the Holy Family of Nazareth

Kostowiec — Franciscan Sisters of the Family of Mary

Kozle — Sisters of the Immaculate Conception of the Blessed Virgin Mary

Krasnystaw — Franciscan Sisters of the Family of Mary

Lancut — Sisters of Charity of St. Charles Borromeo

Laszczow — Sisters of St. Joseph

Lazniew — Sisters Servants of Mary Immaculate (Stara Wies)

Lomna — Franciscan Sisters of the Family of Mary

Lomza — Disrobed Sisters Servants of the Blessed Virgin Mary

Lowicz — Bernardine Sisters

Lodz — Sisters Servants of Mary Immaculate (Stara Wies)

Lublin — Sisters of the Holy Spirit, Sisters Shepherds of Divine Providence, Sisters Servants of Jesus, Sisters Servants of Mary Immaculate (Stara Wies), Ursulines of the Union of Rome

Luboml — Sisters of St. Teresa

Lwow — Franciscan Sisters of the Family of Mary (3 homes), Albertine Sisters, Sisters of the Resurrection, Benedictine Sisters, Poor Clares of Perpetual Adoration, Felician Sisters, Magdalene Sisters, Sisters of the Sacred Heart (Sacre Coeur), School Sisters of Notre Dame

Miechow — Sisters Servants of Mary Immaculate (Stara Wies)

Miedzylesie — Franciscan Sisters of the Family of Mary (3 homes)

Miedzyrzecz Podlaski — Sisters of Divine Providence

Mielec — Sisters of St. Joseph

Miejsce Piastowe — Sisters of St. Michael the Archangel

Milanowek — Grey Ursulines

Minkow — Albertine Sisters

Mirzec — Franciscan Sisters of the Family of Mary

Mszana Dolna — Franciscan Sisters of the Family of Mary

Nieborow — Franciscan Sisters of the Family of Mary

Nowe Miasto — Disrobed Pure Heart of Mary Sisters

Nowy Sacz — Sisters of the Immaculate Conception of the Blessed Virgin Mary

Olsztyn — Sisters of the Holy Family of Nazareth

Ostrowiec Swietokrzyski — Franciscan Sisters of the Family of Mary

Otwock — Sisters of St. Elizabeth, Disrobed Pure Heart of Mary Sisters

Piotrkow Trybunalski — Sisters Servants of Mary Immaculate (Pleszew), Sisters Servants of Mary Immaculate (Stara Wies)

Pludy — Franciscan Sisters of the Family of Mary

Podhajce — Franciscan Sisters of the Family of Mary

Pruszkow — Benedictine Samaritan Sisters

Przemysl — Felician Sisters (2 homes), Albertine Sisters, Sisters of Divine Providence, Sisters Servants of the Sacred Heart

Przesmyki — Sisters Servants of Mary Immaculate (Pleszew)

Pustelnik — Franciscan Sisters of the Family of Mary

Rabka — Magdalene Sisters

Radecznica — Franciscan Missionary Sisters of Mary

Radom — Magdalene Sisters, Disrobed Sisters of Mary Immaculate, Sisters of Charity of St. Vincent de Paul

Radosc — Grey Ursulines

Rawa Mazowiecka — Disrobed Sisters of Mary Immaculate

Rawa Ruska — Albertine Sisters

Rzaska — Albertine Sisters

Rzepince — Sisters Servants of Mary Immaculate (Stara Wies)

Sadowa Wisznia — Felician Sisters

Sambor — Franciscan Sisters of the Family of Mary, Albertine Sisters

Siedlce — Albertine Sisters

Sitnik — Disrobed Pure Heart of Mary Sisters

Skalat — Sisters of St. Joseph

Skarzysko-Kamienna — Albertine Sisters

Skorzec — Disrobed Pure Heart of Mary Sisters

Slonim — Sisters of the Immaculate Conception of the Blessed Virgin Mary

LOCATIONS OF WOMEN'S RELIGIOUS ORDERS

Soplicowo — Franciscan Sisters of the Family of Mary

Sosnowiec — Carmelite Sisters of the Infant Jesus

Staniatki — Felician Sisters

Stara Wies — Sisters of the Resurrection

Szymanow — Sisters of the Immaculate Conception of the Blessed Virgin Mary

Szynwald — Sisters Servants of Mary Immaculte (Stara Wies)

Tarnopol — Albertine Sisters

Tarnow — Albertine Sisters, Sisters of St. Joseph, Sisters Servants of Jesus, Sisters Servants of Mary Immaculate (Stara Wies), Ursulines of the Union of Rome

Trzesowka — Sisters of St. Joseph

Turka — Franciscan Sisters of the Family of Mary

Turkowice — Sisters Servants of Mary Immaculate (Stara Wies)

Walendow — Magdalene Sisters

Warsaw — Sisters of Charity of St. Vincent de Paul (8 homes), Franciscan Sisters of the Family of Mary (5 homes), Sisters of the Resurrection (2 homes), Disrobed Pure Heart of Mary Sisters (2 homes), Magdalene Sisters (2 homes), Sisters of the Immaculate Conception of the Blessed Virgin Mary, Sisters of the Holy Family of Nazareth, Grey Ursulines, Ursulines of the Union of Rome

Wawer — Felician Sisters

Wielun — Antonine Sisters

Wilno — Dominican Contemplative Sisters, Magdalene Sisters, Disrobed Sisters of Mary Immaculate, Disrobed Sisters of the Holy Name of Jesus, Disrobed Pure Heart of Mary Sisters, Sisters of Charity of St. Vincent de Paul

Wlodzimierz Wolynski — Sisters of St. Teresa

Wlodzimierzow — Sisters Servants of Mary Immaculate (Pleszew)

Wola Golkowska — Franciscan Sisters of the Family of Mary

Wolomin — Albertine Sisters

Wrzosow — Sisters of the Immaculate Conception of the Blessed Virgin Mary

Zamosc — Franciscan Missionary Sisters of Mary

Zablocie — Sisters of the Holy Spirit

Zakopane — Grey Ursulines, Franciscan Sisters Servants of the Cross (Laski)

Zbikow — Benedictine Samaritan Sisters

INTERVIEWS WITH NUNS

Mother Superior Tekla Budnowska
(Franciscan Sister of the Family of Mary)

June 16, 1984 in Warsaw

During the war I was mother superior of a home in Lomna. I had 115 children in the orphanage, of which twenty-three were Jewish—one a boy, the rest girls, for the orphanage was for girls. Only later did I get boys.

Sometimes there was a note with the child saying that it was Jewish, but most of the time the children came to us with birth certificates. Some of the girls said openly: I am a Jew. Others did not admit to their Jewish background, and that's the way it stayed. For instance, Teresa B. She did not look Jewish; nothing betrayed her. One day an older girl came to me, her name was Glancman, and she said:

"Mother Superior, Teresa B. is a Jew."

"She is no Jew," I replied. "Blue eyes, the nose and everything; she does not look like a Jew."

"I tell you, Mother Superior, she is! I can feel it!"

Literally: I can feel it.

The fact is these children could somehow tell. For example, if some older Jewish girl was cleaning up, then the younger Jewish girls were immediately drawn to her. They didn't help anyone but the Jewish girl.

Returning to Teresa B.: Teresa came to us when she was eleven. Certainly, she had a certificate. As it turned out later, she had not been baptized. However, she was receiving the sacraments all the time. She was a rather pious, practicing Catholic. Only after the Warsaw Uprising in 1944—she had probably taken some oath—did she turn to an old nun and ask to be baptized. We baptized her in secret, so that nobody knew.

When the Germans would come, the Jewish children would be

the first to go to the chapel, for they were afraid of them. They had a certain feeling, an instinct of self-preservation. They did not exhibit exceptional piety. They probably just felt safe, and that was the reason for their normality, as far as matters of faith were concerned. We took great pains so that the children would not lack for anything. When the children at Lomna went out, I always reminded the sisters to make sure that no Germans or strangers were standing by the chapel.

Once the following thing happened: The children were going out, everyone was looking at them, including a German officer, who finally said to me:

"There are a lot of different faces in your group, sister!"

"What else do you expect," I answered him in German. "Do you want them all to look like you? Everyone has a different mother and father!"

I gave him a look, and that was the end of that. The officer did not think anything more of the matter.

I also remember the daughter of a doctor from Turka. He was needed by the Germans for something, so he was kept alive and walked around with the Star of David. His daughter was being hidden by our sisters in Lwow, but they feared keeping her, for she was too well known. So I told them: "Give her to us; we already have many, so one more won't make a difference."

The little girl had very long tresses, so I said to her: "You have to make a sacrifice, my child."

I cut off her tresses, and we found a birth certificate for her. A sister went to St. Antoni's Church in Lwow; the priest gave her a baptismal book, and after a two-day search she finally found a girl whose age coincided with the age of the doctor's daughter. The priest wrote out a certificate in the name of O., a name which was used after the war by the father of the child also.

Not one of the Jewish children we had was killed. The majority of our children are grateful, and maintain contact with us.

We received children mostly from Warsaw. All the sisters at Lomna knew about the Jewish children, but no one was allowed to differentiate between the children, and no one did. At most, the children did so among themselves.

One day Sister Paulina arrived with some children, and a boy came over to me, and said:

"I beg your pardon, Mother Superior, Sister Paulina has brought some children from Warsaw, all of them Jews!"

"They are not Jews, but all are baptized children, so there are no Jews here!" I replied.

We tried to create an atmosphere where the children would feel safe and secure. After the Ukrainian attacks in 1943, we left Lomna, and together with the children moved to Warsaw. In Warsaw we lived in a small place on Wolna St. until the uprising. All of us left Warsaw in August of 1944.

The children came from Warsaw in groups. There were situations where the conductor, seeing our nuns with a group of children, among which he could see Jewish children, closed the compartment and drew the curtains to assure the safety of the sisters and children. These conductors were Polish, but one time a German conductor did this also.

After the uprising, we stayed for some time in Kostowiec, then in Wegrocia; finally we found ourselves in Lublin Kujawski.

Reclaiming Jewish children started as early as 1945. When someone called at the convent, they gave a name and collected a child. But sometimes it was different.

[See Wojtasik-Jarzabek story, Chapter VIII.]

Then there was a girl I've already mentioned—Bozenka. A very pretty, intelligent girl. She could not remember her real name. She only knew that her father had been a doctor and that her family had lived on Zlota St. She also knew that her parents were not alive. One day a man, a Jew, came over to us, and said that this was his child and he wanted to take her home. Then he began to look her over. He looked at her fingernails, at this and that.

Finally I said to him: "What's going on here? You don't recognize your own child? You have to look at her fingernails?"

Bozenka threw her arms around a sister, and said: "You baptized me, and now you want to give me back to the Jews?"

We did not baptize her, for she had already come to us baptized.

In the end I told this man: "This is not your child. Absolutely not. Besides, she knows that her parents are dead; she's an orphan. Don't do this again."

It seems that certain Jews took these children as their own, and later sold them to some other Jews, or something of that sort. I could not understand how Jews could behave that way.

Then there was Basia. After the war, her aunts came for her. They had hidden themselves someplace, and lived in Lodz. Basia told her aunts: "It is your fault that my parents are not alive, for you could have warned us. I will not go with you." She did not go, and finished her schooling with us....

Sister Roberta Stanislawa Fiedorczuk (Samaritan Sister)
October 14, 1985 in Pruszkow

During the war I was a teacher in the educational institution for boys on Szkolna St. in Pruszkow.

In Wlochy, a three or four-year-old boy, wrapped in pillows, was thrown out of a transport train taking Jews to Oswiecim. The child was taken care of by an old couple in Wlochy, but when he started to arouse suspicion, the couple turned to us with the request that we take him in.

The boy was circumcised.

He was very attached to me; after the war his adoptive parents took him, for they loved him very much—and he them. The boy, today a grown man, doesn't know his ancestry. He finished school, lives in Warsaw, and that's why I don't want to reveal his name.

The Germans used to come to us, but there was never any trouble. We had more than a hundred boys. In each group—and there were seven—we had several Jewish boys. I don't remember their names today.

Aside from a few exceptions, the children were sent by the Social Welfare Department. If it wasn't obvious, if the child wasn't circumcised, we didn't know if he was Jewish. In my group there was a blond boy. No one, not even I, knew that he was Jewish. After the war a Jewish man turned up with a full wardrobe for the child (the size was just right!), and said that the boy was his son. As proof, he identified the scars on the boy's body. The boy left with his father.

Sister Ligoria Grenda (Sacred Heart Sister)
October 22, 1985

My story deals with the years 1943 and 1944. During that time I was a teacher in the orphanage organized around the middle of 1943 by Sister Emilia-Jozef Malkowska, the mother superior of our order, with the help of the Polish Welfare Committee (RGO) that worked in the area. The orphanage was in Przemysl on 80 Mickiewicz St.

The children were mostly orphans whose parents had been killed during the Ukrainian attacks on Wolynia, as well as children lost or escaping from the surrounding area. In the beginning the children usually came from the refugee camps. Through the efforts of the Polish Welfare Committee they were sent to the orphanages.

Sister Emilia Malkowska initiated the help for Jewish children. She had a special love for these children, particularly the orphans, and I believe it was precisely that love which caused her to take on such a dangerous assignment.

I don't really know how these Jewish children got to the orphanage, because the mother superior did not let me in on this. I can only make guesses. I know that one boy, Stas, was brought from the ghetto. He was barely eighteen months old and was circumcised. The ages of the other Jewish children ranged from four to fifteen-years-old. One fourteen-year-old girl turned up at the RGO, saying that she was lost and needed help. She was directed to the orphanage. Later it turned out that she was a Jewish.

Most likely some Jewish children managed to make their way from transports to refugee camps, and from there wound up in the orphanage.

The Jewish children that came to the orphanage either received fictitious names or had them already. They took part in the life of the orphanage and were treated just like any child, both by the nuns and other children. Only the mother superior and I knew about their Jewish ancestry, though the nuns could have suspected. The children went to church, which was just across the street. Besides this, they did not go out in the city. They spoke Polish, but a few had obvious Semitic features.

The children in the orphanage were supported by the meager donations from the RGO and whatever contributions the mother superior could get. The Jewish children were placed on the lists just like the other children. The contacts between the children were normal. The relationship with the nuns was sincere and warm, like that of the other children, who for the most part had also gone through tragic experiences. They eagerly gathered around the nuns, and in a variety of ways showed their love. The following is a fragment of a letter I received last year from a "girl" in Israel: "I hope that I will be able to once again embrace those who were for me a symbol of everything good and worthy, a symbol of boundless sacrifice and sisterly love."

The older Jewish children were more aware of their situation; they were careful; they withdrew from the other children and discreetly took care of the younger ones. It seems that some knew about each other's ancestry. Perhaps they had known each other before? I didn't ask. They prayed gladly, especially the older girls. Several of them asked to go to confession when the front was getting close to Przemysl in 1944. I told them that I could not arrange this, but we all prayed together a lot.

In our orphanage we saved at least eleven Jewish children. The "girl" from Israel that I spoke of specifically named eleven children and mentioned "others," of whose whereabouts she is unaware. Eight are living in Israel.

After the liberation or already after the war (I don't remember when), family members turned up for certain children, and several were taken by the Jewish Community to the Jewish Children's Home in Przemysl. The reaction of the children was rather calm, only the youngest, Stas, cried and shouted as he was being taken, and tore himself away, crying out "Auntie Gina," which meant "Mother Longina." The boy was loved by everyone.

One boy, Edzio, got very sick. To the best of our ability he was taken care of in our home. Because his health worsened, we had to put him in a hospital in order to save his life. After much difficulty, and only thanks to the efforts of a nurse friendly with the nuns, he was admitted. He had pronounced Jewish features, but he had not been circumcised. Almost in his death throes, he was baptized by that nurse. From that moment a change for the better took place, and he regained his health. When he was taken to the Jewish Children's Home, he was barely seven years, but he knew that he had been baptized; he was an intelligent boy.

After the war, Hania was sent to the Children's Home run by the Sisters of Divine Providence in Przemysl, because our orphanage had been converted to a home for boys. An uncle from America turned up for her. She didn't want to go with him. She was thirteen then. The matter wound up in court, and I was called as a witness. Hania said at court that she did not want to go with her uncle, that her life belonged to the people who rescued her. Hania remained with the nuns and after several years she was baptized. I was invited to the ceremony. The nuns gave her a secondary education, she got married and lives now in Przemysl. The other children were not baptized.

144

During the time period of which I speak, I lived in constant fear for the safety of the children—particularly after the death of Mother Superior Emilia, who died on April 12, 1944. The most dangerous time came when soldiers of a country in league with the Germans came to stay in our home. One day a woman from that group took small Stas by her hand and wanted to take him to her comrades; she was already out on the street. Thankfully a nun noticed this and quickly retrieved the boy. He was, after all, circumcised.

Once a convoy of Germans stopped on the street before our home. They got out and surrounded a civilian, who said something to them, pointing in our direction. Witnessing this through a window, I was certain that they had caught someone who was betraying us. I prayed, but remained silent, not telling anyone. Thankfully, after a long, tense moment, they left. I heard about an incident where the Germans had discovered that a Jewish child had been at the home of the Sisters of Divine Providence, and was taken away. Nothing happened to the sisters, because it was declared that they didn't know the child was Jewish.

I am deeply convinced that only through the great mercy of God were the children and the nuns protected. It is difficult for me to say precisely what my motives were in hiding Jewish children. Our mother superior was in charge.

I only know that I could not do otherwise.

Sister Magdalena Kaczmarzyk
Aid Given to Jews by the Albertine Sisters During the Second World War (Archives of the Albertine Sisters, Cracow, 1961)

The following information is gathered from the statements of fifty surviving nuns. Many individuals who were part of the action of saving Jewish children have died, and therefore the whole history of that period will never be known. In many cases even the real names of the saved children are not known. During the war, the children did not want to reveal their names, and in instances when they did, the passage of time has frequently erased the memory of those names.

CRACOW—a shelter on 47 Krakowski St.
A stranger brought to the shelter two girls, ages around ten and eleven.

It turned out that one of the girls was, in reality, a Jewish boy.

Since both diligently attended chapel services and prayed piously, they did not raise suspicion, and despite various German inspections, they survived the war and later were taken, most probably, to Sweden.

A girl named Marysia, the daughter of a Jewish doctor from Cracow. This girl did not want to go to the chapel, and openly stated that she was Jewish and didn't need to pray. Some women who were staying at the shelter betrayed her to the Gestapo. She was probably killed.

Zosia K., a young girl. It was not known whether she was Jewish, since she never told anyone anything. But she was frequently questioned by the Germans, who used to come to take her to the ghetto. But she would stubbornly refuse to go and say that if she was to be shot, let it happen there, at the shelter. Sister Urban defended her, saying that she was certain the girl wasn't Jewish. Zosia was very hardworking and intelligent. She went to school and later finished her secondary-school education. Now she is a teacher in Warsaw, and remains in periodic contact with the nuns, grateful that they took care of her.

CRACOW—an orphanage on 10 Koletek St.

The mother superior was Sister Hermana. The anti-Semitic policies of the Germans increased the number of children being sent to the orphanage. One could tell that these were Jewish children, since the boys were mostly circumcised or had Semitic features.

One evening at nine o'clock, a woman and a man brought a one-year-old boy and said that while going across the Wisla River on a boat they heard a splash and later saw a white object in the water; heading in that direction, they took the child from the river. The boy was completely soaked, blue and unconscious. Sister Fidelisa spent four hours with the boy, before she was able to return him to consciousness, but the child got pneumonia, which thankfully he overcame. During the most dangerous moments of the illness, he was baptized with water and given the name Jozio.

When the Germans retreated, the Jewish community took the Jewish children to its own establishment. Jozio went also. After a time a man—a Jew—came to us from Warsaw, looking for his son. From what he said, it was apparent that his son was Jozio. The father told us that he had given the child to some woman for safekeeping and that this woman later disappeared out of sight and all trace of the child was lost. He probably found his son in the Jewish community.

The police brought a four-year-old boy to the orphanage, who had been found wandering the streets. The boy was intelligent, knew the "Hail Mary," but would not reveal his real name. Whenever he was questioned, he answered that his name was Wroblewski, and sometimes would add: "I have to be Wroblewski or else the Germans will kill me."

We tried to guess his name, but he would not admit to any name, so he was given the name "Thomas." He did not allow anyone to undress or bathe him; only the sisters could do this. Of course, he was circumcised. And his features were Jewish. He was terribly frightened of the Germans. When the Germans inspected the orphanage, looking for Jewish children, the nuns would hide him in a room, lock it and tell him to be quiet. He knew what was happening and didn't move from his place. When the convent was moved to Romanowa in 1942, he went with all the other children. After the war he went to the Jewish community and was there until the Germans withdrew.

There was a circumcised three-year-old boy in Romanowa. We had a lady doctor at that time who was very shy. Once she asked the nuns whether there were any Jewish children at the orphanage, and the mother superior replied that she did not need to know, for the matter did not concern her, and, besides, all the children were suitably documented. This is why, when the Jewish children were sick, the mother superior did not let them be examined by a doctor, in fear that they would be betrayed, and she took care of them by herself. Thank God none of the children died.

Chris. He had been officially taken in as a Jew from the Social Welfare Department as a child born out of wedlock with the name of Eisenberg. He was hidden from the time he was little, and was very quiet and likeable. When orders came from the authorities that Jewish children had to go to the ghetto, the mother superior felt sorry for him and asked the director of the Welfare Department not to send the child there. The boy, however, had papers which clearly stated that he was Jewish. After much persistence from the mother superior, the director decided to destroy the child's papers, and from that time he was called Christopher N. When the boy was seven years old, he went to the convent of the Sisters Servants of Mary Immaculate in Pradnik Czerwony. He could not be baptized at the time, for it was too dangerous, so the sisters did not even know he was Jewish. They made out papers for him in his Polish name, and Chris studied the organ. When he was eighteen, he needed his birth certificate. He came to us to get it, and then he learned that he had not been baptized—so he received baptizm. Today he is an organist in the neighborhood of Tarnow.

A woman who lived on Mostowa St. brought in a one-year-old child as a foundling. We gave him the name of Stas. The child was very sickly and caused a lot of fuss and trouble. When he was three, Stas was adopted by a couple, who became very attached to him and spent a lot of money to get him healthy.

After a while, the older brother and relatives turned up. The mother superior eventually had to admit that the child had been taken by someone else. And now a real tragedy began. The new family was too attached to the child and did not want to give it back, so the Jewish family took the matter to the court. After much unpleasantness, and despite the fact the the boy did not want to leave his adopted family, he was taken by his relatives.

Once a woman came to us and asked what could she do to save a child, Ignas, from the ghetto. She was told that she should simply abandon the child. And so she did. The father of the child went out through the sewers and handed the one-year-old child over to her, and she took him to the orphanage. As the guardian of the child, she used to come to visit him, and sometimes brought money for his upkeep. The boy got sick. The parents became very worried, and not believing either that woman or the nuns, they wanted to see with their own eyes whether the child was still alive. The father wanted to come to the orphanage in the guise of a plumber, but the mother superior did not agree to this because of the lay people working in the establishment, of whom she wasn't sure. Because of this the father took back the child through the same manner that it came.

At that time the boy was two-years-old and was taken in a rush to the ghetto, still dressed in an orphanage shirt that had a seal which read: "The St. Joseph Orphanage for Children," and a likeness of the saint. When the Jews were being transported out of the ghetto, the parents were with the child and also two relatives. At a station the Germans ordered all the Jews to get out and leave their things to the side. Little Ignas, unaware of the danger, ran with outstretched arms toward the commanding German. The parents became paralyzed with fear, and the German asked whose child it was. Shaking with fear, the father moved forward, and said that the child was his.

"How many more in your family?" was the next question.

"Four."

"To the side!" the German ordered.

All four, along with Ignas, stood in fear, certain that because of the child's whim, they would all be shot.

Meanwhile, all the rest of the Jews went to meet their doom, while they remained standing on the platform with their things. The German let them go.

Perhaps he was moved by the gesture of the child, but the fact is that a miracle happened. The entire family reached Westfalia and survived the war.

Wojtek. A pleasant, quiet boy, he did not like to play with the other children. Sometimes he would say that his father forbade him to pray to holy pictures and cross himself. He was transferred to another convent.

There were also about ten other children that were saved. Among those that had been abandoned during the anti-Semitic actions, not one went back to the ghetto, and after the war the nuns sent the children to the Jewish community in Cracow. On the other hand, eight Jewish children, who had been in the orphanage before the war and who had Jewish papers, could not escape the pressures from the authorities and were sent to the ghetto, where they probably perished.

CZESTOCHOWA—14 Wesola St.

During the occupation we ran a hostel in Czestochowa. During the time that the Jews were being transported out of the ghetto, a young, thirty-year-old woman came to us. She was slim, intelligent, of medium height, and had blond hair and blue eyes. She had two children: seven-year-old Ludwik, and three-year-old Adusia. The children were attractive and mature for their years. At first the woman passed herself off as a cousin of one of the nuns and received a separate little room upstairs. She went to the chapel with everyone else, and the boy carefully observed what to do in a chapel and followed suit. She had been the owner of a small factory in Czestochowa.

After a while we got her a work permit under the name of Switala

Janina. Her two children were officially taken in under her new name. Later she and her children became baptized behind closed doors. She spoke excellent German and did not have typical Jewish features. So she moved about freely, even going out to make some money.

Once one of the nuns asked little Adusia what was her name, and she answered that it was Horowitz. At which point her brother turned red and said in a disconcerted voice: "Adusia, that was before, but now you are Switala."

When the Jews in our establishment were later betrayed by a lay worker, Mrs. Switala took her children to the private house of her brother, who also was hiding in Czestochowa. During the Feast of Weeks, a German plain-clothes policeman called the boy over, saw that he was Jewish, and all three were shot in the Jewish cemetery in Czestochowa. Her brother managed to escape.

We made out papers in the name of Karolina Wisniewska for a woman of about thirty-eight, who had blue eyes and a Semitic nose. She and her five-year-old daughter, Lola, stayed with us. For some time she worked in our home as a portress, but after a betrayal she moved out and later was caught by the Germans.

Another young woman, with the fictitious name of Racinska, hid with us.

She also had a daughter, Genia, who stayed with us. Racinska worked in our laundryroom.

At the point when a woman brought over what was certainly her son, seven-year-old Jedrus, we had four adult Jews and four Jewish children staying with us. One of the girls who worked in the kitchen had been threatening for a long time to betray the Jews. We did not think she would do this, and told her that she was mistaken in thinking that there were Jews hiding in our place. We felt safe because everyone had Polish work permits, which we had gotten with the help of St. Zygmunt parish, to which we belonged. They even gave us birth certificates. Nevertheless, this girl went to the Gestapo and told them about the Jews staying with us, giving the exact names and rooms were they lived.

The Germans came and took all the Jews with them, but they were astonished when, before leaving the home, all the mothers knelt in the chapel and prayed.

At German headquarters, after answering various questions, the women had to recite Catholic prayers. Since they had learned them every day at the chapel, they were all released, but not feeling safe anymore, they soon left our home.

At her examination, Racinska was told that she should work outside the home in a factory. She fell into despair. After a while she made a bundle for her child and left it on our street, while she threw herself into the Warta River. She was pulled out and sent to the hospital, but the Germans took her from there, and we didn't hear anymore about her. The child wandered for some time before someone took her in as one of their own.

Irena Bochenek, a young girl, a blonde. She knew how to sew. The police came for her and asked for her registration. She was registered, but Sister Isadora hid her in the bathroom and told the police that she was not at home.

When they left, Sister Isadora dressed her and sent her to Warsaw that very day. The following day the Germans came again. This time they didn't believe that she wasn't there. They had been told to ask the portress, a lay person, who said that the girl they were searching for had not come back, and they gave up.

More Jewish people were saved, but Sister Wita, the mother superior at the time, has forgotten their names.

BOCHNIA—an orphanage

Pacula Wojciech, a ghetto guard, brought over a five-year-old girl, Halinka, born in 1938. She was blonde and had blue eyes, and was given the name Kubicka. She was the daughter of the owner of a tannery, Eliasz Ekstein.

A very intelligent girl, she went to school with the other children, and learned the Catholic religion without revealing her heritage. At her own request she was baptized in June 1947, and took her first communion. After the liberation she was secretly taken from the school by her aunt. Apparently her father survived the war and took her to Palestine with him and was thankful that the nuns had hidden his child.

Rozyczka N., the daughter of a lawyer from Cracow, spent three years in the children's home in Bochnia. She was quite pretty and intelligent, but her features betrayed her Jewish roots, and she spoke to other children about her parents, so it was thought that she would be betrayed by the older boys in the establishment. She was returned to her parents. Her further fate is unknown.

Her little brother, Wladyslaw, was also with us a short time. He also was taken back, as he was circumcised and brought attention onto himself.

Jas Moskowski hid with us until the Germans left, and then he was sent to Cracow.

On May 1943 we received an abandoned one-year-old Jewish girl. She was listed as a foundling, and safely stayed with us.

Nine-month-old Eliza from Bochnia, last name unknown. In 1945 the four-year-old was taken by her adoptive parents, but when her real family turned up later, they took her with them.

TARNOW—6 Nowodabroska St. Orphanage and infirmary for children.

A Polish policeman in the company of a brother of a missionary order brought to us a four-year-old boy who had been found in a church. The boy was very attractive, well-dressed, well-fed and very intelligent. He had a medal with the Heart of Jesus around his neck, crossed himself exquisitely, frequently kissing his medal and saying prayers. He said that his uncle had left him in the church and told him to wait patiently until he would come back, for he was going to buy a fiddle. The uncle did not come back, and a priest became interested in the boy, and they sent him to the orphanage. The boy said that his name was Jurek Gorski. Later he told a nun in secret that his real name was Norek. He was very intelligent and learned quickly. He went to the chapel with the other children. He adjusted very quickly to his new surroundings. After the liberation, four Jewish men came with an order from the district authorities to turn Jurek over. When he was told this, Jurek took his prayer-book and hid behind the altar in the chapel, so that no one could find him for a long time. He did not want to go for anything in the world, but finally was taken by force.

LWOW-ZAMARSTYNOW—an institution for boys

During the occupation three Jewish boys hid in the establishment; I've forgotten their names. Two of them were taken after the war by their relatives, and one of them left for the West by himself, as he had no one left in his family.

BAWOROW

A ten-year-old girl sent by the parish priest of Procyk admitted that she was Jewish. She became baptized. A two-year-old girl found by people in a field near a forest was in the home, too. Given to the Ukrainian police, she was handed over to the sisters for several days, after which she was to have been sent to the ghetto in Tarnopol. Through the efforts of the nuns she remained in the establishment and was baptized on June 13, 1943 and given the name Antonia. After the Germans left, her mother turned up and took her away.

TARNOPOL
During the time of the greatest action against Jews, a policeman came to the institution one day with a little boy in a small basket, who weighed no more than four kilograms. The policeman claimed that he found the child in an empty home. The child was taken in, bathed, fed and cared for. Because of the lack of beds for babies, he was placed in a new laundry basket, and the children surrounded the basket like angels around the Bethlehem manger. After several days a Catholic couple, who were childless, turned up and wanted to adopt a child. When the little boy was shown to them and they found out that it had been found, they took it gladly. They baptized the boy, giving him the name of Tadeusz, and surrounded him with true Christian love, even though the child was not that attractive. No one ever found out that the child was not theirs.

SANDOR
A two-month old Jewish baby was cared for by one of the sisters for about a year. When it started to walk it was given to the Basilian sisters in the town, since our home was for the elderly.

BRZEZANY—a home for the elderly
Aside from adult Jews, for a month we hid Helena Uchman, a daughter of a Jewish neighbor of ours. One Saturday she did not come to us. At the time there was an action against Jews, and the girl died with her parents.

A girl by the name of Zosia was given to the RGO (Central Welfare Council) by a peasant's widow, who, going to the West with two of her own children in 1943, could not take the girl with her. The RGO sent the girl to the nuns, where she was raised.

During the anti-Jewish actions, we hid for a day and a night a woman with her eight-year-old son. When she met the sisters later on the street, she knelt down before them, thanking them for saving their lives.

RAWA RUSKA

A boy found on the street was sent to our home. All he could say was that he had a letter with him and money, and some woman took them from him. His name was Zygmus. Some time later he was in our home in Cracow on Podbrzeze St., then he left for some other destination.

DROHOBYCZ

In 1942 a woman from the Polish Committee brought to our home a two-and-a-half year old boy who was circumcised. We learned from him that his name was Tadeusz, but he wasn't able to tell us his last name, so we named him Galewicz. When the Russian-German front moved and the situation became desperate, out of fear for the soul of the child, we had the boy baptized with water.

When in July, 1944 the Germans left, an aunt came to the home with a photograph of the boy. The father was waiting outside. It was Major Mieczyslaw H. of the Polish Army. The child's aunt assured us that the father was thankful for us for saving his child. Indeed. When the entire establishment moved to westward and reached Wroclaw, the nuns were homeless and went out to the city to look for a place to live. In their walk they met a Jewish man, who asked them what they were looking for. They replied that they were in poverty, and he told them that they had an important protector in the major, whose son the nuns had saved, and he gave them his address. When we turned up at the major's, he gave us his two-story home on Serbska St., while he himself moved to Karlowicka St. After some time he turned up for his son's baptismal certificate. When the home on Serbska St. was taken from us in 1950, we went to see Major H. for help.

BUSKO-ZDROJ

We were going to give a night's lodging to a Jewish woman with her two children. She stayed with us for half a year, however, and through that time was on our upkeep. After the liberation, we attired her in warm clothing, and she left with her children to Czestochowa.

SKARZYSKO-KAMIENNA—a home for the elderly

We hid a small girl, whose mother had been captured. When the liberation came, she took the child.

Also, a child found on the street was brought to the home. It had a card on its person, saying that it was nine-months old and not baptized. A childless couple took the child in and had it baptized in the name of Barbara.

After the war, Jews came for the child.

WOLOMIN—an orphanage

We hid two Jewish girls. One was adopted by a Polish family, and the second, older one was sick and became baptized. After the war, her brother turned up for her, but she did not want to go with him. But the authorities demanded that she be turned over.

During the Warsaw Uprising, a five-year-old boy wandered around the children's home in Wolomin. He was shabbily dressed, dirty, verminous and malnutritioned. The boys of the establishment chased him away several times, and even threw stones at him. When one of the sisters noticed this, she took the child in, bathed and fed him, and dressed him in new clothes. He stayed in the convent. He couldn't say anything about himself. Because he had dark skin, he was called a Gypsy. At first he was scared and never smiled, but after a few days he changed and the other boys began to like him very much. He was in the orphanage until September, 1946. At this time a nun, who had been caring for him, was transferred to a home in Siedlce, and a Jewish woman in Siedlce was looking around the convents for her child. She showed people his photograph, and the nun recognized the "Gypsy" from Wolomin. The grateful mother took her child from there, and in thanks offered the nuns leather for shoes.

SIEDLCE—orphanage

In 1943 a farmer brought a Jewish child, a six-year-old girl. The girl stayed in the home until the Germans left, then her father took her, saying that his wife died in Warsaw, while he had been hiding with the Albertine brothers. He was thankful that the nuns had saved his daughter.

During the time of the liquidation of the ghetto in Siedlce, the orphanage received a young Jewish child, whom the sisters had to hide before the lay personnel of the establishment. He was taken by a guardian of Jewish children.

Around 1943, two women came to the orphanage asking us to accept a child.

Since the nuns could not do this without going through a legal process, they advised the women to abandon the child at night. That's what was done. The several-month old Jewish girl was in the home for some time, later she was taken by a friend of her mother's.

A girl named Roza Zoik was also abandoned. After the Germans left, the father turned up for her; he had been hiding with a Catholic woman in Warsaw, whom he married, as his previous wife had perished in the ghetto.

A farmer brought a three-year-old girl, as he feared keeping her longer.

The girl was deathly afraid of Germans; she didn't even want to look out of the window in case someone would see her. After a short time someone told the Germans that the nuns were hiding Jewish children. When they came, a nun hid the girl in bed, as her features betrayed her, and she showed the Germans a boy, saying that perhaps they were looking for him. That child had Germanic features, so they patted him on the head and said that someone had been lying and left.

MINKOW

During the occupation we had displaced persons from Warsaw. A Jewish woman with her young child, and two older women.

CRACOW—6 Podbrzeze St.

Two children—ages seven and ten—were admitted into the home. One of them was named Jurek. Their mother came to visit them three times a week; she brought various things; she was very rich. One day the boys went out into the street, and the Germans caught them and took them away. Because of this, the home had much difficulty from the Germans, including protocols and commissions.

RZASKA

Hania Raj, a ten-year-old girl, was brought by her aunt, who said that the girl's parents had been in camp and later left for England. Hania went to school, had good grades, and even at the request of the aunt, was prepared to take first communion. As soon as the

Russians came, the aunt took the girl and placed her in a Jewish children's home in Cracow.

CRACOW—Pradnik Czerwony

A woman came to our mother general asking us to admit Jas, a son of our neighbor in Rzaska. The family was Catholic, but of Jewish ancestry. Under the name of Noskowski, Jasiu was sent to our home in Bochnia, and returned to his family after the war.

Sister Ludwika Malkiewicz (Elizabethan Sister)
October 20, 1984 at the Otwock orphanage

When on October 10, 1940 the Germans kicked us out of the children's home in Grabia, near Torun, and sent us to the General Government (to make room for the Hitlerjugend), the Social Welfare Dept. of Warsaw picked us up at the station in Warsaw and placed us with the Sisters of St. Teresa in Swidrze on Mickiewicz St. The living space was too small for all of us, so we requested the mayor to let us have the Jewish boarding school in the neighborhood, which was empty since the Jewish population was already in a ghetto. By ourselves we painted the interior and created a chapel, and the mayor gave us the necessary furniture from that furniture that had been left behind by the previous boarders. I received desks from a Jewish school that had been closed in Otwock.

The owner of the boarding school, as we found out, was Jozef Kaplon, a Jew, who was at the time in the ghetto in Otwock, about a kilometer away. We decided that since we were using his establishment, it was only proper to see if he needed food in the ghetto. I sought him out. It was 1941.

Kaplon was without any family and already very old and also ill. He was happy to see me and asked me to visit him regularly. He had something to eat, but every Sunday I brought him a warm dinner and a bit of this and that. Thus I became acquainted with Jews.

I always entered the ghetto under the barbed wire, for there was no entrance from the side of Swidrze. Except for Kaplon, the Jews looked at me with suspicion. But this didn't last long. The ghetto police themselves proposed that when I would be going from Otwock to Swidrze, I should shorten my way by walking through the ghetto. With time they began to trust me completely, so much so that they gave me their savings for safe keeping, and, needing money, they came for it at night. Later I started going to the ghetto on Saturday, right after school lessons, to see how the Jews prayed and observed the Sabbath.

And that is the way I began my contact with Jews and how it came to be that I wound up helping both Jewish adults and children.

The decision to help Jews belonged solely to the mother superior of our house, Sister Gertruda Marciniak, while I was the person who carried out her instructions, with the stipulation that in case of immediate danger the decision rested with me.

Jewish children were brought in through the requests of hiding parents or Mr. Adamowicz, who worked for the Welfare Department of Warsaw at 72 Zlota St.

The director of the department was Antoni Chacinski.

In our home there were several Jewish children. They came with fictitious names, some of which I don't remember. I will only tell you about those I do remember:

1) Alfred Karol (Leopold Blitzylberg, phonetically spelled), born in Baden-Baden. His mother was German, his father was a Jew. When the father was killed in the Warsaw ghetto, the mother escaped with Alfred to the Polish side, taking nothing with her. She begged for bread from some German soldiers but did not present herself to the German authorities in fear that they would take her child away to the ghetto. An Austrian woman, Marta Harf (likewise phonetically spelled) saw her on the street. Seeing a sick and teary-eyed woman in front of her, she decided to help. The mother was taken to a hospital, and Marta Harf took the child to her place. The mother died in the hospital, but before she died she asked Marta Harf to send the child to its family in Baden-Baden. The German authorities didn't allow this, and the child was to return to the ghetto.

Marta, a decent human being, looked around everywhere to save the child's life. Finally, Sister Gertruda sent me to Marta. Once there, after examining the situation, I was to decide whether to take the child back with me or not.

There was a fear, which Director Chacinski expressed, that this was a ruse on the part of the Germans, since Marta had assured the Welfare Department that the child was of pure German blood, in the face of which the question became why send the child to a Polish home for children? If I didn't take the child, it would have to go to the ghetto. So I took this seven-year-old boy to our home in Swidrze. This was in 1941. The boy remained with us to the end of the war.

2) Daniel Lancberg (phonetically spelled). In 1941 his parents begged us to take him. At their request the child was baptized and received the baptismal name of Wojciech. The child was barely three. The boy's father died in the Otwock ghetto; the mother survived the war and became baptized.

Daniel was a very thin child; he looked half-starved. He constantly had to eat, so he would go by himself to the kitchen to get a bite there. One day he got on top of a table to take a look out the window. Two German soldiers who were passing by saw him and rushed to the kitchen very angry and accusing us of hiding Jews. I ran to Mother Superior Gertruda Marciniak, who knew German quite well. (In those days the populace in the General Government did not know German.) The mother superior entered the kitchen calmly, and with a smile on her face, said:

"How can you possibly think that we have Jews here?"

Daniel, who was called Wojciech at our convent, did not understand what was being said, and at the sight of these faces looking at him with such anger, he went into a panic, crying and cuddling to the mother superior, who took him by the hand and said to him in Polish and to the soldiers in German:

"So you are the one who is supposed to be a Jew? What a joke! Don't cry, Wojciech; see how nicely these gentlemen are dressed and how good they are. They like children a lot—won't you like them?"

The boy, though he was still crying, extended his hands out to one of the Germans so that he could hug him. The soldiers were speechless. The mother superior, ignoring their confusion, asked them if they wanted tea and something to eat, all the while acting very calmly and smiling. The Germans were so dumbfounded that all they wanted to do was to leave our convent as quickly as possible. And yet it would have been very easy for them to see if Daniel was circumcised. Apparently they thought our mother superior was German.

3) Ruth Noy, the daughter of Max and Roza Noy. She was accepted to our home on Swiderski St. in Otwock in November, 1942, at the request of her parents, who were hiding after the liquidation of the ghetto there. With the agreement of the convent I made out a fictitious birth certificate for her under the name Teresa Wysocka.

We arranged the "abandonment" of the child: Without being seen, the mother left the child in the courtyard in the evening. The little girl began to cry, at the sound of which the nuns, and the personnel of the convent, came rushing up, and everyone saw the abandoned child. The girl had a small pouch about her neck, and inside was her fictitious certificate and a letter requesting us to keep the girl for a short time. The mother wrote in the letter that her husband had been taken to Germany to work and that she herself was spending a lot of time trying to make a living and didn't have a place to keep Teresa. In her difficult situation she counted on the mercy of the nuns. Of course, the mother signed her name as Wysocka.

The child was in our home for almost two years. Her parents saved themselves, hiding in Warsaw on Pelplinski St. After the war they wanted to give whatever money they had left to the convent for saving their child. The mother superior refused to take the money, so they offered it to me, and I likewise refused to take it.

4) Salome Rybak. In 1941 or 1942, I don't remember exactly, thirteen-year-old Salome (I don't know if that was her real name) was hiding under the stairs in the empty Jewish boarding school in Swidrze. At night she used to come to our children's home on 1 Mickiewicz St. and take from a barrel before our building the remnants of food left as fodder for pigs. Caught in the act, Salome was placed by us in our farm building and given a place to sleep and something to eat. When winter came, we took her in with the group of children in the children's home where, unfortunately, she could only remain for a few months. One of the wards, the son of an Ukrainian, wanted to tell the Germans about her. Here, once again, Mr. Adamowicz helped out and found another children's home for her, this one run by the nuns in Starowce. I took her there myself, though I've forgotten the name of the street.

Her Semitic features gave her away. To take her to Warsaw, I bandaged her entire head, leaving just an opening for one eye. I don't know what happened to her afterward.

All the children that were hiding with us were of the Hebraic religion. The only one who was baptized was, as I have already mentioned, Lancberg, and this was done at the request of his parents.

My attitude toward baptizing Jewish children was based on canonical law, which states that in regard to the baptism of children, one should get the approval of both or one of their parents. Furthermore, the baptized child should have a Catholic upbringing. There was no such certainty with the Jewish children we had because their parents could survive the war and bring them up in the Jewish religion.

Sister Zofia Makowski
July 16, 1985 in Labunie

During the war there was a swarm of children at our home. Anyone—policemen, neighbors—who met a child on the street or on the road brought the child to us. We had a house on Zdanowski St. in Zamosc. There came a time when even our hallways were overflowing with children. We had a rather large chapel in the old building we used, so finally we converted it to sleeping quarters for the children. We made the chapel so small that we had to hear Mass in the hallway. All this was not enough, and finally we occupied a school on Lukasinski St. Not being able to house all the children even there, we began to give them, if possible, to Polish families.

I worked at this school on Lukasinski St. Those were very hard times. I was in charge of the infants and the infirmary. There were three groups of children. I worked day and night. No one was paid. The women who peeled the potatoes got a bowl of soup. We did not get any subsidies for the children.

We collected contributions. Our entire treasure was the children.

Our mother superior was an Irish woman, Katherine Crowley. She trembled in fear for the children. We accepted everyone. We never thought about whether a child was German or Jewish or anything else. Our only consideration was that it was a child and we took in children.

Sister Ewelina Nienaltowska (Passionist Sister)
July 21, 1984

I've been a member of our congregation since 1930. The war found me in Janow Lubelski, where we had a home for old people and orphans. When the war broke out we had 200 senior citizens and 30 children. In the spring of 1940, the Germans moved us to Laczka Zaklikowa. Through the entire occupation we had a Jewish boy with us—Janek Burak.

He came to us before the war. His parents had gone to Germany, where they later died, but before that happened they gave the child to us. A nun went to pick up the child at the border. When she brought him over to us, he still did not know how to walk. We did not know if he had been baptized, so he was baptized in November, 1943 by Father Zielinski behind closed doors of Holy Spirit Church in Krasnik Lubelski. During the entire war the nuns hid Janek Burak from the Germans, as his features betrayed his Jewish heritage. When the war broke out, Janek was eleven years old. One day I sent him with some girls to Zaklikowa for meat. The Germans were riding in a car, when they saw him. They jumped out of the car and shouted: "Jude!"—that is, Jew.

Then the girls fastened onto the Germans and started to shout: "He is not Jewish! This is our Janek! This is our Janek!" Finally, as the girls continued to scream, the Germans got back into the car and rode away. Janek was so shaken up, that he never wanted to leave our home again. And after that I never sent him out.

Sister Janina Osmolska
(Sister Servant of Mary Immaculate—Stara Wies)
Archiwum Glowne Zgromadzenia SS. Sluzebniczek Starowiejskich (The Main Archives of the Sisters Servants of Mary Immaculate—Stara Wies)

During the war I was a teacher at the Children's Home in Piotrkow Trybunalski. In October 1941, two men brought us a several-month-old baby found on a parkbench with a beautiful linette by her side and a card bearing the name Helenka. She looked well. We determined that the baby was left behind not because the parents were poor, but in an effort to save her, and so she was probably Jewish, as Jews were being taken to the ghetto at the time.

I took her to a doctor to get examined. The child was healthy and, according to the doctor, must have been six or seven months old. We took care of the child because she needed help. She was under the care of the doctor, and we weren't concerned about her ancestry. Suddenly, after several months, we got a letter ordering us to show up with the child at the German command to determine her race. We were surprised, for we didn't know who or how anyone could have known about her. We talked about what we should do, for if it was determined by the Germans that the child was Jewish then death would await her. This we could not allow, even if it meant death for us also for hiding a Jew. We went through a lot of turmoil thinking about what would happen to the child, but I knew that I could not go to the Germans with her.

And then, suddenly, this healthy girl got sick. The doctor came and said she had diphtheria. The Germans greatly feared any contagious diseases, and that must have been the reason why they did not carry out their examination.

The child was baptized and taken to the hospital, and there the doctor said she needed serum immediately or else she would die. The hospital did not have it. Without thinking, I rushed to the drugstore, but I heard the same thing: "We don't have it." In order to get to the second drugstore I had to go to the other side of town, and time was running out, for the medicine was needed immediately. Not paying attention to anything else, I ran as fast as I could. I finally got to the drugstore, and with racing heart I asked and got the answer: "It is here!" Overjoyed, I waited for the medicine; then I remembered that I had no money on me. I tried to figure out what to do and suddenly came upon a good idea. I was wearing a new pair of shoes, so I decided to give them as security and run back to the hospital in my bare feet.

It was the end of April and already warm; the life of the child was more important. The injections were brought to me. I said that I didn't have the money but that I will give my shoes up as security. I was told: "I don't need the shoes because I know that the amount due will be paid." Once again I ran, this time back to the hospital; the doctor said that unless some complications would arise, Helenka should be alright. In the home we all waited, while I related what had happened. The following days we learned of Helenka's health by telephone. Because of her contagious disease, we could not visit her. We had fifty-six children of various ages at our home, and could not risk the danger of bringing the disease back with us. Finally we received by telephone the happy news that the girl was feeling better, though she was still breathing through a tube placed in her trachea. We were able to visit her. I went; she even looked well; the tube had already been removed and there was a bandage about her neck. We visited her frequently, which was important in order that she not forget us. In the hospital she began to take her first steps. After we took her home, she blossomed nicely, both physically and psychologically. She was already walking well.

When the war ended, a man with Semitic features turned up at our home and presented himself as Helenka's father. When he was asked for proof, he began to explain. Helenka had been left behind, because he and his wife were to be taken to the ghetto; they wanted to save their child. He knew that she had suffered from diphtheria and had a tube placed in her throat; he knew other things also—everything checked out. They had people who observed what was happening to the child, and after their return they found out from them everything that had happened. With tears in his eyes, he thanked us for our solicitous care of the child, particularly during the time of her life-threatening illness. We were very happy to have saved the child from death. He told us about his and his wife's experiences in the concentration camp, and how they were tortured. Somehow they managed to survive, and after the war they wound up in Sweden.

At first, Helenka did not want to go with her father, and she would not accept anything from him. The father was heartbroken. We told him to come everyday, for the child had to get used to him. The mother came also. One cannot describe the moment when she saw her child so grown up and looking so well. She embraced her, crying from happiness. She nestled her, kissed her and thanked us. She was overwhelmed with joy. The child's heart warmed up, and she began to respond to them differently. The father was a tailor by profession and had already rented an apartment, so they wanted to take the child. The child needed some convincing before she would go. All the children bid her good-bye and cried for her, just as we did, and she said: "I will come here everyday." And so it was. They all came one day and said: "That Helenka has put us through the mill; we have to get down on our knees and pray before we can go to sleep." We told them that the child had been baptized, to which they replied: "Let her be a Catholic, it is good that she is alive!" During the entire time that they stayed at nearby Piotrkow, they came to us every Sunday after church. In 1946 they left for Palestine, saying that there was no work for them in Poland. Once there, they wrote us that they had arrived, and it ended in that. I do not remember their names.

Sister Charitas Soczek (Samaritan Sister)
October 14, 1985 in Pruszkow

After the war the Jewish children were reclaimed by the Jewish Committee—I don't know the particular details because the office took care of this. As a token of their gratitude for keeping the children and adults, the JDS presented us with a considerable amount of food. Remembering what we did for them, the rescued Jews who had attained positions in society after the war helped us when we were in danger of losing our home....

During the war I maintained contact with the underground and also was one of the chief persons involved in helping persecuted people. I was the second in charge to the Mother Superior in these matters. Among other persons, I occupied myself with Iwona Szenwitz and her parents. The girl, who was twelve or thirteen, used the name Jankowska during the occupation. She was a difficult and moody only child who suddenly found herself in the ghetto. She was one of the first to leave the ghetto and was taken in by people who only wanted to make money—they used to give her to other people under the pretext that she was being sought by Germans. The girl was a witness to many horrible scenes in the ghetto. I became aware of the perfidious game of her guardians and determined to take this distraught girl from them. I had a lot of trouble with her; I had to go with her everywhere because she was so frightened.

I placed her with the Ursuline nuns and provided for her. The nuns knew her background. One day I found out that I had to take the sobbing girl out of the boarding school. I took her to Pruszkow, but I couldn't keep her there long because a lot of illegal work was already being done in our home. I found a boarding school in Warsaw with some secular women, but they did not really want to take the girl and questioned why it was that I was taking care of her.

Not thinking it over, I said that the girl had an aunt in Pruszkow, and gave the name of a woman doctor I was familiar with. In trepidation I returned to Pruszkow, not knowing how the new "aunt" would react. The "aunt," however, immediately went to Warsaw and fussed over the food and the inadequate conditions at the boarding school, which had the effect of making the women think that they were really dealing with the girl's aunt. After that, the "aunt" took care of matters for Iwona, and the girl remained in the boarding school until the Warsaw Uprising. I provided for Iwona from her family's money, which I had difficulty obtaining. I also took care of Iwona's parents.

Once, I arranged a meeting between mother and daughter (both looked like typical Semites), for they missed each other very much. During the uprising the father took the girl from the boarding school. I was able to find both of them in a camp at Pruszkow, and thereafter they lived in our home. The father (who had a good Slavic look) remained with us to the end of the occupation, while Iwona was taken in by her adoptive aunt. After the war, the entire family went to Lodz. We remain great friends even to this day, though Iwona now lives in Canada.

Sister Roberta Sutkowska (Sister of St. Joseph)
June 2, 1985 in Tarnow

During the war I worked in Trzesowce, which is near Kolbuszow. On April 12, 1942, Palm Sunday, a girl came to us. The weather was horrible, the child was poorly dressed—shabby boots, a crumpled dress of shepherd's cloth, a coat made from a blanket. She said she came to work for us, and would do whatever we liked, if we would only keep her.

She was taught to say these things by the people who threw her out and ordered her to go to the nuns. She had been taken in by some people near Mielce, who had received money and linen from her parents. They had a girl her age. Later, as she began to trust me, Rachela told me everything:

"How did you get to those people?"

"That man from Mielce came for me in Lwow, where I was staying with a woman. That woman said she could not keep me any longer."

The girl did not know who the man was who took care of her.

"Where are your parents?"

"They also were hiding because the Germans were looking for them," she replied thoughtfully. "My parents were very rich. My mother is not alive, and I don't know about my father."

"And how did it happen that you came here?"

"That man told me to go because he was afraid of the Germans. And he took me to a field and said: 'Go straight to that tall building; don't talk with anyone along the way. There you will find nuns who will take you in, for I can't have you at my home anymore.' And so I came here."

She came to us between ten and eleven in the morning—tired and dirty. We took pity on her. Before the war, we ran a nursery in the village. We couldn't do that during the war. Older sisters arrived from Lwow to be with us, so there was a good number of nuns, from ten to twelve. I went to seek the advice of Father Dunajewski in Kolbuszow. (He has since passed away.) The priest advised me to go to Bishop Lisowski in Tarnow, who said:

> You are not the first person to show up here on such a matter. It is good that you took this child in. God will take care of this, so that nothing will happen and no one will interfere. One has to gradually learn from this child her history, and then later we will have to deal with the issue—for its possible that we will have to baptize the child. In the future the child has to go to school. But let's take things a step at a time. Somehow everything will work itself out. One just has to make certain that the girl does not contact anyone and talk. If someone takes an interest in the child, tell them she has been accepted into the convent, and that's that.

Three, four years went by. To the end of the war. The girl constantly demanded we give her some work. I laughed—she helped us in all our chores.

After the war, Father Dunajewski went with Rachela to Bialystok. It turned out that the child had spoken the truth. The priest at the notary took out all the documents on the girl. Today I refer to her as Rachela, though we never called her by that name—she had a different first and last name, but I don't know if she'd want me to reveal it.

After the war we sent Rachela to school. The head mistress, after giving her an exam, admitted her to the fourth grade. She went to grammar school in Przemysl—our sisters took care of her there. I helped her as best I could, though she did not want anything special. On holidays and on vacation she stayed with me. She learned well, very well. Later she went to Krakow to study medicine. I used to go to see her in Krakow. When Rachela met her future husband she feared telling him about her ancestry, but I advised her that she couldn't keep it a secret from him. She told him. When they would write to me later, they signed themselves, as always: 'Your children.'

After the war, there came a time when Jews came to find Rachela. A very smartly attired man came and said that he wanted to talk to the mother superior. When I entered, he said:

"Mother Superior, you took in this girl."

"How do you know?"

"We know everything now," he said, telling me who he was. "This child interests us very much. I am a representative of the Jewish Committee, and have the task of finding this girl and taking her with me. We want to relieve you of the burden of taking care of her; such a girl needs protection and care and material goods."

"My dear sir," I replied, "the fact that I took in the child and have taken care of her till now is my affair. One can always do an act of kindness."

"But you are aware that this is a Jewish child?"

"Yes."

"Could I see this child? Could I talk with her, one on one?"

I was taken by surprise. "Very well," I said, "But I would request to be present at this talk, because the child will be intimidated. She'll be reassured by my presence."

I went to get Rachela. The girl was afraid of everyone. Everyone. Whenever a stranger would come to our home, Rachela would immediately run to me and ask with fear in her voice: "Who is that? Who has come here?"

So now I had to calm her down, telling her that no danger threatened her, that she should not be frightened. But the girl asked:

"Why should I go to this man?"

"He wants to talk with you."

"I don't want to talk to him, I don't want to talk to anyone. For sure, he is a Jew."

Before Rachela spoke with this man, he told me:

"Mother Superior, you should know that we intend to take this girl out of the convent. I will give you half-a-million zlotys today if you will help me in the matter."

"You are strongly mistaken," I said to him. "I am not a dealer in people, I don't deal in children. Anyway, when the child comes, you will see."

The girl was very intimidated when she came to see him.

"Ah, so you are Rachela?"

"No, my name is N— N—," she replied.

"Your name at home was Rachela."

The girl lowered her head.

"Is it good for you here?"

"Yes," she said, cuddling up to me more and more.

"What do you do here?"

"I help when I can, but aside from that I do nothing except learn."

"You learn? Listen, the nuns here have meagre conditions, while we will give you everything. You will go to whatever school you want."

"But I am a Catholic."

"That's nothing. We will not interfere with that. You will be able to sing religious hymns whenever you want. We will not stop you."

"I will never go! I will never go!" Rachela shouted. "I just came to the sister, and she is my mother! She is my mother!"

Nothing came out of that talk. That man came to us once again. He had seen Father Dunajewski. I tried to persuade Rachela to return to her own people, but she always answered that she would not go to the Jews, that she didn't want to know them. I tried to explain that perhaps some member of her family was alive, that perhaps she had someone.

In the meantime, a package arrived for Rachela, probably from her aunt in Belgium. The aunt wrote that if she wanted something, she would send it, that she would take care of her. Rachela refused it all, saying:

"I don't want anything! I don't need anything! I have no aunt! I won't go to any aunt. I will not write back to thank any person! I don't need anything; you, sister, have given me everything!"

Sister Janina Watychowicz (Seraphite Sister)
September 8, 1985 in Nowy Targ

During the war I worked in Drohobycz in a orphanage called St. Jadwiga on Polna St. Jewish children were not admitted officially, but were delivered to us, usually by some anonymous person from the Social Welfare Department. Sometimes we had three Jewish children staying with us, sometimes five or six; the number changed whenever a child would be taken away by an acquaintance. Once we got new-born twins wrapped in a sheet.

We were never told the names of the children because they were supposedly missing persons of war. There was no talk of payment; the Social Welfare Department provided for their food.

Once we learned that the Ukrainians were to attack Wojtowska Gora, where our order was situated. A German told us: "You have to arm yourselves with knives, you have to save yourselves." Our fear was great, and not only because of the Jewish children; the Ukrainians would not have spared Polish children either. Thankfully they did not come, for there was an air raid.

Our duty to our order led to our work in the East, both for God and the people there, be they Polish, Ukrainian or Jewish—everyone who needed our help.

INTERVIEWS WITH SAVED JEWISH CHILDREN

Franciszka A. (Saved by the Sisters of Charity in Ignacow)

November 12, 1987 in Herzliyya, Israel

When the war broke out, I was living with my family in Stanislawow, near Minsk Mazowiecki. I was twelve years old. My father was taken prisoner by the Germans....

[...]I knew that no one in my family was left alive, for when I was escaping from Stanislawow it was clear that on the following day the Germans would deport any Jews who returned to their homes. Then I met a neighbor—she now lives in Israel—who had escaped from the transport train. She had been in a car together with my mother and sister. I knew then that I had no one. I thought that there was no reason for me to suffer longer. I went out onto the road. I always used to take back roads, so that no one would see me. This time I went out onto the main road so that the Germans would catch me and my sufferings would be over.

If I were religious I would say that some angel was watching over me....

It was February, 1943. I was dressed in a blouse with short-sleeves and my legs were bare. Suddenly an older woman stopped me and asked where I was going. I told her that I was displaced and that I was looking for work.

"You're looking for work?" she asked. "Do you have some documentation?"

"No," I answered.

"If you don't have documents then no one will take you," she replied.

"But you know what? Do you see that church steeple? There are nuns there, and a convent and an orphanage also. Maybe they will take you in. When you get to the convent, say, 'Praise the Lord,' and kiss the nun's hand and ask her whatever you want."

I went off the main road and went to the convent. When I went inside, it was just like the woman said.

The mother superior, Sister Marcjanna, came out. I said "Praise the Lord." She didn't ask me much. She asked me my name, where I was from, how old I was, and what kind of work I wanted to do. She said she was sorry but that dinner was already over, and there was only bread and milk left. She called the postulant, Regina, to take me to the kitchen and give me something to eat.

In the kitchen I was given bread and milk. I ate. Then I was taken to the bathroom, where I was washed and given clothes. They were not new clothes but they were clean, from one of the children, for there were 150 of them there. Regina asked me what job I wanted to do and if I liked children. I replied that I liked them, so Regina led me to the so-called "barn." This was a separate building in which one group of children stayed.

The work was not hard—simply helping out with the children. One had to help them make their beds, wash their cups, lay the table, etc. For some time I helped the teacher nuns, and later I was transferred to working in the hen house. I worked with an awful woman there, Janowa, who was cross-eyed, hunchbacked and very unpleasant. No one wanted to work there, but I never complained to the nuns. In the hen house there was also Adela, a handsome older woman, who had been raised by the convent. She wanted me to serve her after work was done. I told her I wouldn't do this, and she cursed me to the high heavens....

Once, when I was still working with the children, I came down from the bedroom and saw that the courtyard was filled with German soldiers. Whenever I saw Germans I always felt that they were there for me. I continually thought that someone would betray me and that the Germans would take me away. In this "barn" slept Sister Bronislawa, the nun in charge of education (she had a room next to mine), and two other workers besides me. When I heard this nun coming out of her room (one could not enter the room of a nun) I went up to her and said: "Sister, what should I do?"

At the time I still didn't have my work permit but only a piece of paper showing that I had registered at the police station. This police registration always worried me, for I feared that someone would try to verify the false information I had given. I always felt that something bad could happen around the corner. At the time, there was a round-up of Jews hiding in the woods.

So I asked Sister Bronislawa what I should do. The sister replied that she would go to the big house, to the mother superior, because she didn't know what to do. She opened the door.

"Halt! Who is there?"

Sister Bronislawa came from the German border and spoke the language well; so she answered in German:

"A group of children live here, along with me and three helpers—two grown-up and a young one."

The Germans demanded documents, but when the sister said that I still didn't have any, they had me summoned. When I came into the room they said that they had to take me to the big house to make sure that I hadn't come to the convent just now at the time of the round-up of Jews. Then I showed them my police registration and Sister Bronislawa translated it, the result being that they said I didn't have to go with them. It was said that the Germans caught a lot of Jews in the forest that day.

The following day Sister Bronislawa came to me and stated that I had to go to Minsk Mazowiecki to get myself a work permit.

"How can I get a permit?" I asked. "I don't even have a birth certificate!"

"I will take care of everything at the office," she replied.

Everyone who applied for a work permit got it after two weeks. With me it took three months. When I finally received it, I felt relieved. I stayed with the nuns until the liberation in 1944.

Throughout the entire time I was in the convent I was considered Polish.

The sisters never asked about anything. Even Sister Joanna, though we were such good friends.... The sisters did not know that I was a Jewess. They could only suspect it. In the convent, however, there was an old priest, who, every time I went to confession, always mentioned something about Jews.

Obviously, since I was in a convent, I went to confession. This priest was served by Jozka Mankowska, and when she went to visit her family, I took her place. I brought him food and cleaned his room. One day the priest asked me why I wasn't writing a diary.

"Why should I write a diary?" I asked him.

"Because your life is more interesting than other peoples," the priest replied.

I think that he knew who I really was.

In the convent all the children belonged to the "Association of the Children of Mary," and every Sunday after dinner we had a meeting with this priest, who taught us and explained certain religious matters. At every one of these talks he would add something about Jews. Not against Jews, but he always put in a word on the subject. He would say that it was a great sin for someone not to confess to which religion he belongs and to accept holy communion without being baptized. We sat and listened. Irka was there too.... After that lesson we both came to the conclusion that we were committing a sacrilege because both of us were Jews.... It was, in truth, this Irka who took me to the woods and told me that she was committing a sin because she was Jewish.

How could she not be afraid to tell me about it? After all, if she had told someone else.... Irka told me that she sensed that I was Jewish also, and that is why she told me about herself.

I remember one more incident. The day after I came to the convent, Sister Bronislawa sent me to get coffee for breakfast. Outside I met a teacher I knew from Wolka Czerniejowska, Irena Cudna, who knew me and my parents very well. I pretended not to see her. Through the entire time of my stay in the convent, she saw me everyday; despite this, she did not tell anyone about me to the end of the war. Only after the liberation did she tell her family that Szpigner's daughter had been staying at the convent.

After the war I met my future husband, and I got married. I got married so young because I had no one and nowhere to go. Upon my departure from the convent I told the nuns that I was going to look for my family—to the end I did not tell them that I was a Jew. I just couldn't. I had lied too much and was, quite simply, ashamed. After a certain time I wrote them a letter and explained myself and that I did what I did because I wanted to live. When I was in Poland in 1984, I visited these nuns. I asked the mother superior what she thought when I arrived at the convent, whether she guessed that I was a Jew. She told me that she did not want to think about it at the time, she was only interested in helping people and saving lives.

As far as I know there were ten Jewesses living in Ignacow. In my group there was a little girl, perhaps four-years-old, who did not know who she was.

She was called Marysia. I remember a game she played one day with the children. She placed all the chairs in a row and sat the children down, after which she crawled under a chair. When I asked her why she wasn't sitting on the chair but hiding underneath it, she replied:

"Quiet, Miss Frania! If the Germans catch me, I'm dead!"

When I asked her why she said that and from where she came, the girl told me her story. She told me that she was once walking down a street in Warsaw with her aunt and when they came to the doorway of her building, the aunt told her to remain on the street and if a policeman asked her any questions she was to say that she knew nothing. Marysia wound up in the Boduen house, and then Ignacow. I told her not to tell anyone what she had told me, but this was a child.... She always hid under the chair, so that the Germans would not kill her....

During the war one of the convent buildings, the "barn," burned down. The Germans stationed in nearby Janowa proposed that the nuns use one of their barracks. The children were without a roof over their heads, so the nuns transported them to Janowa. Marysia did not go, however, but was placed in the "big" house. She was too Jewish-looking for the nuns to allow her to live among the Germans.

Aside from various inspections, the Germans would come to Ignacow for their walks, while the children cuddled next to the nuns for they needed a mother, and they didn't have any.... One day a German officer came to Ignacow for a walk with his wife. Marysia was holding onto Sister Bronislawa. Then that German woman—I was standing nearby—pointed to Marysia and said to Sister Bronislawa:

"That girl looks Jewish!"

"We have absolutely no Jewish girls here!" the sister replied categorically. "We know where each child comes from."

She was lying, of course, for there was no way for her to know from where each child came.

In any case, Marysia was kept hidden a lot, for she looked very Jewish.

Apparently, so was another girl, the slightly older Marysia Kuczynska, who couldn't go to school with the rest of the children because she also looked Semitic. The nuns brought over a teacher to the convent to teach Marysia.

In the convent there were fourteen nuns, the old priest, 150 children and 50 other people, among whom were farm-hands and so-called "ladies"—women who were hiding. When I went to work in the sewing room, I moved to the bedroom of these ladies. Among them was an older woman named Maria Kowalska, who when she entered the chapel seemed to speak to God Himself, she was so religious.

After the liberation I joined the army and worked in the army hospital in Lublin. One day a doctor, a Jew, asked me to accompany his aunt from Szojadel. You can imagine my surprise when I saw that the aunt of my doctor was the lady from Ignacow, Maria Kowalska, the woman with whom I had slept with in one room! When we finally reached Lublin, Maria said to me:

"Frania, let us go to church to say a prayer in thanks for our successful journey."

I found this very funny, for she already knew that I was a Jew and that I knew she was a Jew, too, and yet.... I'm laughing at Maria now, but I myself had in the convent a praying-desk by the main altar, and every free moment I would sit in the chapel and pray.

I came from a very religious Jewish family. Despite that, I believed in Jesus Christ. Because, firstly, a young person is very susceptible. Secondly, being in a convent will make a believer out of anyone! To be in those surroundings, a part of that life, of that wonderful life. The nuns lived so nicely! It was a peaceful life.

Materially? The war was on and not much was expected. But everyone had enough.

I valued life in the convent above all because I knew how I had lived before. I knew that I lived well here, that I got everything I needed. I did not get money, but I didn't need it. I had enough to eat, a clean bed and a kind word—everything I needed at that time, everything that a person could need.

Coming from a religious family, it was not easy. When we were escaping the first time, we stayed with the Czapski family, and Mrs. Czapski gave us potatoes with pork cracklings. I cried, and though my mother told me to eat, I couldn't put it down my throat, I gagged. I was hungry but I couldn't eat.

Later, when I was in the convent, I ate pork and liked it very much. After the war, I couldn't eat pork once again. I wasn't religious any more, any religious feelings in me had died out, but I still couldn't eat pork, and I can't to this day.

In the convent I was very religious. I began to believe in Christ when that old woman on the road pointed the convent out to me and had me go there.

I went off the road then, knelt and prayed to Christ to help me. That was the first time I prayed to Christ. I promised Him that if they accepted me in the convent and I survived the war, that would mean that he was the real God and I would never leave Him. I did not keep my word, but through the entire time I was in the convent I prayed, went to confession, took holy communion—I did everything, believing in it! I believed in it!

After the war, I couldn't decide whether to be baptized and change my faith, for I was brought up in the Jewish faith and all the people close to me were dead because they were Jewish. When I was older, I thought differently.

The Germans didn't ask what a person believed in; if you were Jewish you were dead.

The Germans also killed Poles, but they did this in a different way.

Perhaps if the war had lasted longer, the same fate that met the Jews would have eventually met the Poles, because Hitler wanted a pure race. The Poles were also arrested, after all, even if they were innocent....

Lea B. (Israeli citizen)
March 1984 in Brwinow, Poland

Before the war my parents lived in Ostrow Swietokrzyski and owned a furniture factory. We had an accountant named Gluchowski, and my father, when the Germans were taking him to Oswiecim, gave him the key to the factory and asked him to hide me. He sent my mother to Russia. I'm sure it was this Gluchowski who took me to the convent in Brwinow, but I really don't remember much from that time. My father doesn't like to speak about this; he's very old. He doesn't even know that I'm in Poland at the moment. My mother died in Warsaw in 1944; I think she used to come to the convent on occasion, and once she brought me some white bread. I was at the convent until 1945.

I remember that I was very sick. I had some type of growth and an infection. There was heavy bombing going on, and a nun took me by the hand and ran with me one night to the hospital, in which there were soldiers. The nun sat with me and told me through the entire time that if I behaved she would buy me a doll larger than the one in the convent. They operated on me, and I returned to the convent.

I also remember that during the bombing we would go to the cellar, whose ceiling was made not of concrete but of earth. We laid there with the nuns; I remember the smell of potatoes. I remember the type of life we led, and Christmas, and a Christmas tree in some room to the left, with candies on the tree. Candies during wartime! St. Nicholas would come on Christmas; he would come through that big gate and go up the steps. This was during the war! We did not have potatoes to eat; we ate offals—and the nuns ate offals! Just like the children. And yet we would get candies at Christmas. The Christmas tree was enormous, and covered with balls and candles. There was much joy at the time. Now I have come back to my childhood, and it was not a bad one at that!

All in all, my war experiences were not tragic. I think that if during the war it was possible for me to be on a bed of roses, then the bed was prepared for me here. And that is why the war is not so terrible for me.

But I never really understood why they were hiding me. They did not explain it to me; they only said that there was danger. I remember one more thing. The Germans used to come to the convent and take eggs, or sometimes pigs. There was a garden there, fruit and vegetables were growing—and the Germans came and took them. One day, there was a large basket full of eggs and straw. Perhaps there were hens in the convent? I do not remember.

The Germans came in so suddenly that I was left inside the room and could not be taken out through any door. Sister Helena—she was tall and slim, her face was like that of the Madonna; she was beautiful—took those eggs out so quickly! She put me inside the basket and covered me with the eggs and straw.

A German came in, kicked the basket and asked what was in it. She calmly answered that there were eggs in the basket. The German said he was taking the eggs. The sister started begging him, saying there was a seriously ill nun in the convent who had to have those eggs. The German persisted, but then started paying her compliments, for she was very beautiful. Finally he left the basket where it was and went away.

There was a lot of straw lying on the floor. I could not stay in that basket, for the straw prevented me from breathing properly. I had to hold my nose shut the entire time. Nowadays I think I must have been co-operating with the nun. A five-year-old girl, that's all I could have been at the time. Not more than five. To be aware of the terrible danger we were in! Both she and I, and the entire convent!

When the Germans left, the sister took me out of the basket and began to clean my nose. She kissed and hugged me. I was well-liked in the convent; I always felt that somebody loved me, and this was very important.

I remember one more thing. When we went to church, I always went with a blanket over my shoulder. A nun had explained to me that if a German came up from one side, I was to place the blanket on that side so that it would hide my face. I always listened to what she said, for I was a good, obedient child. If there had not been this attention to every detail, I don't know if I could have survived the war.

Before I left for Poland on this trip, I visited to the Yad Vashem Museum. There is a map of Poland there. Written in black numbers are the number of Jews in Poland before the war and how many survived. Before the war there were 3,700,000 Jews in Poland. After the war—this is what the map says, but it is not accurate because it doesn't count those Jews who saved themselves in Russia—20,000 survived. Of that number, 5,000 were children. I was one of 5,000 children that survived out of 3,700,000 Jews! That is a miracle. Truly, if it had not been for the nuns, it would have been impossible for me to have survived. Impossible.

But I don't understand what a short memory we have, here in Israel, too.

I said the same thing on Israeli radio. People have such a short memory. Just as one should not forget acts of evil, one should not forget acts of goodness.

We talked about that before coming here, that the entire world did not help the Jews during the German occupation. People partied, danced, went to cafes. No one helped. Only a small group of people saved Jewish lives. And my life was saved....

Nina E. (Israeli citizen, saved by the Felician Sisters in Staniatki)

September 28, 1986 in Warsaw, Poland

In September of 1939, Polish radio informed all Jewish men to leave Cracow. It was assumed that the Germans would treat women and children benignly and do them no harm. My father escaped with his brother—he left our house on September 2, and it was December of 1945 before I saw him next. He was in Siberia, then in Central Asia. I remained with my mother and brother, who was eight years older than I.

We had a large house. The Germans assigned it as living quarters to a prostitute, most probably a woman of German descent, on November 5, 1939. My mother was ordered to cook and clean for her. After about two days, the prostitute left for Katowice, and at that time my mother packed a few things and took me and my brother to my aunt's on Kazimierz St. We lived at my aunt's until the ghetto was opened.

When the ghetto was created in Cracow, we were not allowed to live in it since my father was not with us. We lived in Gdow. In September of 1942 all the Jews from the neighboring villages were sent to Wieliczka. The majority of them were later packed into lime-strewn wagons and transported to the gas chambers. In Wieliczka my mother sent telegrams to her Polish acquaintances, in which she asked them to come for me. There is a big marketplace in Wieliczka. We stood there. After a while my mother said: "Look, the Latawcows are coming!"

My mother waved to them. They came up to us, they were not afraid. My mother said: "Take my child!" They took me. The husband on one side, his wife on the other. I don't know if they understood at that time what they were doing. They were a childless couple who lived on Grzegorzecki St.

They took me home with them just as I was, without anything. At first it was very hard, but they became used to me. They were very orderly people, while I was ten-years-old and had been living in the country for the last two years—a free child.

My mother was able to escape from the transport train and she reached the camp in Plaszow, from where she made contact with the Latawcows. I visited my mother several times in Plaszow, and my adoptive father visited my mother in Plaszow every Friday.

I was with my adoptive parents, the Latawcows, from the summer of 1942.

In the spring of 1943 someone recognized me. I don't know if it was some cleaning lady or washerwoman, in any case soon the entire apartment house knew that the Latawcows had a Jewish child at their place. There had been, of course, some suspicion, because I was not going to school and stayed in the house. In that same building lived another family. That family said that they could not take the chance of my presence because they had a child my age. We had to get away. By the spring of 1943 most Jews were already not around, but one still heard of captures and that the remaining Jews were being betrayed.

So from that moment on we looked for lodging every night, but no one was ready to keep us longer than a day or two.

It was a desperate situation. My adoptive parents could not do anything with me, and they became so attached to me that they did not want to give me back to my mother. My mother knew of this situation and told my adoptive father on one of his visits to Plaszow that she wanted me with her in the camp. We would share the same fate, she decided. My adoptive parents did not want to agree to this. My adoptive mother, a practicing Catholic, frequently went to church and prayed. According to her, St. Anthony inspired her one day to place me in a convent. She went to the Social Welfare Department and said that she had a niece from the Poznan area whom she wanted to place in a boarding school. They gave her the name of the Felician sisters in Staniatki and obtained a birth certificate for me, and we left for Staniatki. This was the beginning of 1944. My adoptive mother had had me baptized with water earlier. I was accepted as a Polish girl in the convent until the end of the war.

The nuns did not know, therefore, that I was Jewish. My appearance was good, my Polish likewise. I behaved properly and was a practicing Catholic.

When I was ready to take my first Communion, though, I was afraid that I would commit some sacrilege. In truth, though my adoptive mother had me baptized, it was not a real baptism. One day I approached the mother superior and asked to have a talk with her. I told her that I was a Jewish and begged her to have me baptized before I took Holy Communion. She fixed her eyes on me and said:

"Daughter of the Chosen Race, good child, let's try to figure this out." The next day the mother superior made a trip to my adoptive mother and asked her by what right had she placed a Jewish child in the convent without telling her. She said she already had several Jewish children and needed more Polish children to hide the presence of the others. Meanwhile, each new child she was getting was Jewish! (There were not many children in the school, about eighteen. Taking that into consideration, six Jewish girls was a lot.) My adoptive mother swore that I was not a Jew, but rather her niece. The sister replied that that was nonsense, for I had admitted it myself. When she next saw me, my adoptive mother said: "Nina, what have you done!"

So I became baptized. In the meantime I befriended the other Jewish girls there, and thanks to me all six became baptized. Of course, everything happened in secret, though with much ceremony.

Every Saturday we received fresh underclothes and two little bars of soap: one for our toilet and the other for washing clothes. During one such occasion, Krysia said to me: "This *lejbik* has so many holes in it!"

This word was of Germanic origin and meant undershirt.

Afterward, I went up to her and said: "You are Jewish, isn't that right?"

She swore that she was not.

"I am Jewish also!" I revealed.

We started to hug each other and promised to help each other.

Later, Krysia said: "You know, Hania is my cousin; she is also a Jew!"

We then went to church and, hiding there, started to tell each other about ourselves. There were three of us. As for the rest of the Jewish girls, everyone knew that they were Jewish because of the way they looked. We tried to protect them somehow because they were constantly being bothered. The other girls bullied and frightened them, saying that if they misbehaved they would be denounced. Of course, no one betrayed them, but they were terribly bullied.

When I organized this baptism, we were all very happy because we felt that if something happened we would go straight to heaven.

I was treated very well in the convent. My adoptive parents paid for me during the entire time I was there. My adoptive father supported me from his meagre post office pension. Aside from the mother superior, not one of the nuns knew that I was Jewish. I was there until the liberation of Cracow in January 18, 1945. My adoptive parents came for me the following day and took me home with them. I returned home, and they enrolled me in school.

My mother survived Buchenwald; she returned from camp at the time I was with my adoptive parents. I did not want to go back to my mother. My father returned, but I did not want to go with them. I wanted to remain a Pole.

What I lived through after the war! I cannot compare those times to what happened during the war, for there was no fear or threat to one's life, but the battle between these two women, these two mothers, my biological mother and that mother who had saved me, was terrible!

I was in Cracow until 1949, but I did not live with my parents. I did not have the courage to go out into the street with my parents, for I feared that someone would see me and realize that I was a Jew. So I remained with the Poles.

I always steered the middle course between both mothers to get a surplus of love and care... In truth, I was with the Poles to the end. Only when my biological parents decided to leave Cracow—above all because of me—only then did I leave my Polish family. That was a very hard time for me, you cannot imagine. I knew perfectly well that I belonged to these parents. But I did not want to belong! I did not want to be a Jew, I wanted to remain a Polish girl.

I've already mentioned that my adoptive father visited my mother in Plaszow once a week. One day he asked her to write a will in case of her death. In the will it said that if she should not survive the war, then no one else—no relative, uncle or aunt—had a right to me but them. She wrote that in case of her death, I am theirs, the Latawcows' daughter. My adoptive father kept this will the entire war. Not too long ago, when one of my friends visited my adoptive mother, she heard her say of my real mother: "She went to her doom, and look, she came back and took my child away!"

After the war I did not want to leave my adoptive parents. I felt safe beside them. But there were other reasons....

Before the war my parents went to the synagogue only two times a year, and in our house we ate ham. So the Catholic religion was my first real religion.

I remember that when I went for the "Aryan papers" I was told: "Keep your head up." Because Jews, in order to hide their faces, kept their heads down.

Since that time, I have always walked straight and carried my head high. When one observed the Poles during the war, in a line or someplace else, all the Poles would glance at your face. Everyone was looking. This was some kind of obsession, this was madness, you cannot imagine it—everyone was looking for Jews!

My adoptive father was dark-haired and had a large nose. How many times was he pulled over and checked to see if he was a Jew! This was some kind of national sport. I myself do not know how to describe this. This was a continual search—one had to be careful of every gesture, so as not to betray oneself.

I had a medal of the Holy Mother of Czestochowa about my neck. I remember that when I found myself in the convent, after that nightmare life on the outside, I felt a great relief. I felt like I was in paradise. The prayers and everything else suited me very well. I was probably even more eager than other children to hush up my ancestry. My marks in religion were perfect, while my marks in math were only passable, because one could not have good marks in math, for only Jews knew how to count well.

It was good in the convent. The nuns protected us. They tried to dress the girls who had an "inappropriate look" in such a way as to cover up their "Jewishness." The nuns were very orderly and tried very hard. Particularly, the mother superior, Sister Filipa Swiech.

The convent in Staniatki was a Benedictine convent. The Felician nuns who had been thrown out of their home in Cracow by the Germans were taken in by the Benedictine sisters. And it was there, in the Benedictine convent, that the Felician nuns ran the boarding school, where I found myself. The Benedictine sisters also had children, but no Jewish ones. There was only an adult Jewish woman, who was hidden behind a wardrobe. One had to take out her refuse, and nobody wanted to do this. Therefore I did it, for I apparently have it in my genes—I like to help.

There were only three Felician sisters. Mother Superior Filipa Swiech, Sister Klementyna and Sister Marcelina. The teachers were secular, and they did not know that we were Jewish. When in 1946 one of our teachers came to Mrs. Latawcow and found out the truth, she nearly fainted. She was angry and couldn't get over the fact that she had taught Jews.

One of our girls, Irka, lives now in Israel. She is in a psychiatric hospital. Perhaps as a result of the war?

There were different stages in the convent. Toward the end of the war we suffered from hunger, for there were no food supplies and nothing to eat—but love and warmth were not lacking. Sister

Marcelina was an exceptional person in this regard. For me she was not only a mother, but a friend. She worried over us and cherished us. And then there were the Latawcows, of course. Every Sunday they came to me with a toy, a blouse, sugar or something else. Through all the years of the war I did not lack love and warmth. I was fortunate.

Rachela G. (Saved by Sisters of St. Joseph)
July 22, 1985

Everything began when I was five-years-old. My family lived in Bialystok. The deportations began to Siberia. My parents, fearing that, as members of the bourgeois, they would be sent there, moved the family to Lwow.

We passed the Soviet occupation [1939-1941] pretty well, living in a rented apartment. My father worked as a laborer.

When the Germans came, the tragedy began. At first there was complete peace, then came the Star of David bands, but at that time we still passed as Polish. My father did not have Semitic features, neither did my sister and I.

Only my mother looked Semitic. For some time we managed to live outside the ghetto; my father worked as a Pole. Eventually too many people took an interest in us, and the ground began to burn under our feet, so my father put on the Star of David.

But we didn't go to the ghetto. At first I was sent to some farm people near Debica, while my parents and younger sister hid in Tarnobrzeg under assumed names.

Then it started to get really bad. There was talk that they were Jewish. At that point my father escaped. To this day I don't know where he went or what became of him. The people with whom I was staying were in fear—great fear. Then the campaigns against the Jews started—I don't remember the exact details, but I do remember seeing Jewish children running away to hide someplace. Just like animals being chased by dogs. These children were refused entry into homes; they ran through the fields, the Germans shooting after them. I had been ordered not to admit my Jewish heritage, not to say a word—so I was just in a stupor. All of this happened in Rzochow, near Debica.

In a panic, the people with whom I was staying decided that I had to be sent to a convent.

Then a real tragedy happened. It was probably 1942, before the

Holy Week. First they took me to Tarnobrzeg, where my mother and sister were hiding. My father was already gone. My mother decided to commit suicide with the help of the farmer. Suicide by drowning. Together with my little sister. She was three-years-old then.

I was left by the river and told to wait. I was completely stupefied. This was not normal. First I met my mother, who greeted me with unusual emotion. Then I greeted my sister. I did not know what was happening. Some time passed. Finally the farmer came back and said that everything was over, and that we should be on our way.

Dazed, I was taken to Trzesowka. The convent was visible from a distance, for it was the only two-storied stone building in the village. The farmer left me in the field, and said:

"Go there; they will take you in."

It was Palm Sunday. Like an automaton I went to the convent. Sister Roberta was not there at the time. Sister Adolfina was the nun in charge. She was so fat and so—well, strict—but she greeted me warmly and had me say a prayer. Of course, I knew how to pray. I rattled off a prayer, and then I heard:

"You can stay here."

This was an intelligent woman. She was aware of the truth, and the following day baptized me with water. People began to take an interest in who I was and how I came to be in the convent. But nobody ever suspected that I was Jewish. (After all, I had blonde hair and blue eyes). They thought I was the child of some acquaintance, or an orphan—and it was left at that.

In the convent I was treated like a normal village child. I worked at everything and even enjoyed it. After all I had gone through, my stay in the convent was stabilizing. I knew that I would remain there, that it was good for me there, that I was safe. I even knew that should the Germans come, nothing would happen to me because the nuns would be able to take care of everything.

None of the nuns ever tried to set me against Jews. God forbid. The nuns did not talk on this subject.

I liked the Christian religion because it is attractive to a child. The sisters sent me to First Communion, they dressed me in white—a child is influenced by these things. Besides, I was growing up among Polish children, I had a lot of friends—even before the war I had Polish girlfriends. I came from an assimilated family. My parents were Polish in their sensibilities—that I remember. I always loved Christmas and Christmas trees. As a child, I used to visit families that celebrated Christmas. I also went to church with my girlfriends, though, of course, I went to the synagogue with my parents.

But all this was before the war.

When I found myself in the convent, among the nuns, in that Catholic environment, I liked it a lot. Besides, I considered it a miracle that I was alive. I was a very religious child. I observed Lent and fasted, I went through the Way of the Cross. I read the Old and New Testament, and cried at the suffering of Christ. By the way, I never had the feeling that the Jews were bad because they were responsible for His death. That attitude was not present in the convent.

The reason I chose to stay with the nuns was, above all, that I liked Christianity. As I child, even as a teenager, I was very, very religious.

Also, I have to admit, I chose to stay because of fear. I thought it was a miracle that I knew how to pray, that my parents had taught me how to pray before we parted. So I thought that God had managed things in such a way to save me. That is, I thought that it was a sign from God that I should remain among Christians, for they had saved me. I felt I owed it to the Christian religion to stay with it.

I did not want to return to something that had been so tragic for me.

Being a part of Christianity, of Poland, gave me a sense of safety. I was a child so terribly damaged psychologically and so shook-up, that anything that would bring me back to my other, Jewish life, was frightening. Here I was safe. Because of psychological reasons, I could not got there under any circumstances. I did not consider why I should go back, that we were the chosen people, and other such arguments. In the convent I felt safe, although I also saw Poles die. But this was a different sort of dying! A different sort of dying!

I knew only one thing: that as a Jewish child I did not have the right to live. I did not feel any safer after the war, particularly as there was a certain amount of anti-semitism around. I always heard: "That's a Jew." "I will take in a child, but a Jewish one—no." I heard and experienced everything personally, and thought: I will never go back to that.

It may be cowardice that I do not admit to my ancestry. Yet why should I? Why? Let my children have peace. I still don't know what will happen.

Why should someone say to them that their mother is a Jew, or tell them that they should be denied something because of their ancestry or even be exterminated. Yes, my fear from the war has remained with me to this day.

That is why I want my account to be anonymous. I've lived through so much, that I truly have had enough and don't want any more.

But to return to the convent—I felt at home there. I treated the nuns—particularly Sister Roberta—as my mothers.

I don't remember exactly what occurred when, after the war, the two people from the Jewish committee came and wanted something from me. That is, they wanted to take me, and I became frightened and said that under no circumstances would I go. Later Sister Roberta talked with them.

The decision to stay with the nuns was mine. Sister Roberta talked to me, and brought me to the two people and said that they wanted to take me, and asked me what I wanted to do. So this wasn't imposed on me. This was my decision. I had been born in 1934. These people came for me probably in 1945—so I was eleven. I already knew what I wanted. Of course, if these had been my parents there would have been no question as to my decision. For, after all, I had been waiting for my father during the entire war. But these people who came—whether it was an uncle or an aunt—were strangers to me. I didn't know them at all. They were introduced as my uncle and aunt, but I didn't know them!

My parents wanted to save us and themselves. Since they couldn't save my younger sister or themselves, they at least saved me. My life, therefore, has meaning.

Maria Klein (Israeli citizen saved by the Sacred Heart Sisters in Przemysl)
February 15, 1986

I was born in Przemysl on August 31, 1930. I entered the orphanage when I was ten-years-old. I want, however, to shed light on certain things that happened before I came to the orphanage.

I was led out of the work camp in Przemysl, as the ghetto was being liquidated. People were being burned alive, murdered, robbed, while children were shot or grabbed by the legs and smashed against a wall. I can see their spattered brains to this day. The Polish populace was generally quite set against the Jews and gladly gave them over to the Gestapo. I ran away to Mrs. Romankiewicz, who lived near the camp, and that woman brought me, as well as milk, to the orphanage. Along the way we came across our maid and I thought she recognized me. I was very frightened that she might give everyone away.

But the prayers of the nuns helped, and she didn't give us away.

The nuns accepted me with love and great understanding. There were children from the ghetto already there. In those days one Jewish child initiated another into the life of the convent, and we could talk with each other if no one else overheard us.

In the orphanage there were children whose mothers worked till two o'clock. There were orphans, whose parents had been killed in Volhynia and thirteen very frightened Jewish children, some orphaned and unwanted by anyone. These children were accepted with grave risk. Everyone was loved and assured a feeling of safety.

The fact that I was Jewish was known by Sister Emilia (the mother superior), Sister Ligoria and Sister Bernarda. I came from a non-religious Jewish family; my father belonged to the PPS (Polish Socialist Party) for many years and was a shoemaker by trade. The Polish children did not know that I was a Jew.

Hunger reigned in the convent, for the war was on. There was no electricity; various diseases caused by malnutrition were prevalent; and we were all verminous. Medicines for fighting lice were lacking. The infected children conveyed the lice to others. Those children from Volhynia were in no better condition. Furthermore, their parents were murdered by the Ukrainians right in front of their eyes, and one of the girls, Tekla, was wounded in her belly with a knife and was very weak.

The nuns' attitude toward Jewish children was more indulgient and full of underthanding and patience. If they got some dainty for supper, they often shared it with me in secret.

The conditions in the convent were quite meagre; the sisters lived through the efforts of the Social Welfare Department and the contributions of various good people. Food and clothing was lacking, as well as everything else.

Despite this, I felt safe in the convent, since the nuns were always looking after us. I had a key to the church, and if the Germans made a search, I was to hid inside the altar where the holy relics were kept. Sister Bernarda had given me this key. I felt surrounded by the care of people and God.

I did not get baptized in the convent, even though I very much wished to.

During the bombardment of Przemysl I asked a priest who was with us in the shelter to baptize me but he refused.

When I came to the convent I did not even know how to cross myself. I took Sister Ligoria's advice and knelt at the very back of the chapel and mimicked praying. Sister Ligoria said I should do it in order not to differ from the others, but she also said that each of us had our own faith; the war would end someday, and if my parents survived I would remain Jewish, but one's faith is not a pendulum and one cannot change it. So when I became twenty-one, I would have the right to do what I wanted.

The nuns in no way tried to influence me to receive baptism. Somehow a Hebrew prayer-book found its way to the convent. Keeping something like that jeopardized one's life, just like hiding us did. I could even differentiate and read some letters when Sister Bernarda asked me what they were. So she locked me in her room every other day so that I would not forget how to read those few letters that I knew. She said: "Pray to the Jewish God, and we will pray to Lord Jesus. If we all pray, then perhaps we will survive the war."

My parents and brother survived the war. When my brother first came to the orphanage, I did not want to speak with him. I did not want to go back to my parents. I did not want to have anything to do with Jews. For me, being a Jew meant death and hell, while Christianity meant safety and heaven.

It was very difficult for me to leave the nuns. I had become attached to them and I will always love them. My separation from the nuns is only physical. Spiritually I always want to live my life so that I could look them in the eye with a clear conscience.

Luby L. (Saved by the Sacred Heart Sisters in Przemysl)
November 5, 1987

In the convent where I was staying there were thirteen Jewish children and more than forty Polish ones. The Jewish children were not put under any pressure in regard to religious matters. Yet the quiet one finds in church, the life one led with the nuns, their spiritual peace—all this had to have had an effect. The nuns said that we had to go to church and take holy communion with the others so that we wouldn't stand out. But that was all we had to do.

I did not get baptized in the convent. The nuns were very good to us. They were very good to all the children.

It was very difficult for us, since there were lice, but this did not really bother me. Perhaps the younger nuns were bothered by this, those that were picking the lice off us and working over us.

The children helped the nuns; they carried the water for the wash. I don't remember other details very well. In any case, the convent was another reality. After all I had lived through—it was like the difference between night and day. In the convent I had soup and a piece of bread; I was not hungry and I felt safe. I stopped being frightened. The nuns were so quiet and good; they were an example to us all.

Irit R. (Saved by the Sisters of Charity in Ignacow)
November 12, 1987 in Herzliyya, Israel

When the war broke out I was nine years old. Before the war I lived in a tenement in Minsk Mazowiecki. Our neighbors were the Izbrechts, a Polish family consisting of father, mother and four daughters. The youngest girl was named Jozka, and I played with her all the time despite the fact that my grandmother beat me good so that I would not play with her. My grandmother did not allow me to play with Jozka Izbrecht because she was Polish and she feared that if I went to her home I would eat something with pork in it. So my grandmother beat me, but I still played with Jozka. This continued on until the war. When the war came we still played with each other, until the Germans threw the Poles out from those blocks where the ghetto was to be. The ghetto was sealed off; I was there for a year. What a horrible time it was! There was such hunger! My Jozka lived someplace else at that time, but she would pretend to be Jewish and bring bread to me in the ghetto. She would say it was for me. When I wanted to share it with her, she would say that she had already eaten at home and what she brought was just for me. Once I told her that when we would be grown-ups and I would be working, I would give her everything back. "Oh, forget about it," she replied.

Later my mother gave me to a peasant whose wife, at a certain moment, turned me out, saying that I should go home because my mother was waiting for me. That woman didn't tell me that at Minsk there was no one, for all the Jews had been transported by the Germans. This was at the end of 1942. I went to Minsk and met Jozka on the street. She pulled on my sleeve and asked:

"Ita, where are you going?"

"Home," I replied.

"Are you crazy? There is no home! Come with me!"

She took me to her home, squeezed me under her bed, covered it with something, and had me stay there and told me not go out; she fed me during that time. I don't know how many days I laid under that bed. When everyone was asleep, I left for the toilet. One day her mother found me, and ordered me to leave and never come back, and she beat Jozka. Jozka cried and went after me.

When we were out on the street, Jozka said to me:

"Come, we have a cellar here. Stay there; I will bring you food; my mother doesn't know anything about this."

I don't know how long I stayed in that basement, but one night I heard Germans talking (I knew Yiddish so I could make out what they were saying), and they said that the next day they would search the cellar. I fled and began wandering from village to village.

In 1943 I was at the home of a peasant, who told me: "The entire village says that you are a Jewess! So I will kill you now. But not by myself. I will hand you over to the Germans and get a kilo of sugar and two kilos of bacon for you."

He listed the items he would get for me. I was older then, I was twelve, while he—he was so tall! He probably was two meters high! And he was so shrewd, but I told him:

"You pig! Don't you fear God! You will get this and that for me? Let's say that I am a Jewess. But I am not a Jewess!"

When I cried this out, he sat down and looked at me. I was shouting, and the entire village rushed over to see what was happening.

Then I told everyone: "Look at him! He wants to hand me over to the Germans! This is a human being! No, this is an animal!"

While I was shouting this, one of the peasants said to me: "And who exactly are you?"

"I am Polish, I am not a Jewess!" I continued shouting.

"Oh, if you are Polish, we will see.... If you are Polish then go and bring your birth certificate tomorrow."

"Very well," I said. "I'll go and bring it here."

When everyone went home, my peasant sat down, looked at me and said: "You bitch! Tomorrow morning if you don't bring me the certificate, I will kill you!"

I replied that, very well, tomorrow I will get the certificate.

I could not sleep the entire night; I only thought about whether he would let me leave. But he let me go! At first I went slowly, but when I saw that he was not following me, I began to flee. I ran and ran, and suddenly I stood still and asked myself: where am I going? I began to think it over and thought that, more or less, every third or fourth Pole was named Kowalczyk, and in Minsk Mazowiecki there were probably fifty Kowalczyk families. So I would go to my own town. When I was in Poland recently, I realized that it was not far, but I considered it a great distance at the time. I walked, and it seemed to me that I was walking without end. Finally I arrived at my destination.

Minsk Mazowiecki was the town in which I was born. I walked around the marketplace and eventually saw a church. I kept on looking at the church, and finally I thought: every Polish child, when it is born, is registered with the priest and is baptized. When I thought about this—I don't know how, but my legs moved by themselves. The church was by the marketplace, and it had a small gate. I opened this gate and entered. At that moment I saw a priest. I approached him and said:

"Praise the Lord. Please, Father, in the village they all say that I am a Jewess, and I want to prove to them that I am not. So I ask you to give me my certificate."

The priest asks me: "What is your name?"

"My name is Irena Kowalczyk, I was born in Minsk Mazowiecki, only I don't remember if it was in 1928 or 1929. My father's name was Wladyslaw, and my mother's Zofia."

The priest took a piece of paper and began to write, saying: "Tell me everything again."

So I repeated everything, and then the priest went to his shelves, started to take out books and read through them: "Kowalczyk, Kowalczyk—not here!"

I thought at that moment it would be impossible for him to find anything considering the convoluted story I had told.

Finally the priest said to me: "Listen, my dear child, I don't have time now because I'm in a rush. Come back here tomorrow at ten in the morning and I will give you your certificate."

I said thank you and left.

I mulled about the marketplace, and at night I went to sleep in the ghetto ruins. In the morning I got up, shook the dust off of me, smoothed down my hair, and when it must have been ten I went to the church and said:

"Good morning, Father. I've come back."

"Ah, you are here. Well, thank God I found your certificate."

He handed me the certificate and said that he needed two zlotys, for he had to register it in a book, but that the money was not important. I told him that I had two zlotys. I gave them to him, thanked him and left.

Suddenly I wanted to return and ask him if he had given me the certificate because he knew I was Jewish, or if what I had told him was in the book. But I was afraid to do this, so I didn't go back and ask. I grabbed the certificate and ran to the peasant. Along the way I stopped only to read what the priest had written. On the certificate it said that Irena Boleslawa Kowalczyk had been born in the village Cudna to an unmarried woman, Zofia. I was old enough already to understand what the priest had done. Apparently he knew that I was a Jewess. If they let me live in the village, it would mean that I am a foundling. And if I was a foundling then I could not be a Jewess!

I returned to my peasant and said: "See, I am not a Jewess. Look!"

The peasant looked at the certificate, he did not know how to read but he took it, and said:

"Now I will go to village mayor and will break his head! It was he who told me you were a Jewess!"

This was the truth. I had this cousin, but that is another story.... In any case my peasant went to the mayor with the certificate, showed it to him, to which the mayor replied: "Do you know, she looks so much like a Jewess you'd think she was one!"

My peasant returned home, sat beside me, nudged me and said with a laugh:

"So, foundling, who is your father?"

I knew exactly who my father was, but I started to mutter something.

"Foundling, stop it!"

Suddenly the entire village knew that I was a foundling. That was a wonderful thing! Because no one was talking about a Jewess anymore, but a "foundling." The entire village had something to talk about. When I used to go with the cowherds, people called out to me: "Foundling! Come here!"

Yes, it was very good, but ... my peasant began to drink. At about one or two at night he would get up from his bed, pull me from my bedding (I slept on the floor, on a straw mattress) and, drunk, would ask me who my father was.

I feared that he would beat me... This began to happen with greater and greater frequency, until finally his wife (they were childless) called me over and said:

"I like you a lot. I thought of even adopting you as my daughter because I like you so much. I thought many times that you would become my daughter... but he will kill you! You have to leave me!"

And I cried so much... I did not want to leave her because it was good for me with her. After I had brought the certificate, she went to church fair and bought me an overcoat and boots! But when he wouldn't let me alone at night— he assumed that because I was a foundling that my mother was a whore and other things—his wife then said: "Listen, you will not be able to live here with him, you have to go. Take the road to Minsk until you see the convent. Go there, the nuns will accept you, for sure."

When I came to the convent, I went to an older nun and said nothing, but just handed over my certificate. By that time I was much wiser and I knew that my certificate said everything. The nun also did not ask me anything, but told me that I would work in the kitchen, where I would be comfortable and where it would be warm. She had me go to another sister for boots. But the most wonderful thing about the mother superior was that she did not tell anyone in the convent what my certificate said, but she said that the priest from Jakub had brought me. (The village of my peasant was called Jakub, and it was five kilometers distance from Ignacow.)

In the convent I worked in the kitchen. I washed pots, served food. At the time it seemed to me that the kitchen was enormous. When I visited the place a year ago, it turned out to be very small....

All the children in the convent belonged to the "Association of the Children of Mary," and every Sunday after dinner the priest used to talk over religious matters with us. One day the subject matter of the meeting was sacrilege. So I was sitting and listening—I had been out of my home since 1941, and at that point it was perhaps

1943; I was already so hardened to everything, so that I didn't even react when the conversation turned to Jews—the priest was talking about sacrilege, which had no effect on me, but opposite me sat Frania, and I could see that she was upset by the entire conversation.

I thought that she was a Jewess for sure. And also that she is a Jew, and I am a Jew—but how could I tell her this? How could I convince her about this?

How would she believe me?

After the meeting I asked Frania to take a walk with me in the forest.

Once there, we sat down; I took her by the hand and said: "Do you know that I committed a sacrilege?"

"You committed a sacrilege?" Frania said, shocked.

"Yes, for I am a Jewess from Minsk Mazowiecki. Frania," I said finally, "you also are a Jewess."

"Go away from me! I am not a Jew," shot out Frania.

At that point I was very, very certain that she was a Jew. I was thinking of what I could say to make her stop being afraid of me. What could I tell her that would make her believe that I also was a Jew? The war was on. At the time every word, even a remembrance of Jews, could mean death. I feared that Frania would think that I wanted to draw out information from her to betray her.

So I told her who my parents were, where they lived in Minsk, everything.... I saw that she was softening. I finally told her who my grandfather was. With my grandfather it was a totally different story. My grandfather was Icia Majer, a well known figure in Minsk and the neighborhood.

My grandfather—today I say he was ill—was crazy; he walked about the streets and shouted. My grandfather was a great problem for my grandmother, who was very pious. My grandfather ate ham, which for her was a matter of life and death. In any case, when I told Frania that I was related to Icia Majer, she started to believe me, and asked me if I knew Yiddish. I knew it, and we started to talk the language. Then we both were certain. Today we can laugh about it, and frequently do, but at that time—every move could cost one one's life.

I worked in the kitchen in the convent. On Sundays I gladly went to work in the garden. Not because I was ordered to, but because there were apples and pears in the garden. Sister Irena worked in the garden. She was so quiet, so orderly, she always asked me where

I was from, what I was doing here and when my birthday was. On my birthday she brought me a blouse that she embroidered herself. That blouse was and is the best gift I have received in my life.

Think about it. At the peasant's home they did not cherish me. Not only did I work hard, but I slept on the floor. Only in the convent did I have a bed and sheets. And when Sister Irena gave me that blouse, I had a feeling that I was a human being once again, for only a person gives another person a gift and does something special for her....

I have nothing against the Polish people. People who were not born in Poland, who do not know the atmosphere there and did not live through it, are not able to imagine what was happening. I know that Poles helped me. I have nothing against them! I remember that I was hungry, I was shaking like a dog, and a woman came out of a house. She gave me bread, a dress and an old pair of boots, and said: "I know that you are a Jew. I'm afraid to keep you in my house. Take this bread, these boots and this dress, and go—but don't tell anyone that I helped you!"

There was terror; people were afraid to help, but they helped. But I also heard when I was in the villages that there were people who said they were going to look for Jews. At that time I did not know precisely what this meant; only later did I learn that they were going to the forest to rob Jews of their watches and other valuables. I remember that there was an old woman who said to them: "Dear God! How can you do something like this! You're not human!"

So I can say that I saw various types of people. But now, forty years later, how can one judge the Polish people? Our youth also judges the Jews as cowards who did not fight. Who has a right to judge those people? Those Jews and those Poles? One cannot judge Poles. Here they say that I like the Polish people, and that's why I take this view. But that is not so. There is no black and white. In between there are other colors, and one has to be aware of this.

A.S. (Saved by the Magdalene Sisters in Rabka)
November 6, 1987 in Tel-Aviv, Israel

I was born in Warsaw, and when the war broke out I was five years old. For the first time in my life I saw death and experienced great terror during the bombing of Warsaw. I remember the great fear that took hold of everyone; everyone was running from house to house; no one knew where to hide. We sat in a shelter, I heard the bombs explode, and then I saw the first bodies.... I remember many of my war experiences, though a few, obviously, I know about only from what my mother told me. I remember quite well, however, that at a certain moment one had to go to the ghetto, which was for me an experience in and of itself.

In the ghetto I learned for the first time what it meant to be hungry. We lived in a small apartment in which there was nothing to eat. I associate the ghetto, therefore, with continual hunger. I remember that I used to always dream about the good times I had before I arrived in the ghetto. I dreamed of scrambled eggs and sausage. I remember that I was afraid of walking out in the streets because in the streets of the ghetto corpses lay around covered with newspapers, foam on their lips. Everyone was begging for something to eat, and yesterday's beggar was today lying under newspapers.... People were indifferent to this because they themselves had nothing to eat.

I don't remember the exact moment I left the ghetto, but I know that we—my mother, aunt, younger brother and I—left with a group that was working outside the ghetto walls. Until our "Aryan papers" were finished, we sat in some room in absolute quiet so that no one would hear us. When the documents were ready, we went to acquaintances of ours, three sisters (Helena Byszewska, Maria Szulinska and Jadwiga Gostkiewicz), who helped us a lot. Their house was our haven.

Because our family was known in Warsaw, it was not possible to remain there. My mother even had a run-in with a blackmailer.

The person who made the documents for us was a member of the underground; he helped us get out of Warsaw. Then began a period of wandering from town to town.

Let me talk for a moment about my father. He was supposed to have left the ghetto at a later date, but a day or two after we left everyone was transported to Treblinka. He escaped from the transport, and hid out for some time at Helen Byszewski's. Later on, I don't exactly remember when, we met him in Sandomierz. Everyone stayed at some small hotel, and one day when we returned from a church fair, my father was not at the hotel. We would never see him again.

There were still Jews in Sandomierz, and when my mother asked around, she was told that my father was shot on the street because he was recognized by a Polish policeman, whose name was Olejnik, or Olejczak—something like that. A Pole helped my father, another Pole killed him....

We left Sandomierz and continued to wander around. We stayed with a peasant couple in Przyglow. They were childless and took a great liking to my brother, Maciek, who was two-years-old at that time; but we had to escape because someone complained about us to the black-uniformed Silesians who were stationed in the village. The Silesians came and one of them took out a revolver, shouting at my mother in Polish: "You are a Jewess!"

My mother had pluck. When that German-Silesian was already pulling the trigger to shoot—I was standing to the side and felt that something terrible would happen at any moment—my mother hit him in the arm, and said: "What are you doing? First check who I am. Who told you that I was a Jewess?"

My mother's courage and audacity sobered him up, for he was drunk. At that moment, if one can believe in miracles, a miracle occurred. Suddenly we heard cries in the neighborhood—a fire had erupted. The Silesians rushed to the fire, my mother ran away to the field, while I grabbed my brother and rushed with him to the attic.

After this incident, my mother knew that we could no longer stay in this village. She also realized that we could not hide as one group, for in case we were caught, all of us would perish, while if we went different ways, perhaps someone would survive.

For Jews, escaping at that time was very hard for there was no place to go. Jews were homeless and moved about from place to place. But we had a "family." Helena Byszewska was our family, and she helped us in various ways.

Among other things, she regularly sent out letters and cards addressed to my mother. On the postcards she signed herself as "Aunt Byszewska," and it was known that such an open card would be read in the village and proclaim our Polish blood.

Thanks to these cards we were not homeless fugitives.

But after the incident with the Silesians my mother and aunt decided that we had to leave. I said, however, that I would not go anyplace with them and would stay where I was. My mother did not have time to discuss this with me, and she left with my aunt and brother, while I remained with these peasants, who were good to me and with whom I felt at home.

The man was particularly good. Michael was his name. The

Germans came from time to time and asked me if I was Jewish, but I categorically denied it, so they finally left me alone, perhaps because I was so young. After some time my mother returned to see how I was doing, and they arranged it so that now my brother could stay with the peasant couple, while I would go with my mother.

He did not have children and loved Maciek very much. My mother did not promise him anything. After the war they received some money, but they did not count on any gain or anything of that sort; they simply loved us.

So I went with my mother to Cracow. We lived on Pilsudski Street, and my mother and aunt worked at a German-owned business.

One of our neighbors had been raised in Rance by the nuns of the Order of St. Mary Magdalene. Seeing that it was very hard for us, she suggested to my mother that she try to place me in a convent she knew. As my mother told me later, this neighbor suggested that she go to the nuns on holy day of Mother Mary, and they would not refuse her.

My mother went and told the nuns that it was very difficult for her. She made up some type of emotional story—my father was in prison, etc.—and when Mother Superior Teresa Ledochowska explained that she couldn't take me in because she already had too many children, my mother fell to crying and said:

"Please don't refuse me; today is the day of Mother Mary, you will not refuse me...."

The sister was moved by this and said: "I see that you are a good Catholic; very well, I will accept this child."

My mother took me to Rabka. To the end of the war the nuns did not know that I was Jewish.

There was a war going on, the times were hard for everyone; it was also not easy in the convent; everyone had to work. The youngest child was a four-year-old girl named Krysia, who teased wool. The convent had cows and two goats. The girls had the responsibility of, among other things, tending cattle, sheering sheep; the older girls spun wool, and various items were made to offer up for sale.

To this day I make use of the many skills I learned at the convent. I know how to crochet, knit, sew, clean and wash clothes, for every child was taught this in the convent; no one ate bread for free. At first my mother paid the sisters for my upkeep. Later Mother Teresa freed her from these payments.

Everyone experienced poverty at that time, and Mother Teresa would frequently relate to us her dreams of owning an umbrella. She would say to us: "Pray to St. Anthony for me to come across some umbrella so that I won't have to get wet in the rain." As luck would have it, the Byszewski family had a shop in Warsaw that sold umbrellas. So I told my mother about Mother Teresa's wish and on St. Teresa's Day, the third of October, my mother turned up at the convent with a huge black umbrella. Mother Teresa was dumbfounded. "St. Anthony heard the prayers, the umbrella is here," she replied, and in gratitude she freed my mother from payments during my stay at Rabka. She knew, besides, that it was hard for my mother.

In the convent there was nothing to eat, for, in truth, we were living only from German rations. We drank chicory-flavored water or coffee, and I remember that when the bread was dry the coffee was sweet, and when there was marmalade on the bread, the coffee was bitter. We always fought over the bread for everyone wanted to get the crusty end of the loaf. My mother used to go to Waksmund on some business and would tell me beforehand when she would go through Chabowka so that I could meet the train. She would give me a loaf of bread, and I was so famished that, not wanting to share it with anyone, I would eat the entire loaf before I reached the convent.

Once, when I was sick, my mother sent me a poppy-seed cake. I had cut the cake up into pieces. Suddenly a nun came into the room and said, "So, you're treating all the girls to a piece of cake?"

I fell into despair. Who told the sister that I was treating everyone? I had not given her one sign that I wanted to do this, for I would have gladly eaten it all myself. And yes, I got only a small little piece.

As to food, only we ate badly. The nuns had something to eat. An incident occurred that alienated me and shook my faith in the entire institution of convents. One day, wanting to tell something to one of the sisters, I entered the refectory unannounced and saw what the nuns had on their table. White cheese, golden cheese—tasty things we couldn't even dream of. I was speechless. When they saw my reaction, they shouted at me to leave at once. I left, but I remembered how Sister Modesta, when I had once asked her for an additional piece of bread, refused to give it to me, saying that I had to suffer for Christ.

That incident was a blow to me. I never forgot that table.

A Jesuit priest used to come to us. Father Ciosek was his name; a very orderly man, a real priest. I would tell him everything, for I knew that one tells a priest everything. I went to him for confession, and he conducted Mass at our place. So I told him about the food, and he must have called their attention to it, and they must have realized who had told him, for later I had a lot of unpleasant incidents with the sisters.

Returning to Sister Modesta, the nun who had refused me that bread. That same sister poisoned a cat all of us girls loved. The cat was dying in convulsions, and we were crying. How could she, a nun, do such a thing?

The methods used in bringing up children in the convent were medieval.

There was a girl, Marcyska, who used to wet her bed at night. The sisters, instead of trying to cure her, had her pray to St. Anthony. Of course the prayers did not help, so the sisters came to conclusion—apparently most of them were simply ignorant—that Marcyska was doing this on purpose and that one had to punish her. They thought that if they confiscated her straw mattress and she slept on twigs, she would know when to get up at night to take a leak.

Marcyska cried a lot, so one merciful nun gave her an ironing board to sleep on. In truth, that night Marcyska did not wet herself. But only because she did not fall asleep the entire night.

The sisters wanted to find out various things about their wards, so they had them write letters to St. Joseph and put them under his statue. I'm a little amused by this because there is a similar custom among Jews, who take letter to God to the Wailing Wall and put them in the fissures there. But in the convent we wrote letters to St. Joseph. I must have been quite cunning in those days because, wanting to ascertain if the sisters read these letters—after my experience with the food on table I did not trust them so much—I wrote a letter to St. Joseph asking him to help me to be good and to do good deeds. After a couple of days I had a reply. I did something, and a sister said to me: "What do you think, that it's enough for you to write to St. Joseph that you want to be good? You have to try to be good!"

The nuns beat us, too. Among the wards there was an older one, Konsulata was her name. Everyone who came to the convent got a new name; I did also and even carry it to this day. So this Konsulata had the strength of a horse, and she did the hardest work. She also had the job of dishing out the punishments or beatings marked out by the nuns. Konsulata's punishments were administered with a belt. The ceremony was held in an elegant guest room. I remember that once I was slated to get a hiding. Upon orders of Konsulata, I took off my underwear and placed myself on a chair, but since I did this obediently, I heard her voice: "Because you were obedient and humble, this time I will not whip you, but next time you won't get away!"

Of course, Marcyska received the most beatings, for wetting her bed.

Once Marcyska and I wanted to take a short cut from school to the home, and we went through a stream swollen by the spring floods. Naturally, we fell into the river and got our clothing wet. The sisters punished us by having us kneel on peas. We had to kneel until we apologized to the sisters. Marcyska apologized and knelt for a short time, but I did not know what I should apologize for, so I knelt for several hours, until they ordered me to stand.

From my stubbornness, and for everything else, they punished me in another way. They did not accept me into the organization of "Guardian Angels," to which belonged all good and polite children.

In the convent I was a believer, but I received my baptism in church long before I came to the convent. The first prayers and Catholic traditions were taught to me by Helena Byszewska right after I left the ghetto, so that I would not make any mistakes on the "Aryan side," which could have ruined me. Before the war our family was atheistic. Yet we only spoke Polish; I did not know Hebrew or Yiddish at all. That helped during the time of the war.

Also hiding in Rabka was another Jewish girl, Halinka Lamet. The nuns did not allow her out of the convent, for they feared that the Germans would capture her. Once the nuns managed with difficulty to get her out of their clutches. After the war I met Halinka in Cracow. I started to talk to her, and she said: "Don't talk to me about those nuns! I don't want to hear anything about them!" She couldn't stand them.

When the front was getting closer, my mother was advised that it would be better if she took me from the convent, for when the

Russians reached the town, it would be better for me if I were with her than with the nuns. I was happy to be back with my mother.

As far as mementos are concerned, I've kept several things: a prayer book, an album with inscriptions from some of the people I met in the convent. I always remember with warmth Mother Superior Teresa Ledochowska. She was a very elegant person; she knew how to behave. Unfortunately, because she had a lot of duties, she didn't have much time for the children. Rather, we were with these other nuns, of whom Sister Julia, the cook, distinguished herself by her goodness and decency. I remember that when we were hungry, she would give us something to eat on the sly.

But Sister Modesta—she was terrible. But, for sure, in every institution there are good and bad types.

I think that the religious upbringing in the convent was very good and that it had a good effect on me, even though in the end I remained an atheist.

It left something positive in me.

Several of my acquaintances from Poland, who know me as a praying and devout Catholic, cannot comprehend, and ask: "How is it for you in Israel? It must be bad for you there?"

They are most amazed when I tell them that I don't believe in anything and am not suffering. But it is true. I don't like to play a game. When I was a Christian, I was a Christian with my whole heart, because what I did, I did with my whole heart and soul, never as a game.

When work camps were being formed, or something of the sort, my mother's desire was to get there, and she was thrilled when she successfully arranged that. My father worked there earlier. Yes, I remember, these camps were called "sheds." Grownups worked beside the machines, while we had to hide in the corners. At night these halls were transformed into bedrooms; everyone spread out their straw mattresses, or whatever they had. In the morning one had to quickly gather everything up, for the grownups would again begin work, and the children would go into the corners. From this time period I also remember best the hunger and the dying people. When my father got a bowl of soup— dishwater with a piece of potato—he shared it with us, though my mother said that he should have all of it since he was working.

MISCELLANEOUS INTERVIEWS AND EXCERPTS

Izajasz Druker
November 9, 1987 in Ramat Gan, Israel

When I began my work in the army rabbinate in 1945, Jews were returning from all points and reporting that while visiting their family villages and towns they had heard of Jewish children who had been saved by peasants. During the war one could not talk about this, but after the war people talked about this openly. I then began an operation to find these children, and this became my main work during the years 1945-49.

This activity was quite difficult. Aside from the religious issues involved, the physical act of taking back children from people with whom they had lived was tragic. It was very difficult and tiresome work.

Mothers would come and tell me about the children they were searching for, children they had given up to the convents.

There was a case where a mother returned to the convent, but did not find her daughter there because the nuns had given her up for adoption. After a thorough search, we found the Polish family that was raising her child. A tragedy. The matter went to the court. In the first instance the court granted the Polish mother the child based on the fact that she had raised it.

In the second instance, taking into account the wartime conditions, the court gave the daughter to the Jewish mother. But the Polish parents did not want to submit to the court's ruling and they fled with the girl, moving from place to place. The adoptive father, though, remained working in Warsaw, and on Saturdays he would visit his wife and adopted daughter. One day I followed him and found out where they lived in Cracow. Then, armed with court papers, the police and I took the child from its adoptive parents and returned her to the rightful mother. The girl went with her mother to Israel. For a long time she resented her mother and the fact that the mother took her away from that family—she couldn't reconcile herself to that and missed the Polish family and wrote them letters.

Then there was the matter concerning Irena, a ten-year-old girl hiding out in one of the Cracow convents. News about her was given by Mr. Baraftik, who later was the minister of religious affairs in Israel and a member of the Knesset. Irena came from the Mendlow family, and her family in America wanted to take the child. Mr. Baraftik went himself to the convent, but they did not want to talk to him. Contact with the child was maintained by Mrs. Aszenbrener, a wife of a Cracow lawyer, but she also could not convince the nuns to hand over the child.

So I began to visit the girl myself. I would talk to her and bring her sweets. I took her for walks. The sisters allowed this for they were afraid.

My uniform frightened them, and they did not want to have anything to do with the authorities. But when the child returned several times from the walks, the sisters stopped being afraid. Talks began on the subject of the child, and a time came when the nuns agreed to give her back. I promised an endowment, and everything was on the right track, for at a certain moment the girl was also disposed to leaving the nuns. I used to tell her that in America, where she was going, she had an aunt and uncle....

It was arranged that I would pick her up one day. When I came, the girl shouted through a window: "I am not going anymore, I am not going! The priest told me not to go!"

If not, then not. I left. But I did not want to leave her. I made an arrangement with a Jewish woman, who had a child the same age as Irena, that at a prearranged hour she would take a walk with her daughter. I went to the convent and asked to take Irena on a walk. During the walk I sat down on a bench near my acquaintance, and the girls started playing with each other.

Then, under the pretext of going for ice cream, I placed the girl in a car and took her to our children's home in Zabrze.

I had a difficult time with Irena, but after several weeks the girl became convinced and went to America.

In many cases, when I went to retrieve the children—and not only from the convents—I pretended to be a member of the child's family, usually the uncle.

I acted this way, because the children had become attached to the nuns or Polish parents; it would have been difficult otherwise.

In the convents impersonating an uncle did not make the matter easier, for it was not a simple thing to convince the nuns....

One of my dealings with a convent was quite typical. It concerned Miriam S., who was in a convent in the neighborhood of Jaslo. At the end of the war Miriam was 17 or 18 years old. She came from a rabbinical family. Miriam's grandfather was at that time one of the more important persons in the Mizrach Party in Israel, and he turned to us with a request to find his granddaughter, who originally came from Lodz. After much searching, I finally found the girl and began a conversation with her. She did not want to leave the convent for anything in the world. She said that she was not a Jew, that she had been baptized and wanted to become a nun. The mother superior of the convent was, of course, on her side. Then I began to show her the letters her grandfather had written to her—nothing helped. I told her that I would make out a passport for her, and that she could go to her grandfather's just to visit. I promised that no one would try to influence her or bother her—she would visit her grandfather and come back. Miriam did not know, and apparently neither did the convent, that in those days if she were to leave on her passport for Palestine, she could not return, because she would leave Poland as a Jew. One could not take foreign currency out of Poland, so I bought her a diamond ring as security for her return—so that if she needed she could sell it and have money for the return trip.

In relating all this I am, perhaps, showing myself in a bad light, but I did this because I was convinced that after the war that small handful of Jews which had remained could not allow Jewish children—particularly those that had close relatives—to remain divested of their Jewish heritage. So I had a telegram sent from Israel with the following message: "I, your grandfather, am standing at death's door and wish to see you before I die." The telegram was signed by the grandfather—a postscript to the telegram said that he would not create any difficulties concerning her return to Poland.

The telegram was sent directly to the convent. I went to visit Miriam and see her reaction. I told the sisters that if Miriam travelled to Jerusalem, she would see the Holy Land, and that her return trip was assured, after all.

At that point Miriam became convinced, and she went with me

to our children's home in Zabrze. She was there for a very short time, before she left for Israel.

Unfortunately her grandfather did not treat her very well. He did not understand her situation, he did not understand the difficulties in changing from being a Christian to a Jew, and the girl became very unhappy. She would go to church in Jaffa and Jerusalem. In 1948 she joined the Israeli army but continued to go to church as before....

Going back to the convents—the nuns did not take money for the children. I myself, of my own initiative, gave endowments to the convents. To sum up, in the convents the issue of money did not play a role.

In carrying out my activities, it frequently happened that I would have to go to church with the children—we tried not to do anything by force. We convinced these children through a gradual process that they were Jews. The children did not want to hear about their Jewish background—they hated Jews.

One of their arguments was that if they were Jewish, then why had they not been saved by the Jewish God, instead of Jesus? It was difficult to convince them.

In our children's home, therefore, they walked around with crosses, prayed, and once in a while hung crosses in their rooms. New groups of children would replace the old, who were transported out of Poland.

I did not take the children in the name of the army rabbinate, for I officially could not do this. But Rabbi Kahane was not only the chief rabbi of the Polish Army, but also the chairman of the Jewish Religious Community. So I was taking back Jewish children in a non-official status, though I was part of the rabbinate. Only later, when I was demobilized from the army, did I become the secretary general for the Jewish Religious Community, but by then Rabbi Kahane had left Poland. If I am not mistaken, he left Poland in 1948 or 1949.

He was permitted to leave Poland under the condition that he would leave a successor. I was promoted to major at the time, and after Rabbi Kahane left the country, I took on the full obligation of chief rabbi of the Polish Army.

Even though I worked in the army rabbinate, we took the children under the auspices of the Jewish Religious Community. We had two orphanages: one in Zabrze and the other in Gieszczepuste, which is in Lower Slask. In the latter home we placed primarily Jewish children from the new eastern borders. In Zabrzu, however, we placed children taken from Polish families or convents.

With the children from the east there was an entire different story because of the rivalry between the Jewish Committee, the Religious Community, and the Coordination—three independent organizations that occupied themselves with retrieving Jewish children.

The Coordination was a union of Zionist Jewish parties, with the exception of the national-religious Mizrachi. As a representative of the Community, I worked with the Coordination. This was in 1945 or 1946, when Grynbaum came from Israel to Poland. Grynbaum came to Warsaw to organize a joint effort among all Jewish organizations to retrieve Jewish children from Polish hands.

With the agreement of the Community, I worked along with Grynbaum. But this cooperation didn't last long. Grynbaum promised a donation of money from Israel for the purpose of retrieving the children, but the money never came.

We, as the Community, had more money, so I returned to work under its auspices. We hired people who went around Poland looking for Jewish children.

The Coordination had its own children's home in Lodz.

The Jewish Committee was formed in 1944. Its first chairman was the Zionist Emil Sommerstein. Gradually the Committee went from the hands of the moderate and Zionist parties to the communists. One of its subsequent leaders was the Zionist Kosower, and later Smolar and Mitter. In 1945-46 the Committee did not concern itself too much with the question of Jewish children. That was a later interest, probably during the time when the Jews, wanting to leave Poland, had to register in Kotec and when the first difficulties were occurring in relation to Jews leaving Poland. The Jewish Committee had its children's homes; some of them were in Otwock, Bytom and Cracow. I don't know if they received many children....The children taken by the Jewish Committee went to Israel. It was difficult at that time for Jews who had no clear commitment to their heritage.

Communists of Jewish descent were at that time high up in the Polish government and hid their ancestry. Among the average Polish Jews there were not many communists; in any case, there were not many communists with genuine communistic principles. That is why the personnel of the children homes, belonging to the

Committee, worked with the Zionist organizations, the result of which was the abolishment of many homes. The children and personnel, without the agreement of the Committee, found themselves in Israel.

The chief rabbi of Israel, Dr. Hercog, turned to the Pope with the request of issuing a bull calling on all European convents to give back the Jewish children they had been hiding. The Pope did not agree to this. I am not certain, but it seems that Rabbi Hercog saw the Pope personally on this issue.

I know this all from Rabbi Hercog himself, who in 1946 arrived in Poland, and I worked with him.

Rabbi Hercog arrived in Poland with the address of a certain child hidden in a convent in Czestochowa. He wanted to go in person to see the bishop there, but the government did not want to take responsibility for his journey, since this was after the tragic pogrom in Kielce. So I went to the bishop—this concerned a girl named Szczekacz, who is now here, in Tel-Aviv. I had quite a long talk with the bishop at that time—I don't remember his name—and he told me that once a person takes the sacraments no priest can agree to return that person to a previous faith.

Rabbi Hercog, upon leaving Poland, took with him a considerable number of children, who were relocated in children's homes in France.

As far as acquiring funds for the Jewish Religious Community, Rabbi Szenfeld [phonetic spelling], the son-in-law of the chief rabbi of England, did much. Szenfeld was in Poland twice, and both times he took transports of children, each containing 100 children, to be adopted in England. Among those children were ones taken from the convents.

Besides this, there was Mrs. Lederberg, who worked for the Aguda. The actions of Mrs. Lederberg were financed by the foundation of Mrs. Szeternbuch of Switzerland. [Both names are phonetically spelled]. The actions of Mrs. Lederberg were very limited—the children taken by her were immediately sent out of Poland.

Besides the above-mentioned people, there were individuals who reclaimed children that belonged to their families.

I don't have a list of the children take by the Community—I only have a list somewhere of the children I was not able to take.

Another one of my post-war duties was taking back women who

during the wartime were compelled to marry the men who saved them and with whom they had children. There were several incidents where, without the knowledge of their husbands, I took the women and their children. This involved the issue of abduction and tricking the husbands, who later went mad, running about and searching for their wives and children....

Before the war I lived in Cracow with my family. On Sept. 3, 1939 I escaped with my entire family and we reached the Lithuanian border—my father and one brother crossed the border, while I and another brother were arrested by the Soviets. We were sentenced to spend three years there, but served only about two years, for after the agreement between Sikorski and Stalin, we were freed. My brother and I wanted to join Ander's army but we couldn't get to the moblization area. The mobilization was occuring only in the southern part of Russia, while we were freed from a camp in the northern part, not far from Archangiel. After the liberation we were offered Soviet passports—but we didn't take them, for we wanted to remain Polish citizens. Then we were once again placed in prison. We sat there for several months when news reached us that army was being organized again. We presented ourselves to the army being organized by Wanda Wasilewska—they sent us to the mobilization occuring in Moscow. They did not want to admit us there, for we were Jews. At the Association of Polish Patriots we were seen by Luna Brystygierow and she told us that this army was not for us and that we should go back where we came from. But there were already several of us by then: my brother and I, the two Zarecci brothers, lawyers, and still one more youth, whose name was Brenholtz.

All five of us insisted that we would join the army and finally we were directed to the gathering point of the 1st Kosciuszko Division. When we reached the area the same story that happened in Moscow with Brystygier. The doctor, who is now a doctor in Tel-Aviv, told us that we should go back and not bother about joining any army. We insisted and finally were accepted to the army—we were mobilized and from Leningrad we started our military career.

After a certain time my brother and I were separated. He went to officer school, while I with the second foot regiment went to Berlin.

After the war we camped out in Siedlach, when I found out that in Warsaw there was an army rabbinate. So I wrote a letter to Rabbi

Kahane requesting him to visit our unit, in which there were a lot of Jews. The rabbi did not come, but he wrote that he would be interested in talking with me. He sent a chauffer for me and I rode to Warsaw, where Rabbi Kahane proposed that I work in the army rabbinate. I accepted the proposition.

In those day the army rabbinate consisted of the Chief Rabbi of the Polish Army, who was Rabbi Kahane, then the two field rabbis, who were Captain Bekier and I. Besides that, there was an army kantor, a chauffer and an orderly. Our place of business was located in a house which during the war was occupied by the gestapo. The army rabbinate concerned itself with matters of demobilization, performing services for Jewish soldiers and generally, maintaining contact with the Jewish soldiers finding themselves in the Polish Army. Of course, these were not officers of the Security Force—that most often hid their ancestry, did not admit to being Jewish, and with the rabbinate, or with Jewish matters, that did not have anything to do with, or want to do with.

[...]On Pradnik St. in Cracow, there was a inn owned by a woman, who was wheelchairbound. She sat in the wheelchair and had a woman who took her outside. During one of these excurtions the woman saw at the river a woman tying a rock to the neck of a small child. She immediately had the her assistant rush over to see what was happening. It turned out that the woman was Jewish, an aunt of the child. (The Germans had taken the mother away to camp.) Not wanting the child to fall into the hands of the Germans, she decided to drown her. The innkeeper took the child, a newly-born baby, and took it home. The innkeeper became friendly with a German and started a rumor that she was pregnant by him; then she left town and returned after a certain while with the child from the river, and everyone thought that this was indeed the child of the German, who, besides, helped in the deceit by taking the little one out for walks.

All this seems like fiction, but these are facts.

After the war the innkeeper was acquised of collaborating with the Germans, and the woman who wanted to drown the child, came and asked the woman to return the child. The innkeeper had become attached to the child and didn't want to let him go. Then certain things began—perhaps these are not nice from the Jewish side—but in those times.... This woman needed an official letter that the information about her relationship with Germans was set out in order to save a Jewish child. We figured that we would give out such a declaration under the condition that she would give us back the child. Without any other possibilities the innkeeper gave up the child to the woman who wanted to drown it.

Rabbi David Kahane
November 7, 1987 in Tel-Aviv, Israel

D: I'll try to answer your questions as best as I can, even though I personally did not take part in the recovery of Jewish children, as after the war I was the chairman of the Jewish Religious Community in Poland, and up until 1950 the chief rabbi of the Polish Army. The Community had a home for children in Zabrze, in which we placed the children we retrieved from Polish hands. We were also interested in the children who had found themselves in the convents; they, too, were housed in Zabrze after they were recovered. In my rabbinate I had an associate who concerned himself with getting these children. His name was Izajasz Druker, and he knows more about these things than I do. Today I can only recollect particular events, while Druker was occupied with the entire affair.

K: When did you first learn that Jewish children had been saved in convents?

Did you know about this during the war, or only after the war?

D: After the war, people were returning from Russia, the camps and other parts of the world. They were returning to their villages and towns, and asking about their families. Sometimes a person would give information that a Jewish child was alive in such and such a place, in this or that convent. People noted down this information and sent it to the rabbinate in Warsaw, and Druker, along with several other individuals from the Community, went out to retrieve the children. There were some difficult cases.

During the war I was in the Janowski camp in Lwow. After the war I remained in Lwow for several months. I had a friend whose wife became pregnant in 1942, and before the liquidation of the Lwow ghetto, in June of 1943, she gave birth to a child at a Polish midwife's on Pelczynski Street. She returned to the ghetto, and left her child at the mid-wife's. Later she and her husband and her entire family perished in the ghetto. I found out about all this in the first days of August 1944. Since Pelczynski Street was well known to me, I found the midwife's apartment without much difficulty, and she told me that, not knowing what to do with the child and knowing that the parents were no longer alive, she gave the child over to a well-to-do, childless couple.

When I went to those people, I saw that the child's age corresponded with the age of the child of my friend. I was, nevertheless, indiscreet enough to tell them why I was there. The man said that it was their own child, while the woman closed the door in my face. I went back several times to see the midwife and the couple, but I got nowhere. Meanwhile, I was called to Warsaw to organize a rabbinate in the army—and that couple must have left for the West.

I have a clear conscience regarding this matter....

K: After the war, did you have any contact with the convents in the matter of taking back the Jewish children they had saved?

D: To answer this I would have to be at least ten years younger. I am eighty-five years old, and my memory of what happened....

There were difficulties with the convents. The mother superiors of these convents would say that the child is baptized and because of religious reasons they could only give the child back if the person taking it would guarantee that the child would be raised as a Christian. Such things were promised, and not just once.

K: Did you personally make contact with the convents regarding the children in the convents?

D: Yes, of course. Some experiences were quite pleasant, very friendly and warm. But certain cases were very tragic. Once the nuns did not want to speak to me, and a certain ten-year-old girl, who was staying with them, told me that she had no intention of returning to the Jewish nation, to that nation which had murdered Christ. And that was the end of that. I had no more contact with her, and I don't know what happened to her.

K: Rabbi, the Polish nuns are certain that after the war people frequently turned up for Jewish children presenting themselves as family members, when in fact they were complete strangers to the children. The nuns then came to the opinion that these people were doing it for money. Do you think that there could have been people showing up for the children who were not related to the them in any way?

D: Yes, that's a possibility. You should know that for the Jewish nation every Jew has something inborn that ties him to his Jewish descent. That is why the Jewish nation takes care that no branch falls off from the Jewish tree. That is why everything must be done to return the child to Abraham's bosom. That is why at the end of the war all the Jewish groups in Poland coordinated an operation to retrieve Jewish children from Polish hands. Very often, then, the people picking up the children said that they were related to the child and asked how much money these Poles who kept them wanted for hiding the child.

K: Don't you think, rabbi, that this pretense of being the parents of the child and offering money could have, in the case of the convents, led to greater confusion in the matter? What were the reasons behind this?

D: A nun is a religious person, and her duty, from a religious point of view, is to make sure the child becomes a Catholic, because she believes it is the one true faith.

The nuns reacted to this based on their own conscience.

K: What, according to you, were the motives behind the nuns rescuing Jewish children?

D: There were times when the saving of Jewish children was guided by two reasons: humanitarian and religious. But among Jews there existed the opinion that nuns were missionaries.

I have, for example, a lot of experience with Ukrainian nuns. When the Janowski camp in Lwow was closed, I managed to escape and reach the palace of Archbishop Szeptycki, a person of high morals. How the Ukrainians acted we don't have to talk about—the whole world knows. But Szeptycki gave an order to his convents to save Jewish children. The mother superior of these convents was a very energetic, religious and educated person. She saved sixty or more Jewish children. But the first thing she did was to get them baptized.

"You have to get baptized," the sisters would say to the children, "so that you will not be different from the others; you will be able to go to Church and take communion."

This was a very serious matter. That is why most of the Jewish children ran away from these convents the first day after the liberation. But there were small children, two or three-years-old, babies—they all remained there.

Now it is part of Russia, so I don't know what happened to them....

K: Do you think that the claim that Polish nuns were motivated purely by missionary purposes was just?

D: No, one can't ascribe missionary motives to everyone. There were such fears in Jewish circles, but that does not mean that the primary reason for saving Jewish children in Polish convents was a missionary one. The primary reason for saving children was humanitarian, to save lives; the secondary reason was a missionary one.

K: Was this the prevalent thinking during the war among Jewish circles?

D: Who knows? But this issue is connected with something that is very close to our hearts and the hearts of the Polish nation. There were about 30 million Poles, and the files of the Medal of the Just in Yad Vashem list around three thousand. What kind of percent is that? It's terribly low. Where was the Polish nation when Jews were being murdered? It stood from a distance and watched. One issue is connected with the other.

K: Rabbi, are you certain that the files in Yad Vashem accurately reflect the actual number of Poles who saved Jews? So far, the medals of honor have been given to just a few nuns, yet many more....

But let's get to another point. I wanted to ask you if you ever heard about the council of Jewish leaders which took place in the Warsaw ghetto and which tried to decide whether Jewish children should be saved in convents?

D: I know that Ringelblum mentions the subject, but at the time I was at the Janowski camp in Lwow....

K: I'm not talking about the event itself, but about the problem it posed.

I'm asking because of my own difficulties in understanding the Jewish religion and the concept of *Kiddush ha-Shem*. On what basis could one decide that it was better that the children perish rather than be saved in the convents? Please tell me this as a man, a Jew, and as a rabbi.

D: I can tell you what it was like for us in Lwow. We had to deliberate on such issues. From the religious point of view.

There are 613 commandments. For example, if you are sick and have to heal yourself, and it is believed that, in the case of consumption, pork helps, then one should forget about all commandments—in this case the very strict rule concerning eating pork—and eat it. All commandments and rules become null and void if death is facing you.

There is only one exception: if, in order to survive, you accept someone else's faith. It would be better in that case if you were killed, for you would be breaking this commandment—which is called *Kiddush ha-Shem*, sanctifying the name of God.

We faced such issues during the war when people came and asked if they could hand over a child to a convent.

The majority of rabbis thought that the children should be turned over.

The reasoning was that if a child survives the war, then he or she can be retrieved. If no one survives, then the child will still be saved. But there were rabbis—in the minority, I might add—who said: Don't hand over the children to the convents, rather let them perish with us. Yet these same rabbis in Lwow protested sharply and prohibited the Judenrats from giving the Germans lists of Jews intended for transportation. As to the children, the majority of rabbis agreed that the most important thing was their rescue.

Father Michal Michniak from W. Bartoszewski and Z. Lewinowna's Ten jest z ojczyzny mojej (He Is My Fellow Countryman)

Krakow 1969

At the end of 1941 the Germans organized a ghetto in Slonim, where I was hiding. In this ghetto they placed about 200,000 Jews. On June 29, 1942, from 7:30 to 20:00, the Nazis liquidated the ghetto in a barbaric manner. Jews in groups of 150 to 200 were taken through the city to a small town, Gora Petrelowicka, about two kilometers away. Once there, they were forced to take off their clothes and were machine gunned into freshly dug ditches. The execution squads, drunk with alcohol, did not carry out there instruction so well. Many people were buried half-alive. On the following day one could see hands stretching out of the ground. I observed everything from a smoke hole in the roof of the presbytery near the parish church. A certain number of Jews managed to escape. They were hidden in the Jesuit monastery in Albertynow. A portion of them managed to make it to the partisans. Father Adam Starki and I provided false baptism certificates to the hiding Jews.

Up until late autumn of 1942 we hid the Kagan family in the convent of the Order of the Immaculate Conception. The husband and wife were dentists, as well as the daughter. Mrs. Kagan was married to a Frenchman, de la Vitte, from Bordeaux. They had one daughter. After much difficulty I managed to get a birth certificate from Bordeaux, and on the basis of that the mother and daughter got "Aryan" papers. On the night of December 1942 the Gestapo invaded the convent. The mother superior, Sister Marta, and Father Starki were arrested. I managed to escape. That day the Nazis caught the Kagan family and many Poles, who had been hiding Jews. Everyone they had caught, including Father Starki, were taken by SS men to Gora Petrelowicka and murdered there.

Also at the same time Sisters Marta Woloska and Ewa Noyszewska were murdered, the former for directly helping Jews, the latter, as a mother superior, the one responsible for the nuns and their activities.

Max Noy, father of Ruth Noy (Saved in Otwock)
May 30, 1987 in New York

During the German occupation, I worked in the Otwock ghetto as a guard.

One day Sister Ludwika Malkiewicz came to me with a piece of paper from the Germans stating that she would be getting some furniture. I don't remember the precise details but she needed ten beds. We started talking and the nun admitted that she actually needed many more beds, but that she hadn't told this to the Germans because she feared that she would get nothing if she asked for too much. I told the sister to take as many beds as she wanted because I didn't give a damn about the Germans—I didn't even know if I would be alive the next day.

Soon our conversation turned around to my family. I told her I had a daughter. At first I feared revealing where Ruth was hiding, but finally I told her that she was in Otwock with relatives, but that it wasn't a permanent arrangement and that is why I would like for her to be in an orphanage. At that time my wife was staying with an acquaintance of hers, a Polish woman.

Sister Ludwika took the beds, as many as she wanted, and from that time we became friends—she used to telephone me, and I her, so as not to lose touch with each other. I remember that I once worked in Zofiowka, in hospital for the mentally ill, where the Germans had shot all the people, Poles and Jews.

Sister Ludwika even found me there; she would make a call to the headquarters and ask for me, and they respected her wishes. Sometimes in the evening I would make my way out of the camp to meet her. My wife and daughter at that time were in grave danger because of the edicts against the Jews.

As I have mentioned, I worked for the Germans, and my wife was hiding with the Polish woman. When it was still very hot in Otwock, the Germans allowed Jews to live in the area around Treblinka. We had acquaintances there and my wife and daughter went there to live in freedom. They weren't there long, they didn't have a permanent place to stay, as Irka, the Polish woman, was frightened because she had her own family. After all, the Germans killed entire Polish families for harboring Jews!

So Irka was afraid, and my wife went with Ruth to Kocowa, if only to stay there for two weeks. After staying in Kocowa, my wife wandered around with my daughter. Somehow we always managed to stay in contact. Then one day we made an arrangement. I sent a Pole I knew, Kobus, to bring my daughter. He couldn't take my wife because there was too much risk involved.

Kobus took my daughter to his place in Otwock, and then she became ill. I don't remember if it was the scarlet fever or something else. She had to see a doctor. Since I had been a student at Warsaw University, I had many Polish doctors as friends. I asked a pediatrician, Stas Wieslawski, to help. He visited my daughter. I met him a few times after that, and he told me that he was in great need of medical books, so I stole these books from Zofiowka and brought them to him. He has them to this day.

It was winter already. I made contact with Sister Ludwika, and as soon as Ruth got well, we gave her the child. It was a winter's evening, cold and snowy. The doors of the orphanage were open and my wife said to Ruth: "Go inside; you'll get some candy there."

Ruth went. We made an arrangement with Sister Ludwika that in case of trouble she would light a candle in a window. If no light shone that would indicate that everything had gone alright. We froze outside for two hours, but no light came, so we left the orphanage.

We visited our daughter only twice. She was under the care of Sister Anna, a brave young nun. Later, when we were in hiding, our link with our daughter was the Polish woman I've already mentioned, Irka.

Sister Ludwika was very careful in her activities, which is why we felt safe having Ruth stay in the convent. We left Ruth with a letter, because that's how it was done in those days. She also had an authentic certificate, with the name of Teresa Wysocka on it, which I got in Otwock from a priest I knew.

Provided with the letter and certificate, Ruth started to cry once she was inside the orphanage. The nuns came down to see what was happening, and then they talked about whether the child was Jewish and if so, whether they could put the other children in danger if they took her in. My daughter went up to the mother superior at that point, and the mother superior reacted with these words:

"If the child has come to me, then I will share her fate."

Luckily, my daughter did not talk Yiddish or Hebrew; she only knew Polish and we only spoke Polish at home. Before we left for the convent, we had taught her what to say—that her mother had been taken by the Nazis to Germany, and that her name was Teresa Wysocka.

We gave Sister Ludwika carte blanche when we sent Ruth to the convent; she could do anything she wanted with the child for its safety, including baptizing it, for a little water would not be bad if it saved the child's life. We also left the nuns a little money. They accepted the money, but it would have made no difference if we had not given it, for Ruth would have been accepted into the convent regardless.

We informed the Polish police commissioner in Otwock of the fact that we had given our child to the convent. He assured us that in case something happened and the child ended up at the police station, he would call an engineer living nearby, Szpakowski, and then his wife would take the child in as her own, so that our daughter would not fall into the hands of the Germans.

When Ruth was already in the convent, my wife and I went to Praga to hide. When the Germans were already losing the war, and the front was nearing Warsaw in 1944, Sister Ludwika managed to inform us that the Germans were moving the orphanage to the west and that she didn't know what would be happening to them. So we sent our liaison, Irka, to pick up the girl, and after that our daughter was with us. She didn't have to hide anymore and no one suspected that she was Jewish.

Roza Noy
Excerpt from letter written to Sister Ludwika Malkiewicz, 1981

My dear Sister Ludwika!
Thank you for your letter. I have a strange feeling. It seems to me

that I have found one of my own sisters. (I had four and all perished at the hands of the Nazi murderers.) You are as close to me as a real sister, for who else would have given us so many proofs of self-sacrifice and also have understood our sufferings? I well remember when after the war I came to the convent to thank you for saving my child, and I presented you some money I had managed to save during the war. Dear Sister Ludwika, our guardian angel, said then:

"Keep the money since the Germans took everything away from you. But if ever someone would need help from you, please help them."

I've always remembered those words; they were like a sacred commandment to me. I tried to help where I could, and when people would thank me, I would relate this story to them and what you said. Anytime I meet a nun, I thank her with tears in my eyes and tell her of my deep regret that I've lost contact with you, my dear sister [...]

NOTES

Introduction

1. Ewa Kurek, *Sredniowieczny kult Dzieciatka Jezus jako inspiracja procesu dowartosciowania dziecka* ("The Cult of the Child Jesus in the Middle Ages as the Genesis for the Evolution of a Child's Worth"), *Summarium*, Lublin 1979, p.248.

2. K. Antosiewicz, *Zakon Ducha Swietego de Saxia w Polsce sredniowiecznej* ("The Order of the Holy Spirit de Saxia in Medieval Poland") *Nasza Przeszlosc*, Cracow 1966, p.195; E. Wisniowski, *800 lat Zakonu Ducha Swietego de Saxia w Polsce* ("800 Years of the Order of the Holy Spirit de Saxia in Poland"), *Nowum*, Warsaw 1976. p.126.

Chapter 1

1. Wladyslaw Bartoszewski, *Warto byc przyzwoitym* (It Pays to Be Decent), Editions Spotkania, Paris, 1986, p.25.

2. Yisrael Gutman, *Polish and Jewish Historiography on the Question of Polish-Jewish Relations during World War II, The Jews in Poland, Polish-Jewish Studies*, Oxford 1986; p.178. On the question of the Jews' attitude toward the Soviet occupation of Poland's eastern territories the author takes an attitude which is rather typical of Jewish historians and Jewish public opinion. Namely, he thinks that the Jewish behavior which added a new element to Polish anti-Semitism should be explained by the fact that for Jews the only enemy were the Nazis, and that to the Jews the Soviets appeared to offer a chance for rescue and getting help, as far as was possible under the conditions of the time.

Yisrael Gutman's suggestion seems to contain only part of the truth about what happened in Poland's eastern territories when the Soviet troops marched in and during the Soviet occupation. To be sure, for some Jews the Soviet occupation eventually proved to be a chance for avoiding Hitler's death camps. But it certainly did not look like that to those Polish Jews who from September 1939 to June 1941, together with Poles, White Russians and Ukrainians, filled the cattle-trucks which transported citizens of the Polish Republic to Siberia. One could often hear Polish patriotic songs, including the Polish national anthem, from the cattle-trucks which contained Polish Jews. For them, at that time, Hitler was far away. It was the Soviets who were their enemies and who violated their rights. We must not forget this. The survival of those who spent the war years in Soviet

Russia cannot make us forget about those tens of thousands of Polish Jews for whom the deportations and the Soviet camps proved to be equally as fatal as the Nazi crematories. Mickiewicz's words, "If I forget them, may God forget me," apply also to them, Polish Jews, who heroically refused to accept Soviet citizenship, and for whom their Jewishness was so entwined with their Polishness that they chose to die rather than be a traitor to either of them.

Yisrael Gutman also silently passes over the other, considerable part of the community of Polish Jews that belonged to the Communist party. One cannot escape the facts that for Jewish communists the invasion of Soviet troops meant, above all, that their ideological aspirations had come true, and that it was just their attitude toward the Soviet occupation which agitated Polish public opinion so much, causing a growth of antipathy and open hostility toward all Jews.

Irena, who was saved by the Sluzebniczki Starowiejskie, and whose parents managed to get from Warsaw to Bialystok at the end of 1939, writes:

> My parents were leftists. [...] They moved to Bialystok not only to run from the Germans, but I assume to primarily run after their ideals. My parents eagerly joined the Soviet order, which was formally, though tellingly, expressed by the fact that they accepted Soviet passports. Mother taught history and Latin in a high school. It is an awful thing to say, but it must be said, that many Poles at that time did not like—even hated—my parents.

Cezary Gawrys, *Turkowice-smierc i ocalenie* ("Death and Rescue"), *Wies* 1987, No. 4, p.25.

3. Szymon Datner, *Las sprawiedliwych—karta z dziejow ratownictwa Zydow w okupowanej Polsce* (The Forest of the Just: A Page from the History of Rescuing Jews in Occupied Poland), Warsaw, 1968, p.8.

4. Emanuel Ringelblum, *Kronika getta warszawskiego* (A Chronicle of the Warsaw Ghetto), Warsaw, 1983, pp. 100 and 139.

5. *Eksterminacja Zydow na ziemiach polskich w okresie okupacji hitlerowskiej—zbior dokumentow* (The Extermination of Jews in Poland During the German Occupation: A Collection of Documents), Zydowski Instytut Historyczny, Warsaw, 1957, p. 26.

6. *Dziennik Rozporzadzen dla Generalnego Gubernatorstwa 1941* (Decrees for the General Government 1941) Oct.25, 1941, nr. 99, p. 595.

7. Wladyslaw Bartoszewski and Z. Lewinowna, *Ten jest z ojczyzny mojej* (He Is My Fellow Countryman), Cracow 1966, p.27.

8. On the strength of the above-quoted instructions for the German operation groups active in Poland, issued as a result of the conference that

had taken place in Berlin on September 21, 1939, the so-called Judenrats were established in the ghettos to administer the closed Jewish quarters. The role that was played by the Judenrats is still controversial among historians. Among others, the following authors discuss the problem of the Judenrats: Isaiah Trunk, *Judenrat*, New York 1972; Leonard Tushnet, *The Pavement of Hall*, New York 1972; Yisrael Gutman, *The Jews of Warsaw 1939-1945: Ghetto, Underground, Revolt*. Bloomington 1982.

9. Emanuel Ringelblum, op. cit., p.354.

10. *Barykada Wolnosci* (Freedom Barricade), Nov. 30, 1941 stated: "From Lithuania and the Ukraine comes news about mass murders of the Jewish population in towns and villages, perpetrated not only by Germans, but by Lithuanians and Ukrainians also."

11. Marek Edelman, *Getto walczy* (The Ghetto Fights), Warsaw, 1945, p.7.

12. *The Nuremberg Document*, NG-2586.

13. Marek Edelman, op. cit., p.9.

14. Emanuel Ringelblum, op. cit., p.426.

15. W. Bartoszewski and Z. Lewinowna, op. cit., p.43.

16. Ibid, p.33.

17. Ibid, p.33.

18. *Biuletyn Informacyjny* (Information Bulletin), January 28, 1943, p.8.

19. W. Bartoszewski, *Los Zydow Warszawy 1939-1945* (The Fate of Warsaw Jews 1939-1945), Puls Publication, London, 1983, pp.40-41.

20. Emanuel Ringelblum, op. cit. p.334

Chapter 2

1. Philip Friedman, *Zaglada Zydow Polskich 1939-1945* (The Extermination of the Polish Jews 1939-1945), *Biuletyn Glownej Komisji Badania Zbrodni Niemieckich w Polsce* (Bulletin of the Chief Commission for Investigating the Nazi Crimes in Poland), 1946, vol.I, p.204; Jozef Kermisz, *Akcje i wysiedlenia* (Actions and Deportations), *Dokumenty i materialy z czasow okupacji niemieckiej w Polsce* (Documents and Data from the Times of the German Occupation in Poland), 1946, vol.II, p.473

2. *Encyclopedia Judaica*, Jerusalem 1972, vol. X, p.978

3. Many Jewish historians point to *Kiddush ha-Shem* as the basis for the Polish Jews' attitude toward the Holocaust, among these is Lucy Dawidowicz (*La guerre contre les Juifs 1933-1945*, Editions Hachette, Paris, 1977, pp. 495, 501, 547.)

Here is one, of numerous examples, a shocking picture of the liquidation of a small Jewish community in Ropczyce, as seen by a Polish witness:

July 24, 1942; ten in the morning. The Jews formed a procession. On both sides of the road were gendarmes, SS troops, Sonderdienst, and the "navy-blue police." All were carrying firearms, some also held long sticks or dogs on leashes. Under the pretext of keeping order, the Jews were beaten as they walked. At the front of the procession were the members of the assembly of elders—Dr. Kaufman, a judge; Dr. Federsbusch, a lawyer, Dr. Arnold Meister, rabbis, and other notables of the Jewish community. The rabbis and several other Jews were dressed in their ritual attire; many had gaberdines and skull caps on, and were holding little scrolls of the Torah. The women were dressed in black, and many of them had their children in their arms. The older children were led by the hand by their parents or grandparents. Families kept together, helping the elderly and infirm. From the rows of those marching came the sound of psalms and prayers, along with crying and groaning...

Eugeniusz Taras, *Zaglada ropczyckich Zydow* ("The Death of the Jews in Ropczyce"), *Znak*, no.396-397, Cracow 1988, p.11.

A corroboration of the fact that the behavior of the Polish Jews during the Holocaust was conditioned by their religion is also found in preserved journals, diaries and memoirs; among these is one by Ephraim Oshry, a rabbi from Kowno. (Rafael F. Scharf, "Saints or Madmen? A Meditation on Ephraim Oshry's 'Response from the Holocaust,'" *The Jewish Quarterly*, London, January 1988.)

4. W. Bartoszewski, *Warto byc uczciwym...*, p. 48. Also: Szymon Datner (*Las sprawiedliwych...*, p. 28) writes:

Acts of treason, like the collaboration of the scums of society with the Nazi occupant, constituted a small number, both in Polish and Jewish society. There is no nation completely free of such scums. War is always a corrupting factor, very dangerous for weak characters.

The Polish nation, which was one of the few nations that did not blemish its reputation by collaborating with the Nazi occupant, suffered from the same denunciators and Gestapo informers no less than the Jews. The attitude of both the Polish and Jewish nations was univocal: traitors of all kinds, szmalcowniks, blackmailers and denunciators were commonly condemned and despised.

5. Szymon Datner, *Las sprawiedliwych...*, p. 8, touches upon the extremely important aspect of the problem of rescuing Jews by Poles, an aspect which often seems to be forgotten by historians of the Holocaust. The author writes:

The fact that the Germans murdered three million Jews in Poland is a commonly known axiom which does not need any proofs. But what about our knowledge of the murdered Polish population, the "Aryan" population as the Nazi "scientists" would say? Unfortunately, this issue is—almost a quarter of a century after the end of the war—investigated only fragmentarily today. The fact is that the extermination of a large part of the Polish population has been overshadowed by the almost total holocaust of the Jewish population, despite the fact that in absolute numbers the difference in the casualties in both nations is small. [...] While in the years 1939-1941 the ratio of murdered Poles to murdered Jews was 10:1, in 1942-1944 it was 2:3. The truth is that as a result of the criminal, studied and deliberate policy of the occupant both the Polish and Jewish nation were dying.

6. In *Encyclopedia Judaica* (Jerusalem 1972, vol.VIII, p.875) we read in the article "The Local Population and the Holocaust" that the risk taken in occupied Europe by people rescuing Jews ranged from the death penalty in the General Government to deportation or concentration camps—at the end of the war—in the Netherlands. To say nothing of the propriety of using the Nazi appelation of General Government to denote occupied Poland (for who among young Israelites, Americans or even Poles knows today what the General Government was?) the above statement is false, since rescuing and hiding Jews was punishable by death in the whole territory of occupied Poland. Strictly speaking Hans Frank's decree did indeed apply only to the General Government.

In reality, however, the death penalty was applied to the whole of Poland. One of the numerious proofs of this is the death of two nuns of the Sisters of the Immaculate Conception of the Blessed Virgin Mary, who were murdered in Slonim for hiding a Jewish family. (Slonim was part of the Reich Commissariat East and had nothing to do with the General Government, apart from the fact that both these administrative units were established by the Germans on Polish soil.

It is also worth noting, in regard to the Encyclopedia Judaica, that in no entry concerning the Holocaust is it mentioned that Poland was the only Nazi-occupied country where the rescue of Jews was punishable by death.

7. Photocopy of the German document, Archives of the Jewish Historical Institute, Warsaw, no. 62a.

8. Poster in German and Polish, Archives of the Jewish Historical Institute, Warsaw, no. 16.

9. W. Bartoszewski and Z. Lewinowna, *Ten jest z ojczyzny...*, p. 74.

10. Emanuel Ringelblum, *Stosunki polsko-zydowskie w czasie drugiej wojny*

swiatowej (Polish-Jewish Relations During the Second World War), Warsaw 1988, p.83.

11. For several years the State University of Arcata, California, has been conducting interdisciplinary research on the personality traits of the people rescuing Jews in the years of the Nazi occupation of Europe. The results obtained so far have been included by the authors of the program, Samuel P. Oliner and Pearl Oliner, in the book *The Altruistic Personality—Rescuers of Jews in Nazi Europe*, The Free Press, New York 1988. The authors pay particular attention to the sociological and psychological conditioning necessary for a person to be able to risk his or her life in order to save the life of another.

12. Emanuel Ringelblum, *Kronika...*, p.391.

13. Ibid, pp.434-436.

14. Emanuel Ringelblum, *Stosunki polsko-zydowskie...*, p.114.

15. Rabbi David Kahane interview; author's private collection.

Chapter 3

1. *Chrzescijanstwo w Polsce* (Christianity in Poland), Wydawnictwo KUL, Lublin 1980, p.301.

2. Karol Pospieszalski, *Polska pod niemieckim prawem 1939-1945* (Poland Under German Law 1939-1945), Poznan 1946, pp.88-90, 168-1758.

3. *Proces Artura Greisera przed Najwyzszym Trybunalem Narodowym* (The Trial of Arthur Greiser Before the Supreme Court), Warsaw 1946, pp.229-395.

4. S. Piotrowski, *Proces Hansa Franka i dowody polskie przeciw SS* (The Trial of Hans Frank and Polish Evidence Against the SS), Warsaw 1970, p.293.

5. *Chrzescijanstwo w Polsce...*, p.313.

6. Four important bishoprics in the General Government—Warsaw, Tarnow, Sandomierz and Siedlce—also did not have their ordinaries.

7. Seven orders started their work in Poland before World War I, twelve in the 1920s and seven in the 1930s.

8. All the homes of the Antonine Sisters, the Franciscan Sisters from Orlik, the Sisters of St. Elizabeth from Cieszyn and the Carmelite Sisters of the Infant Jesus found themselves in land incorporated into the Reich. Other orders had a considerable percentage of their homes in that newly-incorporated area also. 60 out of 65 homes of the Sister of Charity of St. Charles Borromeo from Mikolow were located there.

9. Lucyna Mistecka, *Zmartwychwstanki w okupowanej Polsce* (Sisters of the Resurrection in Occupied Poland), Warsaw 1983, pp.94-95.

10. Sister Maria Ena (of the Sisters of the Immaculate Conception of the Blessed Virgin Mary) interview; author's private collection.

11. As Emanuel Ringelblum suggests in *Kronika...*, pp.434-436, the proposition of saving children from the Warsaw ghetto was made by priests. The possibilities that the Polish priests had of rescuing Jewish children by putting them in convent orphanages were considerable. It should be remembered that, because of their priesthood, they have always enjoyed a tremendous authority and confidence with nuns. As priests, they have many connections in clerical circles. If a particular priest did not know personally the mothers superior of convents, or knew only a few of them, he could easily, through other priests, establish or broaden these connections. It seems probable then that the proposition from the Warsaw priests to the representatives of the organizations active in the Warsaw ghetto was founded on just such a basis, supported by preliminary talks with the superiors of several orders. However, since aside from Ringelblum, no Church source mentions the proposition, it seems reasonable to accept the explanations given by Jonas Turkow in his account given in the Jewish language in Buenos Aires in 1948, and translated and published by Szymon Datner in *Materialy z dziedziny ratownictwa Zydow w Polsce w okresie okupacji hitlerowskiej* ("Materials on Rescuing Jews in Poland During the Nazi Occupation"), *Builetyn Zydowskiego Instytutu Historycznego*, 1970, no.73-76, pp.136-137. Here we read the following:

A whole series of talks was conducted [in the Warsaw ghetto—E.K.]. In their final stages, Irena Sendler, a wonderful person, took part. Despite the fact that as a Polish patriot and underground activist she herself was persecuted, she rescued Jewish children from death with unusual devotion and self-sacrifice. Irena Sendler had even earlier contacted our Ala Golab-Grinberowa, and had come to the ghetto several times, where she told Lejman that she had worked out a plan that she wanted to present to the leading Jewish personages in the ghetto. Besides Ala, she also met with Guzik, the director of JOINT, who became very interested in her plan. She wasn't able to come to an understanding with others because of the recent events in the ghetto. But now she is ready to conduct negotiations again. There are possibilities for saving Jewish children on the Aryan side. A suitable fund should be established in the ghetto for this purpose. On her part, she will make efforts to obtain money from the RGO and from the Social Welfare Department of the municipal council.

Lejman drew into the matter a man named Lubliner whom he had traded with in the ghetto. He himself kept on looking for contacts with prominent Jewish social activists in the ghetto. No one was able to give him proper addresses.

So he is happy—he says—to have met me and that he will be able to save my child also. I was to organize a committee in the ghetto which would find the necessary funds and attend to transferring immediately the children to the Aryan side.

During the war Irena Sendler was connected with the Social Welfare Department of the Warsaw Municipal Council, and on its behalf, and in consultation with the Chief Tutelary Council, she had been rescuing Jewish children since the beginning of the war by, among other things, putting them in convent institutions runs by the Sisters of the Family of Mary and the Sisters Servants of Mary Immaculate (Stara Wies). Irena Sendler, *Ci ktorzy pomagali Zydom* ("Those Who Helped Jews"), *Biuletyn Zydowskiego Instytutu Historycznego*, 1963, no.45-46, p.234.

From the account of Jonas Turkow it appears that Irena Sendler was looking for contacts with prominent activists of the ghetto community, most probably to present them with a plan of saving children by putting them in Catholic convents. Immediate talks, however, probably never came off, and since the whole thing was going on in deep secrecy and must have surely gone through an entire chain of trusted people, it reached the activists and Ringelblum as a plan of the priests and not as a plan drawn up by the Social Welfare Department of Warsaw and the nuns.

12. Adam Slomczynski, *Dom ksiedza Boduena* (The Father Boduen Home), Warsaw 1975, p.117.

13. In *Archiwum Glowne Zgromadzenia Siostr Sluzebniczek Pleszewskich* (Main Archives of the Sisters Servants of Mary Immaculate [Pleszew]), Pleszew Wielkopolski.

14. Sister Jolanta Zienkiewicz (of the Franciscan Missionary Sisters of Mary) interview; author's private collection.

15. In the spring of 1942 the German authorities decided to deport all the Poles from the Zamosc region. The deportations took place from November 27, 1942 to 1943. They comprised 110,000 Poles, including 30,000 children from the Bilgoraj, Hrubieszow, Tomaszow and Zamosc districts. In the period between July and August 25, 1943, 4,454 children from two to eleven years old were transported from the Lublin region to the Reich to be Germanized. The remaining children were deported with their parents, or separately, to the Nazi concentration camps, where some of them were murdered in gas chambers and burnt in the crematories; others were taken to special villages in the Siedlice and Sokolow districts designed for the displaced old people and children. It is still not known what happened to most of the children from Zamojszczyna. They were taken from their parents by force. In order to drown out their crying and the screams of their parents in the transition camp, a special brass band was established. (J. Wnuk, *Dzieci Zamojszczyzny* [The Children of Zamojszczyzna]; L.

Siemion, *Dzieci Zamojszczyzny* ["The Children of Zamojszczyzna"]; J. Rodzik, *Przezycia obozowe zamojskiego dziecka* ["The Camp Experiences of the Children from Zamojszczyzna"] in *Zbrodnie hitlerowskie na dzieciach i mlodziezy polskiej* [The Nazi Crimes Against Polish Children and Youths], Warsaw 1969, pp.54-65, 66-67, 70.)

16. Jadwiga Piotrowska, *50 razy kara smierci* ("The Death Penalty Fifty Times") Kierunki, May 11, 1986; Irena Sendler, *Ci, ktorzy pomagali Zydom,* ("Those Who Helped Jews"), *Biuletyn Zydowskiego Instytutu Historycznego,* 1963, no.45-46, pp.234-244.

17. W. Bartoszewski and Z. Lewinowna, op. cit., p.37; Marek Arczynski and Wieslaw Balcerak, *Kryptonim "Zegota"* (Cryptonym "Zegota"), Warsaw 1983, p.105; Teresa Prekerowa, op. cit., p.211.

18. Sister Jadwiga Skalec (of the Sisters Servants of Mary Immaculate [Staras Wies]), author's private collection.

Chapter 4

1. Cezary Gawrys, *Turkowice—smierc i ocalenie* (Turkowice—Death and Rescue) *Wies,* no.4, Warsaw 1987, p.20.

2. Sister Maria Ena interview, author's private collection.

3. Sister Eliza Malczyk interview (of the Sisters of the Holy Family of Nazareth); author's private collection.

4. Sister Bernarda Sochacka interview (of the Sisters of St. Joseph); author's private collection.

5. Zofia Szymanska, *Bylam tylko lekarzem* (I was Only a Doctor), Warsaw 1979, p.145.

6. Mother Superior Tekla Budnowska (of the Franciscan Sisters of the Family of Mary) interview; author's private collection.

7. A. Slomczynski, op. cit., p.118.

8. Nina E. interview: author's private collection.

9. Z. Szymanska, op. cit., p.148.

10. Lei B. interview, author's private collection.

11. Maria Klein interview, author's private collection.

12. Account of Ewa Goldberg, *Archiwum Zydowskiego Instytutu Historycznego* (Archives of the Jewish Historical Institute), Warsaw, no.5518,

13. Aleksander Donat, *The Holocaust Kingdom,* New York 1985, pp.322-355.

14. *Kronika Domu Dziecka sw. Antoniego w Czersku nad Wisla* (Chronicle of the St. Antoni Children's Home in Czersk), *Archiwum Glowne Zgromadzenia Siostr Sluzebniczek Pleszewskich* (Main Achives of the Sisters Servants of Mary Immaculate [Pleszew]), Pleszew.

15. Lei B. interview, op. cit.

16. Rachela G. interview, author's private collection.

17. Sister Eliza Malczyk (of the Sisters of the Holy Family of Nazareth); author's private collection.

18. Maria Klein interview, op. cit.

19. Lei B. interview, op. cit.

Chapter 5

1. Teresa Fracek, *Zgromadzenie Siostr Rodziny Marii w latach* 1939-1945 ("Sisters of the Family of Mary in the Years 1939-1945"), *Kosciol Katolicki na Ziemiach Polski*, Vol. XI, Warsaw, 1981, p.300.

2. Tatiana Berenstein and Adam Rutkowski, *O ratownictwie Zydow przez Polakow* ("On Rescuing Jews by Poles"), *Biuletyn Zydowskiego Instytutu Historycznego*, 1960, no.35, p.29. The authors state: "In some convents the Jewish children had a double burden of secrecy: hiding from the occupant and from their superiors." The suggestion that the children were forced to secrecy by the nuns' negative attitude toward them is not supported by the sources. I believe that it was their parents' distrust that forced them to it. The war and the cruelties they had experienced probably shook their trust in people to such an extent that they considered it safer not to trust anyone. Moreover, in the case of pious Jews, the fear of possible baptism of the child played an important role. Of course, the fact that the parents did not inform the child about his situation, or that the child kept the information from the nuns, did not mean that the nuns did not know or guess the truth.

3. Account of Katarzyna Meloch, in T. Prekerowa, *Konspiracyjna Rada...*, p.211.

4. Icchak Kacenelson, *Piesn o zamordowanym zydowskim narodzie* (A Song of the Mudered Jewish Nation), Warsaw 1982, p.23.

5. Rachela G. interview, op. cit.

6. Sister Bernarda Sochacka (of the Sisters of St. Joseph) interview; author's private collection.

Chapter 6

1. J. Piotrowska, *50 razy kara smierci...*, op. cit.

2. Wladyslaw Bartoszewski, *Polacy z pomoca Zydom 1939-1945* ("Poles Rescuing Jews, 1939-1945"), *Doswiadczenia lat wojny i okupacji* ("The Experiences of the War and the Occupation Years"), Cracow 1980, p.376.

3. See notes 2 and 3 in Chapter 2.

4. Sister Syksta Niklewska (of the Sisters Servants of Mary Immaculate (Pleszew) interview; author's private collection.

5. Oswald Rufeisen, who would later become Rev. Daniel, ended his account about the circumstances of his rescue in the convent of the Sisters of the Resurrection in Mira, which he gave in 1948—with the following words: "It is indeed hard to understand what tricks the sisters employed in order to make my stay there possible, and even pleasant, especially in winter and late autumn. That is what compassion born of God's love can do. And He will surely reward them for this. I would like my account to be a public homage to God and His servants." (Archiwum Zydowskiego Instytutu Historycznego

Archive of the Jewish Historical Institute], no. 3726. Cf. with the accounts in "Child Development Research," New York State University, Sygn. MG Warsaw 02-27-85HX; C. Gawrys, Turkowice—smierc and ocalenie [Turkowice—Death and Rescue], *Wies*, 1987, no.4, pp.21-30; Rev. Michal Kot interview, author's private collection.)

6. Jan Dobraczynski, *Tylko w jednym zyciu* (Only in One Life), Warsaw 1977, p.243.

7. One of the institutions that Jan Dobraczynski drew into collaborating on saving Jewish children was the one run by the Sisters Servants of Mary Immaculate (Stara Wies). According to the accounts given by the saved children, the nuns did not baptize them during the war, and after the war only those who were mature enough to make such a decision or those whose parents decided for them were baptized.

8. Sister Maria Sawicka (of the Franciscan Sisters of the Family of Mary) interview; author's private collection. Sister Barbara Bojanowski (of the Grey Ursulines) interview; author's private collection.

9. Mother Superior Tekla Budnowska (of the Franciscan Sisters of the Family of Mary) interivew; author's private collection.

10. Account of Zuzanna Sienkiewiczowa in W. Bartoszewski and Z. Lewinowna, op. cit., p.809.

11. Mother Superior Tekla Budnowska interview, op. cit.

12. Sister Michaela Bienkowska (of the Sisters Shepherds of Divine Providence); author's private collection.

13. A. Slomczynski, Dom Ksiedza Boduena..., p.121.

14. Sister Gregoria Klaczynska interview (of the Sisters Servants of Mary Immaculate [Pleszew]); author's private collection.

15. Account of Sister Blazei Tomalak in *Archiwum Glowne Zgromadzenia Siostr Sluzebniczek Pleszewskich* (Main Archives of the Sisters Servants of Mary Immaculate [Pleszew]), Pleszew; *Kronika Generalna Siostr Karmelitanek*

Dzieciatka Jezus (General Chronicle of the Carmelite Sisters of the Infant Jesus) in *Archiwum Glowne Zgromadzenia SS Karmelitanek Dzieciatka Jezus* (Main Archives of the Carmelite Sisters of the Infant Jesus), *Sosnowiec*; *Lucyna Mistecka, Zycie i dzialalnosc siostr zmartwychwstanek w okupowanej Polsce* (The Life and Work of the Sisters of the Resurrection in Occupied Poland), doctoral thesis, Catholic University of Lublin, Lublin 1979, p.172-179.

16. Sister Maria Sawicka interview, op. cit.

17. Sisters Eliza Malczyk and Rozmaria Werbinska (of the Sisters of the Holy Family of Nazareth) interviews; author's private collection.

18. Sister Magdalena Kaczmarzyk, *Pomoc udzielana Zydom przez Zgromadzenie Siostr Albertynek w czasie II wojny swiatowej* (Aid Given to Jews by the Albertine Sisters during the Second World War), manuscript in Archiwum Glowne Zgromadzenia Siostr Albertynek (Main Archives of the Albertine Sisters), Cracow.

19. Sister Ewelina Nienaltowska (of the Passionist Sisters) interview; author's private colleciton.

20. Maria Klein interview; author's private collection.

21. T. Berenstein and A. Rutkowski, op. cit., p.33.

22. Stanislawa Bieda, *Zgromadzenie Siostr Franciszkanek Misjonarek Maryi w latach 1922-1969* (Franciscan Missionary Sisters of Mary in the Years 1922-1969), master's thesis, Catholic University of Lublin, Lublin, p.139.

Chapter 7

1. S. Datner, *Las sprawiedliwych...*, p.32.

2. In the oral tradition there are hints that Jewish children were hid by the Sisters of the Family of Bethany, the Daughters of Divine Love, the Sisters of St. Hedwig, the Pallottine Sisters, the Sisters of Mary Immaculate, and the Sisters Servants of Mary Immaculate (Debica).

3. Adult Jews found refuge with the Disrobed Sisters of Angels, the Missionary Sisters of St. Benedict, Sisters of the Blessed Soul of Christ Our Lord, the Sisters of the Lord Jesus' Nativity, the Sisters Servants of the Mother of the Good Shepherd, and Sisters of Common Work.

4. More detailed information about each of the orders that participated in rescuing Jews and their children is found in a seperate index.

5. T. Prekerowa, *Konspiracjna Rada...*, p.215.

6. As the Jewish children's guardians said in their declaration, in the Father Boduen Home alone the Sisters of Charity saved about 200 children. This is confirmed by the author of a book about that convent, Adam Slomczynski, op. cit.

7. It seems that the number given by Teresa Fracek (*Zgromadzenie Siostr Franciszkanek Rodziny Maryi w latach 1939-1945* [Franciscan Sisters of the Family of Mary in the Years 1939-1945], *Kosciol katolicki na ziemiach Polski w czasie II wojny swiatowej* [The Catholic Church in Poland During the Second World War], Warsaw 1981, vol. X) is a bit overestimated. Not all the information given by the author is confirmed by the archival sources and the accounts of the nuns still alive. Moreover, it seems that in her calculations, the author did not take into consideration to a satisfactory degree the possibility of Jewish children moving from one convent home to another. The same child could have stayed in two homes—for example, once in Samborze and another time in Pludach—but be listed as two children saved.

8. E. Ringelblum, *Stosunki polsko-zydowskie...*, p.110.

9. *Zenskie Zgromadzenia Zakonne w Polsce 1939-1945* (Women's Religious Orders in Poland 1939-1945), Wydawnictwo KUL, Lublin, 1982-1987, vol.I-IV.

10. Weronika Duszkiewicz, *Katarzyna Margolska and Maria Strzalkowska, Zgromadzenie Siostr sw. Feliksa z Kantalicjo w latach 1939-1947* (Sisters of St. Feliks of Kantalico in the Years 1939-1945), Zenskie Zgromadzenie Zakonne w Polsce 1939..., vol.I, pp. 57-62, 120-126, 198-201; Jadwiga Szachno, *Zgromadzenie Siostr Franciszkanek Sluzebnic Krzyza w latach 1939-1945* (Sisters Servants of the Cross in the Years 1939-1945), ibid., vol.II, pp.93-131; Waleria Syksta Niklewska, *Sluzebniczki Niepokalanego Poczecia Najswietszej Maryi Panny* (Pleszew), (Sisters Servants of Mary Immaculate [Pleszew], ibid., vol. III, pp.155-165; *Wladyslawa Juliusza Tajanowicz, Zgromadzenie Siostr Sluzebniczek Bogarodzicy Dziewicy Niepokalanego Poczecia* (sluszebnicki debickie) (Sisters Servants of Mary Immaculate [Debica]), ibid., vol.IV, pp.139-154; Zofia Elekta Lasko, *Zgromadzenie Siostr Sw. Jozefa* (Sisters of St. Joseph), ibid., pp.282-291.

11. There were several reasons for the cessation of activities in these homes during the war. Either their nuns were deported or removed, or they were liquidated, or their activity was suspended. Another reason was the repatriation occuring before 1944—mainly due to the Ukrainian massacres raging in the eastern territories of Poland since the end of 1942.

12. According to the data of January 1, 1937 (found in Marian Pierozynski and Stanislaw Szczech, *Rocznik Statystyczny Kosciola Katolickiego w Polscew* [The Yearbook of the Catholic Church in Poland], Towarszystwo Wiedzy Chrzescijanskiej, Lublin 1938, pp. 50-53, 57) there were 63 active orders in Poland with a count of 16,820 nuns. The nuns were working in 1,686 homes, among which there were 243 orphanages, 189 boarding schools and 25 reformatories. One should not accept the this data as credible for the period from the outbreak of World War II through the war years because of the

changes that took place between the time the data was collected and the moment which is of interest to us, i.e. the moment of the outbreak of the war. Also, the yearbook contains inaccuracies regarding the number of orders, homes and nuns. (Cf. the results contained in *Chrzescijanstwo w Polsce* (Christianity in Poland), Wydawnictwo KUL, Lublin 1980, pp.301-313.)

13. The Sisters Servants of Mary Immaculate (Pleszew) were running 5 ophanages and boarding schools, the Sisters Servants of Mary Immaculate (Debica)—7, the Sisters of St. Joseph—5, the Sisters Servants of Mary Immaculate (Stara Wies)— 46, the Felician Sisters—17; the Sisters Servants of the Cross were running institutions for blind children and I have not included their homes in the network of orphanages and boarding schools in question. (On the basis of data taken from *Zenskie Zgromadzenia Zakonne w Polsce w latach 1939-1947* [Women's Religious Orders in Poland in the Years 1939-1947], vol.I, pp.17, 103, 176; vol.II, p.57; vol.III, p.83; vol.IV, p.246.)

14. Here I have used the number of convent homes active in Poland at the outbreak of World War II as 2,289. (See note 1 in Chapter 3.) Taking the top limit, 20% of this number are orphanages and boarding schools, and about 50% of these continued their work in the occupation years, which in absolute number would be equal to approximately 230 homes.

15. The documents, on whose basis is drawn the map of the convents rescuing Jewish children, are in the author's private collection.

16. W.S. Niklewska, op. cit., pp.34-36.

17. According to the account of Sister Gregoria Klaczynska (in the author's private collection) the Germans deported the nuns the night of November 28, 1939, together with the children from the orphanage in Gdynia-Oksywie to the General Government. In Przesmyki, in inhuman conditions, the nuns were bringing up the children throughout the war, and among them two Jewish girls.

18. Sister Jadwiga Skalec (of the Sisters Servants of Mary Immaculate [Stara Wies]) interview; author's private colleciton.

19. Sister Janina Gorecka (of the Atonine Sisters) interview; author's private collection. Account of Sister Oktawia in *Archiwum Glowne Zgromadzenia Siostr sw. Dominika* (Main Archives of the Sisters of St. Dominic), Cracow. *Kronika Generalna Siostr Karmelitanek Dzieciatka Jezus* (General Chronicle of the Carmelite Sisters of the Infant Jesus) in *Archiwum Glowne Zgromadzenia Siostr Karmelitanek Dzieciatka Jezus* (Main Archives of the Carmelite Sisters of the Infant Jesus), Sosnowiec.

20. Jerzy Kloczowski, *Dzieje chrzescijanstwa polskiego* (A History of Polish Christianity), Paris 1987, p.248.

21. To understand the situation of the convents in the eastern territories of Poland one must remember that we are talking about land in which Poles had been living for ages among national minorities, or in which they constituted a minority among Catholic Lithuanians and Orthodox White Russians and Ukrainians. For example, according to the census in 1921, in the Bialystok region (with great differences from district to district) there was a decided Polish majority, as, on average, 769 persons out of 1,000 declared their nationality as Polish. According to the same census data, in the Wilno region, 540 persons out of 1,000 declared Polish nationality in the Nowogrodek voivodship, while in Volhynia, in the Poleski voivodship, only 243 and in the Wolynski voivodship 168. For Galicia the same census indicated 560 Poles in 1,000 inhabitants in the Lwow voivodship, 499 in the Tarnopol voivodship, and 223 in the Stanislawow voivodship. (*Skorowidz miejscowosci Rzeczypospolitej Polskiej* [Index of Localities of the Polish Republic], Warsaw 1924; Jan Suski, *Statystyka narodowosciowa Rzeczypospolitej Polskiej* [Nationality Statistics of the Polish Republic], Warsaw 1926.

22. See note 13 in Chapter 2.

Chapter 8

1. Account of Sister Janina Osmolski (of the Sisters Servants of Mary Immaculte [Stara Wies]), *Archiwum Glowne Zgromadzenia SS Sluzebniczek Starowiejski* (Main Archives of the Sisters Servants of Mary Immacluate [Stara Wies]).

2. Information about people receiving money for reclaiming children who were not theirs from convent institutions is confirmed by Izajasz Druker (interview in author's private collection). Of course, this was not any sort of trading of children; these people received money as payment for their work, which consisted of finding Jewish children and reclaiming them from Poles.

3. Mother Superior Tekla Budnowska (of the Franciscan Missionary Sisters of Mary) interview; author's private collection.

4. J. Dobraczynski, op. cit., p.245.

5. As I have already mentioned, Jan Dobraczynski's position on the question of Jewish children was his private one and it did not have much to do with the position of the nuns who were rescuing the children. That is why the nuns, when asking the JDC for help, did not conceal the fact that in their convents there were Jewish children. On the contrary, they made it clear that they were there and could be reclaimed, but that, as Jewish children, aid could be given for their upkeep in the meantime. In the account of Mother Tekla Budnowska quoted earlier, we read that after the war she

asked the Jewish children their real names so that they could leave the convent and join their families. I have never come across a case in which the nuns refused a Jewish child the right to leave the convent when it was known that the child was going to be in good hands, that is, that the person taking the child would secure proper care for the child. Certainly the nuns could not give a Jewish child to any Jew without the certainy of who the particular person was and where he was taking the child. For the simple reason that they also did not give Polish children to any Poles, or Gypsy children to any Gypsies, etc. They rightly assumed that nationality was not a good enough guarantee that the child would not find himself or herself in danger.

6. "Rescue of Jewish Children," *Encyclopedia Judaica...*, vol.XIII, p.78.

7. Izajasz Druker interview; author's private collection.

8. According to Izajasz Druker's account (see above), he himself was delegated to cooperate with the Coordination. According to the *Encyclopedia Judaica* (see note 6), the Coordination was also financed by the JDC.

9. "Rescue of Jewish Children," *Encyclopedia Judaica...*, vol. XIII. p.78.

10. Both names are rendered phonetically on the basis of I. Druker's account.

11. *An Inventory to the Rescue Children, Inc., Collection 1945-1985*, Yeshiva University Press, New York 1986.

12. Ibid., p.7.

13. "Rescue of Jewish Children" (see note 6) is an entry (as a sub-chapter of the entry "Poland") which appears only in a section concerning events after the Second World War. We also do not find the phrase "rescuing children" used in the Holocaust entry (vol.VIII, pp.827-910).

14. See note 7.

15. David Kahane interview; author's private collection.

16. The only case I know of where a bishop was informed about the rescuing Jewish children from convents concerned the Ordinary of Tarnow, to whom Sister Roberta Sutkowska, a Sister of St. Joseph, came during the war to seek his advice. (Sister Roberta Sutkowska interview; author's private collection.)

17. Sister Charitas Soczek, a Samaratin Sister, interview; author's private collection.

18. Compare the accounts of Mother Superior Tekla Budnowska and Izajasz Druker (author's private collection). See also note 2.

19. Interviews of Sister Roberta Sutkowska and Rachela G.; author's private collection.

20. Rachela G. interview; author's private collection.

21. Ibid.

GLOSSARY

Aktion German word for the brutal rounding up of Jews for deportation.

Armia Krajowa (AK/Home Army) Clandestine Polish army organization. Came under the authority of the legal Polish Government-in-Exile in London. Chief underground activities were: espionage, counter-espionage, judiciary trials, sabotage, partisan combat.

Bartoszewski, Wladyslaw Code name "Ludwik." A soldier in the Home Army and an underground leader and one of the organizers of Zegota. By the age of 21 he had already endured 15 months in Auschwitz. Bartoszewski directed the network of couriers. After the war he spent many years as a prisoner under the communist regime for his membership in the Home Army and political beliefs. Professor of the Catholic University of Lublin. Polish Minister of Foreign Affairs in 1994-95.

Biuletyn Informacyjny (Information Bulletin) Clandestine publication issued in Poland from 1939 to 1945. An organ of the Home Army and the Polish Government-in-Exile in London.

Bund Jewish Socialist Worker's Party (1897-1948) Centos A Jewish charitable organization dedicated to the care of children in the ghetto. Dr. Adolf Berman was a director of Centos and later became Secretary on the executive board of Zegota.

Edelman, Mark A leader of the Warsaw Ghetto fighters and uprising.

General Government In September 1939, after the invasion of

Poland by the Germans from the west and the Soviets from the east, Poland was divided into three parts. The eastern territories of Poland were incorporated into the USSR; the western and northwestern territories into the Third Reich; out of central Poland the Germans created a single administrative unit, the so-called General Government. Its area encompassed 96,000 km. After the outbreak of the German-Soviet War in 1941, when the Germans occupied the eastern lands of Poland, this region grew to 145,000 km. The term "General Government" (Generalna Gubernia) was used only by the Nazis between 1939 and 1945.

Grobelny, Julian First chairman of Zegota. He was a member of the Polish Socialist Party and when war broke out he immediately joined the resistance using the code name "Trojan."

Jewish National Committee A coalition of six Zionist parties. The Jewish National Committee was represented on the Zegota Executive Board by Adolf Berman.

Jewish Police or Jewish Service Order (Zydowska Sluzba Porzadkowa) Uniformed ghetto police under the authority of the Judenrats. Only Jewish inhabitants of the ghetto belonged to it. The ghetto police maintained order and made sure German orders were obeyed by the Jewish populace. The Jewish police actively participated in the extermination of Jews by searching for places of concealment, and seizing and leading to wagons Jews who were then sent to the death camps and murdered.

Judenrats Jewish Council of Elders created by the Germans in September 1939 as an organ of Jewish self-government in the newly-formed Jewish ghetto. The Judenrats were saddled with the responsibility of the exact and prompt execution of German orders. The execution of these orders was done through the so-called Jewish police (*Zydowska Sluzba Porzadkowa*).

Kenkarte A special identification card issued by the General Government which every Pole had to produce on demand. It contained a photo and fingerprints. It could only be obtained from the German authorities upon presentation of a birth certificate.

Kossak, Zofia Well-known Catholic writer and a member of the Catholic Front for Reborn Poland. Intensely involved in assisting

Jews. Generally credited with galvanizing a united front in the struggle to help Jews. She was on the Gestapo's most-wanted list.

Rek, Tadeusz A member of the Peasant Party, social activist and editor of many progressive journals. Arrested in June 1940, sent to Pawiak Prison and then to Auschwitz. Released in November 1941, whereupon he immediately returned to his work in the underground press. Recruited by Zegota, he became Deputy Chairman. His code name was "Rozycki."

Ringelblum, Emanuel Historian and chronicler of the Warsaw Ghetto. He recorded the history of the ghetto and stored his archives in metal containers and buried them. Recovered after the war, his remarkable achievement remains the single most comprehensive documentation on the Holocaust.

Szmalcownik In Polish jargon the word *"szmal"* means money. The contemptuous term szmalcownik was used during the war to describe those criminals and collaborators who demanded money from Jews in hiding or the Poles who hid them in exchange for not informing the Nazis where they were. The szmalcowniks did not always keep their word: after receiving money, they would inform on them anyway.

Volksdeutsch A privileged status granted to a Polish citizen of German origin.

Women's Religious Orders Voluntary associations of Catholic women. In the active orders the women commit themselves in their vows to serve God, which is understood as helping people in need, preserving their vow of chastity and complying with the convent regulations stipulated in the constitution of each order. At various times in Poland these orders counted a dozen or so sisters to over a thousand. Each order had its own hierarchy, attire and specific goals. In the contemplative orders the nuns do not participate in active work; rather, they serve God and man by prayer.

Wolinski, Henryk A member of the AK, he was head of the Jewish section of the Underground Bureau of Information and Propaganda. He was the principal AK contact for the Jewish liaison of the ZOB and the Jewish leader in Zegota.

Yad Vashem Holocaust memorial center in Jerusalem, Israel.

Zegota Clandestine cryptonym for Council for Aid to Jews, one of the underground groups in Nazi Europe dedicated toward helping threatened Jews, under the authority of the Polish Government-in-Exile in London and financed through that body. Members included the main Polish political parties and the more important Jewish ones.

Zydowska Organizacja Wojskowa (ZOB) Clandestine Jewish army organization (1942-43) operating in the Warsaw Ghetto. It directed the uprising against the Nazis.

BIBLIOGRAPHY

Documents, Accounts and Memoirs

Berg, Mary. *Dziennik z getta warszawskiego (Warsaw Ghetto Diary)*, Warsaw, 1983.

Bartoszewski, Wladyslaw. *Warto byc przyzwoitym (It Pays to be Decent)*, Paris, 1986.

Birenbaum, Halina. *Nadzieja umiera ostatnia (Hope Dies Last)*, Warsaw, 1988.

Czerniakow, Adam. *Dziennik getta warszawskiego, 6 IX 1939—13 VII 1942 (Warsaw Ghetto Diary, August 6, 1939—July 13, 1942)*, Warsaw, 1983.

Czubakowna, Genowefa. *W habicie (In a Habit)*, Warsaw, 1967.

Dobraczynski, Jan. *Tylko w jednym zyciu (Only in One Life)*, Warsaw, 1978.

Donat, Aleksander. *The Holocaust Kingdom*, New York, 1965.

Edelman, Marek. *Getto walczy (The Ghetto Fights)*, Warsaw, 1945.

Eksterminacja Zydow na ziemiach polskich w okresie okupacji hitlerowskiej—zbior dokumentow (The Extermination of Jews on Polish Land during the Nazi Occupation—A Collection of Documents), Warsaw, 1957.

Gawrys, Cezary. *Turkowice—smierc i ocalenie* ("Turkowice—Death and Rescue"), *Wies*, 1987. no. 4 pp.14-53.

Hirschfeld, Ludwik. *Historia jednego zycia (The Story of One Life)*, Warsaw, 1957.

Ilochberg-Marianska, Maria. *Dzieci oskarzaja (The Children Accuse)*, Warsaw, 1974.

Kacenelson, Icchak. *Piesn o zamordowanym zydowskim narodzie (Song of the Murdered Jewish Nation)*, Warsaw, 1982.

Kermisz, Jozef. Akcje i wysiedlenia ("Actions and Displacements"), in *Dokumenty i materialy z czasow okupacji niemieckiej w Polsce (Documents and Materials from the Time of the German Occupation of Poland)*, 1946, vol.II.

Korczak, Janusz. *Pisma wybrane (Selected Writings)*, Warsaw, 1978.

Landau, Ludwik. *Kronika lat wojny i okupacji (A Chronicle of the War and the Occupation Years)*, Warsaw, 1962.

Moroz, Anna. *W murach i poza murami getta (Inside and Outside the Ghetto Walls)*, Warsaw, 1988.

Oliner, Samuel P. *Restless Memories—Recollections of the Holocaust Years*, Berkeley, 1979.

Pawlowski, Grzegorz. Historia mojego zycia ("The Story of My Life"), *Tygodnik Powszechny*, April 14, 1966.

Piotrowska, Jadwiga. 50 razy kara smierci ("The Death Penalty Fifty Times"), *Kierunki*, May 11, 1986.

Poznanski, Jakub. *Pamietnik z getta lodzkiego (Diary from the Lodz Ghetto)*, Lodz, 1960.

Proces Artura Greisera przed Najwyzszym Trybunalem Narodowym (The Trial of Artur Greiser before the Supreme Court), 1946.

Ringelblum, Emanuel. *Kronika getta warszawskiego (A Chronicle of the Warsaw Ghetto)*, Warsaw, 1983.

Ringelblum, Emanuel. *Stosunki polsko-zydowskie w czasie drugiej wojny swiatowej (Polish-Jewish Relations during the Second World War)*, Warsaw, 1988.

Romaniuk, Stefania. Moja okupacja ("My Occupation"), in *Meczenstwo i zaglada Zydow (The Martyrdom and Holocaust of Jews)*, Warsaw, 1988, pp.218-226.

Rabinowicz, Dawid. *Pamietnik (Memoirs)*, Warsaw, 1987.

Sendlerowa, Irena. Ci, ktorzy pomagali Zydom ("Those Who Helped Jews"), in *Biuletyn Zydowskiego Instytutu Historycznego (ZIH)*, Warsaw, 1963, no. 45, pp. 234-244.

Sierakowski, David. *Dziennik (Diary)*, Warsaw, 1960.

Smolski, Wladyslaw. *Zaklete lata (The Cursed Years)*, Warsaw, 1964.

Szymanska, Zofia. *Bylam tylko lekarzem (I Was Only a Doctor)*, Warsaw, 1979.

Taras, Eugeniusz. Zaglada ropczyckich Zydow ("The Jewish Holocaust in Ropczycz"), *Znak*, 1988, no.396-397.

Uminski, Zdzislaw. *Album z rewolwerem (Album with a Revolver)*, Warsaw, 1984.

2. Other Sources

Abramczuk, Olga. Zgromadzenie Matki Bozej Milosierdzia w latach 1939-1945 ("The Order of the Sisters of Mary Immaculate in the years 1939-1945"), in *Kosciol katolicki na ziemiach Polski w czasie II wojny swiatowej (The Catholic Church in Poland during the Second World War)*, Warsaw, 1981, vol. X, pp.65-264.

Antosiewicz, Klara. Zakon Duch Swietego de Saxia w Polsce sredniowieczne, ("The Order of the Holy Spirit de Saxia in Medieval Poland") *Nasza Przeszlosc (Our Past)*, Cracow, 1966.

———. Zgromadzenie Siostr Kanoniczek Ducha Swietego w latach 1939-1947 (Order of the Canonical Sisters of the Holy Spirit in the years 1939-1947, in *Summarium*, Lublin, 1947, p.190.

Arad, Yitzhak. *Ghetto in Flames: the Struggle and Destruction of the Jews in Vilna in the Holocaust*, Jerusalem, 1980.

Arczynski, Marek, and Balcerak, Wieslaw. *Kryptonim "Zegota" (Cryptonym "Zegota")*, Warsaw, 1983.

Bafia, Jerzy. Druga wojna swiatowa a dziecko ("The Second World War and Children"), in *Dzieci i mlodziez w latach drugiej wojny swiatowej (Children and Young Adults During the Second World War)*, Warsaw, 1982, p.5.

Bartoszewski, Wladyslaw, and Lewinowna, Zofia. *Ten jest z ojczyzny mojej (He is My Fellow Countryman)*, Cracow, 1969.

Berenstein, Tatiana, and Eisenbach, Artur, and Rutkowski, Adam. Ekstermincacja Zydow na ziemiach Polski w okresie okupacji hitlerowskiej ("The Extermination of Jews in Poland during the Second World War"), in *Biuletyn ZIH*, Warsaw, 1957, no. 21.

Berenstein, Tatiana, and Rutkowski, Adam. O ratownictwie Zydow przez Polakow ("On Rescuing Jews by Poles"), in *Biuletyn ZIH*, Warsaw, 1960, no.35. pp.18-46.

————. *Pomoc Zydom w Polsce 1939-1945 (Help for Jews in Poland, 1939-1945)*, Warsaw, 1963.

Boczek, Helena, and Boczek, Eugeniusz, and Wilczur, Jacek. *Wojna i dziecko (The War and Children)*, Warsaw, 1979.

Borwicz, Michal. "Polish-Jewish Relations, 1944-1947," in *The Jews in Poland*, New York, 1986, pp.190-199.

Chamiec, Anna. Zgromadzenie Najswietszego Serca Jezusowego w latach 1939-1947) ("The Order of Sisters of the Most Sacred Heart of Christ in the years 1939-1947," in *Summarium*, London, 1974, p.201.

Chrzescijanstwo w Polsce (Christianity in Poland), edited by Jerzy Kloczowski, Lublin, 1974, p.201.

Datner, Szymon. *Las sprawiedliwych—karta z dziejow ratownictwa Zydow w okupowanej Polsce (The Forest of the Just: A Page from History of Rescuing Jews in Occupied Poland)*, Warsaw, 1968.

————. Materialy z dziedziny ratownictwa Zydow w Polsce w czasie okupacji hitlerowskiej ("Materials Concerning the Saving Jews in Poland During the Nazi Occupation"), in *Biuletyn ZIH*, Warsaw, 1970, no.73-76, p.133.

————. Polki warszawskie z pomoca Zydom ("Polish Women in Warsaw who Helped Jews"), in *Biuletyn ZIH*, Warsaw, 1969, no.70, p.113.

Dawidowicz, Lucy. *The War Against the Jews 1933-1945*, Holt, Reinhart and Winston, New York, 1975.

————. *The Holocaust and the Historians*, Harvard University Press, Cambridge, Mass., 1981.

Dabrowska, Danuta. Zaglada skupisk zydowskich w "Kraju Warty" w okresie okupacji hitlerowskiej ("The Holocaust of Jews in the 'Guarded Country' During the Nazi Occupation"), in *Biuletyn ZIH*, Warsaw, 1952, no.13-14.

Debowska, Krystyna. Les congregations feminines religieuses en Pologne au cours des annes 1939-1945, in *Miscellanea Historiae Ecclesiaticae*, Wroclaw-Bruselles, p.370-373.

Doswiadczenia lat wojny i okupacji ("The Experiences of the War and the Occupation Years"), Cracow, 1980.

Dunin-Wasowicz, Krzysztof. *Oboz koncentracyjny Stutthof* ("Concentration Camp Stutthof"), Gdynia, 1968.

Duszkiewicz, Weronika, and Margolska, Katarzyna, and

Strzalkowska, Maria. Zgromadzenie Siostr Sw. Feliksa z Kantalicjo w latach 1939-1947 ("The Order of the Sisters of St. Feliks from Kantalicia in the year 1939-1947"), in *Zenskie Zgromadzenia Zakonne w Polsce 1939-1947* ("Women's Religious Orders in Poland in the Years 1935-1947"), Lublin, 1982, vol. I, pp.27-212.

Encyclopedia Judaica, Jerusalem, 1972, vol. I-XIII.

Fafara, Eugeniusz. *Gehenna ludnosci zydowskiej* ("The Gehenna of the Jewish People"), Warsaw, 1983.

Fijalkowski, Zenon. *Kosciol katolicki na ziemach polskich w latach okupacji hiterowskiej* ("The Catholic Church in Poland Druing the Nazi Occupation"), Warsaw, 1983.

Fracek, Teresa. Zgromadzenie Siostr Franciczkanek Rodziny Maryi w latach 1939-1945 ("The Order of Franciscan Sisters of the Family of Mary"), in *Kosciol katolicki na ziemiach Polski w czasie II wojny swiatowej (The Catholic Church in Poland Druing the Second World War)*, Warsaw, 1981, vol. X.

Friedman, Filip. Zaglada Zydow polskich 1939-1945 ("The Holocaust of Polish Jews, 1939-1945"), in *Biuletyn Glownej Komisji Badania Zbrodni Niemickich w Polsce* ("Bulletin of the Chief Commission Examining German Crimes in Poland"), Warsaw, 1946, vol. I.

Friedman, Philip. *Their Brothers' Keepers*, New York, 1957.

Garlinski, Jozef. *Poland in the Second World War*, Hippocrene Books, New York, 1985.

Glinska, Alina. Maloletni w obozie koncentracyjnym Stutthof ("Children in the Concentration Camp of Stutthof"), in *Zeszyty Muzuem Stutthof (Publications of the Stutthof Museum)*, 1977, no.2.

Gumkowski, Janusz. *Mlodziez polska podczas okupacji* ("Polish Youth During the Occupation"), Warsaw, 1966.

Gutman, Yisrael. "Polish and Jewish Historiography on the Question of Polish-Jewish Relations during World War II," in *The Jews in Poland*, New York, 1986.

Hertz, Aleksander. *Zydzi w kulturze polskiej* ("Jews in Polish Culture"), Paris, 1961.

Hilberg, Raul. *The Destruction of the European Jews* (Revised and definitive edition), Holmes and Meier, New York, 1985.

Horak, Stephan. *Poland and Her National Minorities 1919-1939*, New York, 1961.

Hundert, Gershon David, and Bacon, Gershon C. *The Jews in Poland and Russia—Bibliographical Essays*, Bloomington, 1984.

Iranek-Osmecki, Kazimierz. *Kto ratuje jedno zycie—Polacy i Zydzi 1939-1945 (He Who Saves One Life—Poles and Jews, 1939-1945)*, London, 1968; New York, 1971.

Kloczowski, Jerzy. *Dzieje chrzescijanstwa polskiego* ("History of Polish Christianity"), Paris, 1987.

————. "The Religious Orders and the Jews in Nazi-occupied Poland," *Polin* (Oxford), 1988, no.3, pp.238-244.

Kloczowski, Jerzy, ed. *Histoire religieuse de la Pologne*, Paris, 1987.

Kowalik, Krystyna. *Opieka nad dzieckiem w Generalnej Guberni* ("Care of Children in the General Government"), Lublin, 1986.

Kubiak, Anna. *Dzieciobojstwo podczas okupacji hitlerowskiej* ("The Murder of Children during the Nazi Occupation"), in *Biuletyn ZIH*, Warsaw, 1956, no. 17-18, pp.60-108.

Kurek, Ewa. *Encyclopedia Judaica*, Spotkania, Lublin, 1985, no. 29-30, pp. 113-116.

————. *Sredniowieczny kult Dzieciatka Jezus jako inspiracja procesu dowartosciowania dziecka* ("The Cult of the Child Jesus in the Middle Ages as the Genesis for the Evolution of a Child's Worth"), *Summarium*, Lublin, 1979. p.248.

Kurek-Lesik, Ewa. *Podajmy sobie rece* ("Let Us Shake Hands"), *Nowy Dziennik*, New York, June 26, 1986.

Lesko, Zofia Elekta. *Zgromadzenie Siostr Sw. Jozefa w latach 1939-1947* ("The Order of Sisters of St. Joseph in the years 1939-1947"), in *Zenskie Zgromadzenia Zakonne w Polsce 1939-1947 (Women's Religious Orders in Poland in the Years 1939-1947)*, Lublin, 1987, vol. IV, pp.189-325.

Lewin, Izaak, *Z historii i tradycji—szkice z dziejow kultury zydowskiej* ("From History and Tradition—Sketches from Jewish Cultural History"), Warsaw, 1983.

Madajczyk, Czeslaw. *Polityka Trzeciej Rzeszy w okupowanej Polsce* ("The Politics of the Third Reich in Occupied Poland"), Warsaw, 1970.

Maly Rocznik Statystyczny 1937 ("The Little Yearbook of 1937"), Warsaw, 1937.

Mendelsohn, Ezra. *The Jews of East Central Europe Between the World Wars*, Bloomington, 1983.

Mistecka, Waleria Syksta. Sluzebniczki Niepokalanego Poczecia Najswietszej Maryi Panny—Pleszew ("Sisters Servants of the Immaculate Conception of the Most Holy Mary—Pleszew"), in *Zenskie Zgromadzenia Zakonne w Polsce 1939-1947 (Women's Religious Orders in Poland in the Years 1939-1947)*, Lublin, 1985, vol.III.

Oliner, Samuel P., and Oliner, Pearl M. *The Altruistic Personality*, New York, 1988.

Pierozynski, Marian. Zakony zenskie w Polsce ("Women's Orders in Poland"), Lublin, 1935.

Pierozynski, Marian, and Szczech, Stanislaw. *Rocznik Statystyczny Kosciola katolickiego w Polsce* ("Statistical Yearbook of the Polish Catholic Church"), Lublin, 1938.

Pilichowski, Czeslaw. *Dzieci i mlodziez w latach drugiej wojny swiatowej* ("Children and the Young During the Second World War"), Warsaw, 1982.

————. *Zbrodnie hitlerowskie na dziecach i mlodziezy polskiej 1939-1945* ("Nazi Crimes Against Polish Children and Youths, 1939-1945"), Warsaw, 1969.

Pospieszalski, Karol. *Polska pod niemieckim prawem* ("Poland Under German Law"), Poznan, 1946.

Prekerowa, Teresa. *Konspiracyjna Rada Pomocy Zydom w Warsaw 1942-1945* ("The Secret Council for Aid to Jews in Warsaw, 1942-1945"), Warsaw, 1982.

Rustow, Margit Wreschner. *Trauma and Identity: Jewish Children Who Found Catholic Sanctuary During the Holocaust*, International Conference, Montreal, June, 1987.

Sakowska, Ruta. *Ludzie z dzielnicy zamknietej* ("People from the Closed Section"), Warsaw, 1975.

Scharf, Rafael F. "Saint or Madmen? A Meditation on Ephraim Oshry's—Responsa from the Holocaust," *The Jewish Quarterly*, London, January, 1988.

Skorowidz miejscowosci Rzeczypospolitej Polskiej ("Index of Localities of the Polish Republic"), Warsaw, 1924.

Slomczynski, Adam. *Dom Ksiedza Boduena* ("The Father Boduen Home"), Warsaw, 1975.

Sosnowski, Kiryl. *Dziecko w systemie hitlerowskim* ("Children in the Nazi System"), Poznan, 1962.

Stopniak, Franciszek. Pomoc kleru polskiego dla dzieci w II wojnie swiatowej ("Polish Clergy's Aid to Children During World War II"), in *Kosciol katolicki na ziemiach Polskich w czasie II wojny swiatowej* ("The Catholic Church in Poland Druing the Second World War"), Warsaw, 1981, vol. X, pp.3-64.

Suski, Jan. *Statystyka narodowosciowa Rzeczypospolitej Polskiej* ("Nationality Statistics of the Polish Republic"), Warsaw, 1962.

Szachno, Jadwiga. Zgromadzenie Siostr Franciszkanek Sluzebnic Krzyza w latach 1939-1947 ("The Order of the Franciscan Sisters Servants of the Cross in the Years 1939-1947"), *Zenskie Zgromadzenia Zakonne w Polsce 1939-1947 (Women's Religious Orders in Poland in 1939-1947)*, Lublin, 1982. Vol. I, pp.213-279.

Szelagiewicz, Agnieszka. Sluzebniczki Najswietszej Maryi Panny Niepokalanie Poczetej—Stara Wies ("Sisters Servants of the Most Holy Mary Immaculate—Stara Wies," in *Zenskie Zgromadzenia Zakonne w Polsce 1939-1947 (Women's Religious Orders in Poland in 1939-1947)*, Lublin, 1984, vol. II.

Szmaglewska, Seweryna. Dzieci w Birkenau ("Children in Birkenau"), *Sluzba Spoleczna*, 1956, no. 1-14.

Tajanowicz, Wladyslawa. Zgromadzenie Siostr Sluzebniczek Bogarodzicy Dziewicy Niepokalanego Poczecia—sluzebniczki debickie ("The Order of Sisters Servants of the Virgin Mary—Servants of Debica"), in *Zenskie Zgromadzenia Zakonne w Polsce 1939-1847 (Women's Religious Orders in Poland in 1939-1947)*, Lublin, 1987, vol. IV, pp. 7-188.

Tec, Nachema. *When Light Pierced the Darkness—Christian Rescue of Jews in Nazi-Occupied Poland*, New York, 1986.

Tomaszewski, Jerzy. *Rzeczpospolita wielu narodow* ("A Republic of Many Nationalities"), Warsaw, 1985.

Wisniowski, E. 800 lat Zakonu Ducha Swietego de Saxia w Polsce ("800 Years of the Order of the Holy Spirit de Saxia in Poland"), *Nowum*, Warsaw, 1976.

Zielinski, Zygmunt, ed. *Zycie religijne w Polsce pod okupacja hitlerowska 1939-1945 (Religious Life in Poland During the Nazi Occupation, 1939-1945)*, Warsaw, 1982.

Index

Also from Hippocrene Books . . .

DID THE CHILDREN CRY?
Hitler's War Against Jewish and Polish Children
Richard C. Lukas

Winner of the 1996 Janusz Korczak Literary Competition for books about children.

Based on eyewitness accounts, interviews and prodigious research by the author, this is a unique and most compelling account of German inhumanity to children in occupied Poland.

"A major value of this book is that it demonstrates both the 'Germanization' process and the Final Solution to be components of the larger population project the Nazis had in mind for the conquered territories of the East."
—*American Historical Review*

"[Lukas] intersperses the endless numbers, dates, locations and losses with personal accounts of tragedy and triumph.... A well-researched book. ..."
—*Catalyst*
263 pages   6 x 9   15 b/w photos, index   0-7818-0242-3 $24.95   (145)

FORGOTTEN HOLOCAUST
The Poles Under German Occupation 1939-1945 Revised Edition
Richard C. Lukas with Foreword by Norman Davies

This new edition includes the story of *Zegota* and the list of 700 Poles executed for helping Jews.

"Carefully researched—a timely contribution."
—Professor Piotr Wandycz, Yale University

"Contains excellent analyses of the relationship of Poland's Jewish and Gentile communities, the development of the resistance, the exile leadership, and the Warsaw uprisings. A superior work."
—*Library Journal*
300 pages   illustrations   0-7818-0528-7 $24.95hc   (639)

All prices subject to change. **TO PURCHASE HIPPOCRENE BOOKS** contact your local bookstore, call (718) 454-2366, or write to: HIPPOCRENE BOOKS, 171 Madison Avenue, New York, NY 10016. Please enclose check or money order, adding $5.00 shipping (UPS) for the first book and $. 50 for each additional book.